WALKING TCU

Other books by Joan Hewatt Swaim

Walking TCU: A Historic Perspective (First Edition, 1992)

WALKING TCU

A HISTORIC PERSPECTIVE

•

2ND EDITION

Joan Hewatt Swaim and Phil Hartman

Foreword by Chancellor Victor J. Boschini Jr.

Fort Worth, Texas

Library of Congress Cataloging-in-Publication Data

Names: Swaim, Joan Hewatt, author. | Hartman, Phil, 1953- author.
Title: Walking TCU : a historical perspective / Joan Hewatt Swaim and Phil
  Hartman.
Description: 2nd ed. | Fort Worth, Texas : TCU Press, [2023] | Includes
  bibliographical references. | Summary: "Founded in 1873, Texas Christian
  University is located on 272 acres about three miles from downtown Fort
  Worth, Texas. Walking TCU: A Historical Perspective, 2nd Edition
  provides an account of the buildings and other campus structures on the
  Fort Worth campus and before that the Thorp Spring and Waco campuses.
  The book, which builds upon the 1st edition written in 1992 by Joan
  Hewatt Swaim, provides an historical account of the various campus
  structures-academic, residential as well as athletic-from the time of
  their initial construction to the present day. Interwoven are accounts
  of the individuals instrumental to shaping the campus as well as those
  for whom the structures were named. As the title suggests, the book is
  organized such that the reader can walk campus, thereby gaining a
  greater appreciation for its inherent beauty as well as learning about
  those who have shaped TCU's past and present. Containing over 220
  photographs, Walking TCU seeks to capture the essence of what make
  TCU-and its campus-a magical place for so many"-- Provided by publisher.

Identifiers: LCCN 2022047060 | ISBN 9780875658353 (hardback)
Subjects: LCSH: Texas Christian University--Guidebooks. | Texas Christian
  University--History. | LCGFT: Guidebooks.
Classification: LCC LD5311.T383 S93 2023 | DDC
  378.764/5315--dc23/eng/20220930
LC record available at https://lccn.loc.gov/2022047060

TCU Box 298300
Fort Worth, Texas 76129

Design by Bill Brammer

DEDICATION

FROM JOAN HEWATT SWAIM:

Especially for

my late mother, Elizabeth Harris Hewatt
my late father, Willis Gilliland Hewatt
—what blessed fortune to have been in your care.

And also for my late husband, Johnny R. Swaim
for my children Michael R. Swaim and Susan E. Swaim
and for my grandson, Asher B. Kurtz

FROM PHIL HARTMAN:

Especially for

my mother, Marjorie Stewart Hartman
my late father, Paul Arthur Hartman
—how lucky I have been!

for Mary Beth, who is my strength and guiding light
for Jonathan (and loving wife Denise) and Tim, who grew up with TCU as their second home
and for Jensen, Cooper, and Kendall, who keep me young.

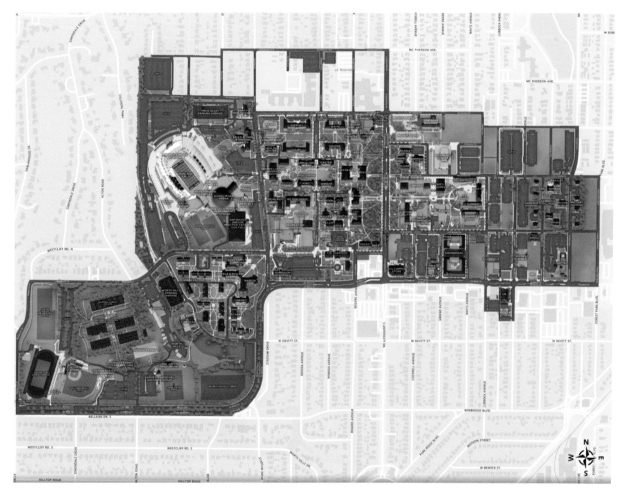

Aerial map of Texas Christian University,
which spans over three hundred acres.

CONTENTS

Foreword

As I read the pages of this second edition of *Walking TCU*, I am amazed by the generous gifts of time and treasure that have transformed the campus of Texas Christian University into one of the most beautiful college campuses in the nation. In taking account of the transformation, I also realize the tremendous impact of TCU on my professional and personal life since I first set foot on the campus to interview for the chancellor position some twenty years ago. First Lady Megan Boschini and I are indebted for the kindness extended to our family over the years and the incredible opportunities afforded to us during this period of our lives. We are truly blessed to part of the Horned Frog nation, and even more fortunate to call TCU and Fort Worth our home.

The TCU campus is a living laboratory and provides the perfect setting for student growth and development as well as community-building initiatives. It is fascinating to see how different areas on campus have become favorite student study spots and gathering centers. The Incubator Lab at Rees-Jones Hall is among the most popular places for collaboration and generation of ideas. The commons area has hosted concerts with big-name entertainers, College GameDay, and the annual Christmas tree lighting event. During the pandemic, leaders of our Student Government Association (SGA) proposed and converted the commons area into a fabulous outdoor space where students could safely meet and study. In 2021, the plaza area by the Mary Couts Burnett Library became the venue for TCU's first Reconciliation Day—a day of community celebration in addressing the past and looking forward to the future. Most recently, the new TCU Music Center (as part of the creative commons on the east side of campus) took center stage in hosting the Van Cliburn International Piano Competition in the Van Cliburn Concert Hall. Suffice it to say, space is utilized in optimal ways on TCU's campus, which spans some three hundred-plus acres.

This year will mark the third year since The Harrison opened. Named for generous donors Brenda and Mike Harrison of Midland, Texas, this new administration building has become the hub of activity for all types of student services, ranging from student financial services and career services to student affairs and the office of institutional equity. The building embodies our hopes and dreams of what we had envisioned in the past—that students would find student services bundled together in one central place.

TCU has come so far. Never could the founders and early TCU leaders predict the expansive campus of today. As we salute the past and toast the future, I hope we will all acknowledge the people and recount the many bold steps taken to reach this remarkable high point in TCU's history. I also salute those scholars who contributed to this excellent updated version of *Walking TCU*.

Victor J. Boschini Jr.
Tenth Chancellor of TCU

Preface to the Second Edition

In 1992, Joan Hewatt Swaim produced one of my favorite books, entitled *Walking TCU: A Historical Perspective*. Interwoven with a rich account of TCU's history and the people who made it, the book's focus was on the buildings and other campus structures. I've long been a sucker for campus architecture, occasionally wandering various campuses and soaking in their ambience while attending scientific meetings or on vacation. And perhaps like you, my many years associated with Texas Christian University have instilled a deep love of the place . . . most certainly for the people but also of the campus itself.

Campus has changed markedly since 1992, so it seemed a proper time—particularly as TCU's sesquicentennial approaches—to update Joan's gem of a book. Much of the material in the now first edition remains an accurate and evocative account of the buildings and other structures. Those sections required me merely to add descriptions of post-1992 renovations and identify recent photography. But of course many new buildings—over fifty in all—have populated campus since *Walking TCU* was published. Their stories are also told on the pages that follow, and I hope my attempt at chronicling them matches Joan's in terms of accuracy and style.

It was extraordinarily fun browsing old TCU *Skiff*s and *TCU Magazine*s while conducting the archival research for the second edition. Many memories, mostly fond ones, were stirred along the way. A bonus round was that the project gave me the opportunity to reconnect with Joan, whose ties to TCU are as strong as they come. I remember her well from days past, in part because her father, Dr. Willis G. Hewatt, also a biologist, was my predecessor's predecessor in terms of heading TCU's Pre-Health Professions Program (now Institute).

They say a picture is worth a thousand words. If so, the second edition checks in at around sixty-five thousand words, but the two hundred-plus photos push it to somewhere in the neighborhood of 270,000 . . . certainly less than the 600,000 of Tolstoy's *War and Peace*, but still quite the read. And speaking of which, I hope you enjoy the read as much as I did the write, or really the revision of Joan's first edition. If walls could talk, they would tell quite a story. Joan and I have attempted to coax them to at least whisper to us.

— Phil Hartman

Acknowledgments for the Second Edition

First and foremost, I would like to acknowledge and thank my best friend and life partner Mary Beth for her cheerful encouragement through this fun but somewhat time-consuming project. Among other things, she unconditionally allowed my escape from many a household chore while I ventured to the library or secreted away in my home office.

Second, thanks to Dan Williams for guiding me through the process of publishing a book. I now much better appreciate the challenges faced by my colleagues in the humanities, social sciences, and fine arts. Also to Molly Spain, Kathy Walton, and Rebecca Allen, who played essential roles in the manuscript-to-book process, and to James Lehr for his marketing mastery.

Third, I direct the reader's attention to the following individuals who provided helpful feedback (including reviewing drafts and offering helpful suggestions) or provided important resources, such as photographs. They are: Craig Allen, Ross Bailey, Victor Boschini (and thanks also for the book's foreword), Jeff Bond, Kris Bunton, Mark Cohen, Kerry Cornelius, Janine Cox, Vanessa Daley, Sam Deitz, John Denton, Susan Roberts Douglas, Ray Drenner, Homer Erekson, Heath Einstein, Lynn Flahive, David Grant, Richard Gipson, Eric Hyman, Tracy Hull, Jay Iorizzo, Bill Koehler, Don Mills, Joel Mitchell, Leo Munson, Harry Parker, Amy Peterson, Ron Pitcock, Liz Rainwater, Tom Rogers, Mary Saffel, Amy Schroer, Jan Scully, Trisha Spence, Jane Torgerson, Elaine Tubre, Kathy Cavins Tull, Kara Vuic, Chris Watts, Susan Weeks, and Newell Williams . . . and probably a few I neglected to mention. Any remaining inaccuracies reflect errors on my part, but this work has benefitted greatly from their input. I was also the recipient of the patience displayed by Anne Dorf and Ann Hodges, both in the library's Special Collections, who carted out numerous issues of the TCU *Skiff* and *TCU Magazine* from the archives for my inspection. Similarly, I thank Robert Carter from TCU Marketing and Communication for freely and repeatedly giving of his time and expertise, assisting me in the navigation of TCU's online photographic archives. As well, thanks to James Anger, also from TCU Marketing and Communication, for filling in the gaps in the photographic gallery. In addition, Emma Graham, in her capacity as an intern at TCU Press, did an excellent job of curating photographs, many of which appear on the following pages. Todd Waldvogel, Jack Washington Jason Soileau, and especially Alan Robinson, all from TCU Facilities, were extremely helpful in providing many of the technical details that found their way into the book.

Acknowledgments for the First Edition

The author wishes to acknowledge those who have made the necessary research for this publication not only fruitful but also pleasurable. Foremost among these are Don Palmer and his staff in Facilities Planning. Jim Pettigrew, John Carter, Richard Mason, Sue Copeland, and Don himself opened to me their well-organized files of plans and blueprints, shared with me their expert knowledge, and buoyed me with their unlimited interest in the cause.

Nancy Bruce of the Special Collections Department of the Mary Couts Burnett Library never flagged in her support and supplied me with difficult-to-find documents and photographs pertinent to the TCU story. Roger Rainwater and Laura Dubiel of the same department were also very helpful.

Harrell Moten, TCU Director of Publications, has literally piles of photographs which he allowed me to sift through; Gerald Saxon in the Special Collections Department at the University of Texas at Arlington Libraries accorded me the same courtesy.

To my manuscript readers for their valued opinion, advice, and encouragement, my heartfelt thanks. These are friend and confidante Mary Lu Schunder; friend and son, Mike Swaim; friend and daughter, Susan Swaim.

And there were so many others who willingly spent time with me and told me what I needed to know: Sara Bartzen, Dorothy Blackwell, Bettye Boisselier, Joe Britton, Bita May Hall Compton, Laura Lee Crane, Chuck Dowell, Ray Drenner, Arthur Ehlmann, Joe Enochs, Kelly Erwin, Lynn Evans, Mary Charlotte Faris, Ellen Page Garrison, Joyce Harden, Helen Huskey, Steve Kentigh, Sarah Normand Kerner, Henri Etta Kilgore, Herbert LaGrone, Suzette Lomax, Mason Mayne, Don Mills, Andy Paquet, Mildred Payne, Libby Proffer, Dwayne Simpson, Emmet and Judy Smith, Darla Smith, Wilma Miller Smith, Kim Spinks, and Andy Williams.

I also turned, as I so often do, to Johnny Swaim and to the "resident memory" mom, Elizabeth Hewatt, for stories, facts, and dates, as well as patience and forbearance.

And finally, gratitude must be expressed to my "boss," Library Director Fred M. Heath, and to my nigh-on-to-perfect staff, who put up with my less-than-full attention to library matters so that I might work on this project.

—Joan Hewatt Swaim

PROLOGUE

The land was yet prairie when they came, the hill rising up to the southwest from the Clear Fork of the Trinity River bottom, still rough and untidy with shrubby brush, grasses, and wild flowers. Jackrabbits, coyotes, and Texas horned lizards still held the territory. Dairies and ranches had been established here, but the land was hardly approachable—not yet tamed, not yet campus, not yet even a part of the city, the center of which lay some three miles distant toward the northeast.

They had come, in that summer of 1910, on a promise, and with a far vision and a dream, leaving the burnt-out shell of an earlier dream standing amidst its ruin in Waco to the south. Fort Worth had promised fifty acres on which to begin again and $200,000 with which to start. In addition, the city would provide utilities, trolley line access, and inclusion in its boundaries. It was an offer they could not refuse.

So they had come. Two of their number, the Clark brothers, had set out from Fort Worth thirty-seven years before, to pursue yet an earlier dream of establishing a strong, lasting institution dedicated to education within the context of a Christian way of life, believing that enlightenment was the sure way to salvation. Their ideals had been taken up by men and women of similar vision, and it would be they who would water the tree of education, the tree of what the 1887 catalogue called "unperishable riches," to be transplanted for a third and final time now on this Texas hilltop.

In January 1911, the school newspaper published a preliminary sketch of the new Texas Christian University campus as envisioned by prominent Fort Worth architects Waller & Field. An accompanying article by Reverend Chalmers McPherson, the university's endowment secretary, explained:

> The Skiff gives to its readers this week a picture of the "Lay-out" of the new T.C.U. This picture is, in part, a dream. The dream is one, however, which will come to pass in the future. A goodly part of it is coming to pass now. . . .

The reason for adopting the ground plans for so many buildings at present is that there may be perfect harmony in the arrangement. The grounds should be properly laid out and every building which is expected to be erected in the future should have its proper place assigned to it.

The sketch includes ten buildings. "So many buildings . . . ," "perfect harmony in the arrangement . . ." "every building which is expected to be erected in . . . its proper place. . . ." Visions can extend just so far.

The "accepted layout" was altered only slightly by the time foundations were laid for the two initial structures, an administration building and a girls' dormitory. Let under one contract to the Texas Building Company, both were to be ready for use at the opening of the fall term that September. Another dormitory, to house men and ministerial couples, was on the drawing board, and it, too, would be completed by the start of the 1911 semester.

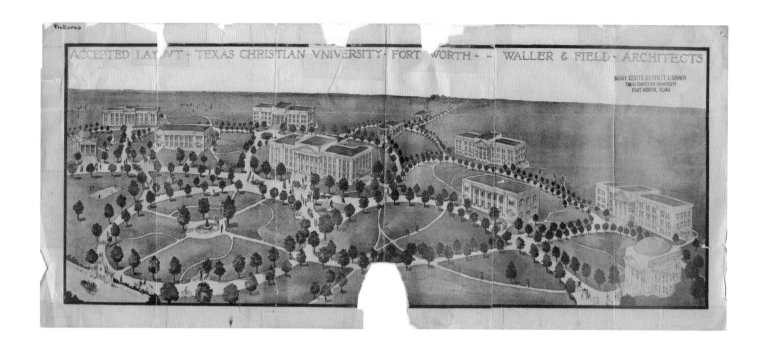

With the car line still a mile and a half away, a cornerstone-laying ceremony was planned for May 9, 1911, to coincide with the twenty-fifth annual assembly of the Texas Christian Missionary Convention, an organization that followed the teachings of Alexander Campbell and his doctrine of nondenominational "Disciples of Christ." It was to be a day given over entirely to university interests and was advertised in the TCU *Skiff* as a "real jubilee day." An invitation was issued to the public, and a call went out for as many as had automobiles or any other vehicles to meet at the end of the Summit Avenue car line to aid in conveying out to the campus and back those celebrants who would take the trolley from town. (In early 1911, the car line probably ended at Eighth Avenue and Weatherbee Street.) With some walking, some motoring, and some riding in buggies and wagons, they made their way across the bare, rough fields toward the two buff-yellow brick structures standing partially finished, solitary in a sea of Johnson grass as far as the eye could see. A crowd of two thousand gathered near the temporary stage erected at the northeast corner of the main building, bedecked for the occasion with purple and white streamers. They stood on the ground amongst the sand heaps and rubble, leaned from windows, and hung from the construction scaffolding to gain a vantage point from which to witness the ceremony

that included a parade of the student body, faculty, and trustees. The band played, the glee club sang, and the students cheered. Speeches were made by representatives of church, community, and college, and finally the cornerstone, with its box of relics inside, was formally laid.

The previous year, Texas Christian University's first in Fort Worth, the school had operated from several leased buildings in temporary quarters downtown. Church and school officials, faculty and students were eager for the move onto their own land and into their own home, at least for the ten years they had promised to stay. The town seemed eager, too, to support its new university, and hurried to complete the laying of wires, pipes, and car tracks out to the grounds.

The ten years pledged were followed by ten more and then many tens more. The city made good its promise of incorporation, and streets were cut, gravelled, paved, named, and renamed. Streetcars came and went. Trees were planted, and Johnson grass and eventually the wildflowers gave way to cultivated lawns and flower beds. Quiet neighborhoods formed on campus peripheries, bringing with them churches and schools. Businesses followed and flourished. The jubilation that had come with birth and new beginnings seasoned and settled.

In time, the new buildings of 1911 became, if they survived, the old buildings of the new millennium. The harmony which Chalmers McPherson deemed essential was continued for long in both placement of new buildings and in the use of the buff brick that would become known as "TCU brick." So well does most of the campus harmonize, that a cursory look does not quickly discern early from late. Upon closer inspection, however, architectural style differs, weathering shows, and subtle seaming appears, where old conjoins new.

If you want to steep yourself in TCU fact and history, a bibliography is provided from which you can read about how the brothers Clark—Addison and Randolph— opened their little school in 1869, in Fort Worth, only a village then on a limestone bluff above the Trinity. You can read about the removal of their Male and Female Seminary from the rough Hell's Half Acre section of the Fort Worth of the 1870s to the peaceful little community of Thorp Spring that lay some fifty miles to the southwest. You can read about how the school was founded there in 1873 and chartered in 1874 as Add-Ran Male and Female College, and how, in 1889, the college was presented to the Christian Churches of Texas, who accepted the challenge of its continuance. In pictures and words you will find the stories of the growing school's move, in 1895, to Waco, a city ninety miles south of Fort Worth, and of its final name change, in 1902, to Texas Christian University; how the main building, and thus the main school, burned there in 1910, precipitating the events—the offers, counselings, discussions, and contracts—that led to its final move, back to Fort Worth. You will find accounts of how the first buildings were begun on this Texas prairie hill in 1911, and how one thing led to another until the small college-become-university now occupies 302 acres of land (that includes 125 major buildings comprising 5.1 million square feet), has a faculty and support staff of over 2,000 with a student body of about 12,000, and with an endowment in excess of $2.3 billion and an annual operating budget of over $500 million.

If you want a deeper sense of place and value, however, take this campus walk with us—perhaps on an early fall morning, when the air is crisp and the light is soft, and before the distraction of people and cars has taken over. Observe the commemorative plaques and statues, the tranquil splendor of nature that permeates campus, the names on the buildings, and consider who Colby Hall, Winton and Scott, Sadler and Waits and Moudy and Tucker, Brite, Meyer, Carter, Neeley, and so many more were and are, and what they did to be so honored. Enter the restored Mary Couts Burnett Library to see the harmony of old blending with new and think about how many have passed there in search of the knowledge an academic library houses. Sit in the elegant simplicity of Robert Carr Chapel and listen to its carillon, as on the hour it plays the alma mater before tolling the time. Sit in the stands of Amon Carter Stadium or Schollmaier Arena. Imagine being there when the home team wins, and feel the pride of the Horned Frog Nation. Attend a concert in the Van Cliburn Concert Hall and soak in the sweet magnificence of the fine arts and their ability to enrich our lives. Venture into a laboratory in Sid Richardson or Winton-Scott and imagine the hundreds of current physicians and dentists whose grounding in the sciences was nurtured here. Climb to the top level of the east stadium stand and look out over the campus, picking out the remaining original buildings and seeing just how far we've come. Walk through Reed Hall and sense the presence of the early administrators, faculty, and students of TCU, for this building was long the active heart of the campus, and a portion of the second floor was for years the Faculty Center, and before that the balcony of an auditorium below, an auditorium that served as chapel, concert hall, meeting place, and the stage for graduation exercises until 1949. For those of us who know, this room fairly rings with the eloquent tones of then-President E. M. "Prexy" Waits, quoting poetry as he was wont to do while conducting chapel services, and it fairly rings with the strains of the alma mater sung by the congregation gathered for baccalaureate. Listen—

Hail, all hail, TCU
Mem'ries sweet, comrades true.
Light of faith, follow through.
Praise to thee, TCU

Enjoy your walk around this very special place we call Texas Christian University.

—Joan Swaim and Phil Hartman

"Frog Bites": Interesting Factoids Scattered throughout the Book

1. Two vestiges of the original Thorp Spring campus now reside on the Fort Worth campus. They are: the thirteen-thousand-pound cornerstone of the Thorp Spring Main building, which was moved in summer of 1992 to its current location at the base of the Clark Brothers statue by the library, and the ceremonial TCU mace, which was fashioned from a red oak beam rescued from the Thorp Spring Main building (see pp. 16 and 169).

2. Add-Ran Male and Female College (TCU's original name) was not named in honor of founders Addison and Randolph, but of Add-Ran, Addison's first born who died and was buried in Fort Worth (see p.13).

3. But for a fire TCU would likely be located in Waco (say it ain't so, SuperFrog!). (See p. 20 for a description of the catastrophic fire that destroyed the Main building and precipitated TCU's move to Fort Worth.)

4. "I'll take a glass of milk, please, Mrs. Dairy Cow." Prior to the 1930s, a dairy farm occupied a portion of what is now the Campus Commons (see p. 30).

5. TCU's campus was land inhabited for many years by the Wichita and Affiliated Tribes (see p. 60).

6. Jarvis Hall and Reed Hall, both built in 1911, are TCU's oldest buildings (see pp. 55 and 65).

7. Memorial plaza has a copse of trees with a gap honoring those who paid the ultimate sacrifice for our country (see p. 65).

8. Until 1960, Reed Hall was simply known as the Administration Building and was once home to virtually every TCU academic program (see p. 65).

9. Reed Hall was once subjected to a plane crash, in 1918, from a young pilot attempting to impress his girlfriend (see p. 69).

10. For almost fifty years the original Clark Hall, named for TCU's founders, sat on the site now occupied by Sadler Hall (see p. 70).

11. Five buildings (Colby, Clark, Waits, Moudy, Sadler, and Tucker) bear the names of former TCU leaders (see pp. 70, 78, 141, 199, 220, and 222).
12. Tennis courts once stood on the lawn between University Drive and Clark Residence Hall (see p. 77).
13. Prior to 1952, all science departments were located in the dark, dank basements of Clark Hall, then an academic building (see p. 78).
14. Dutch Meyer schemed his high-flying offenses that yielded national championships in the then "little gym," now the Erma Lowe Hall occupied by the School for Classical and Contemporary Dance (see p. 82).
15. One hundred percent of TCU's residence halls have either been built in the last fifteen years or have been completely renovated during this time.
16. Seventy-three—that's the number of wells that comprise the geothermal system providing climate control to the Mary Wright Admission Center (see p. 116).
17. Until 1923, University Drive was a dirt-and-gravel extension of Forest Park Blvd., down the middle of which came a streetcar from Fort Worth, three miles to the north. Only prairie was to the south and west of campus (see p. 121).
18. The fire that brought TCU to Fort Worth from Waco was not the only campus conflagration of note . . . in 2006 a fire completely destroyed TCU's bookstore (see p. 123).
19. Perhaps symbolically fitting, given TCU's association with Brite Divinity School, Human Resources and the Opera Program are housed in a former church and funeral home, respectively (see pp. 127 and 206).
20. Winton-Scott Hall is the only building on campus named for TCU faculty (see p. 134).
21. While dwarfed by the parking garages and athletic facilities, Sid Richardson is TCU's largest academic building . . . and it's the easiest to get lost in! (see p. 139)
22. Rees-Jones Hall is TCU's first truly interdisciplinary academic building, not "belonging" to any college or school but to all (see p. 162).
23. In 1923, Mary Couts Burnett made a $3 million bequest (over $50 million in 2022 dollars) to TCU, seemingly "out of the blue," and by far the largest made at that time (see p. 170).
24. Almost 50 percent of TCU's print collection resides about two miles south of campus, making room for more student study space in the library (see p. 180).

25. In 1953 the pink-bricked buildings of Robert Carr Chapel, Beasley Hall, and the Moore Building created some controversy owing to their departure from the TCU buff brick (see p. 181). And then of course there's Moudy's architectural departure from the TCU norm (see p. 199).

26. Standing at 163 feet, 3 inches above the ground, the lighting structures make Amon G. Carter stadium the tallest structure on campus, although Robert Carr Chapel's 137-foot-tall spire is farther from the earth's center by virtue of TCU's gentle downslope between the two buildings. However, both are dwarfed by the 323-foot-tall tower broadcasting KTCU (The Choice) (see pp. 25, 183, and 249).

27. TCU has two Clark Halls (both residence halls) and two Harrison Buildings. Both pairs are named for different individuals (pp. 78, 116, and 188).

28. TCU's student newspaper (the *Skiff*) led an itinerate existence, being housed at various times in a student's dorm room, the Administration Building (now Reed Hall), the little gym (now Erma Lowe Hall), the Bailey Building, Goode Hall (now the site of Clark Hall), Dan Rogers Hall, and finally the Moudy Building (see p. 205).

29. The TCU sundial was designed expressly for the university's exact latitude and longitude and stands on one of few places on the central campus that affords unfettered exposure to sunlight (see p. 217).

30. Colby Hall is named for longtime Dean Colby D. Hall. The use of his first name avoids the awkward moniker of Hall Hall (see p. 222).

31. Until 1930, TCU's home football games were played in Clark field, now the site of the eastern portion of Mary Couts Burnett Library and Rees-Jones Hall (see p. 240).

32. 791,520—that's the number of bricks that went into the 2010 makeover of Amon G. Carter Stadium (see p. 248).

33. TCU once played its home basketball games in the "little gym," now Erma Lowe Hall (see p. 82).

34. Until 1961, Worth Hills was a municipal golf course, opening in 1923 as Fort Worth's first public golf course (see p. 273).

35. Some of us old folks remember when the individual rooms in residence halls lacked telephones because they were thought to be an extravagance. Completing a circle of sorts, the residence halls in Worth Hills lack landlines because, of course, now nearly everyone has a cell phone (see p. 280).

36. Checking in at 391,441 square feet, the Worth Hills parking garage is TCU's largest structure using square footage as a metric (see p. 300).
37. One—that's the number of trees on campus when the decision was made to relocate TCU to Fort Worth (see p. 307).
38. Ca. 3,200—that's the number of trees currently on campus; over forty species in all (see p. 308).
39. The TCU buff brick, now supplied by Fort Worth-based Acme Brick, was likely chosen not out of the desire for aesthetics but because it wouldn't burn and was the least expensive option (see p. 310).
40. The red slate roofs so common on campus were mandated by the unavailability of asphalt-based shingles owing to petroleum rationing during and shortly after World War II (see p. 310).
41. There would likely be no extant TCU were it not for the efforts of T. E. Shirley, for whom Sherley Residence Hall is named. For it was Shirley who as chair of TCU's Board of Trustees refused to honor a motion to discontinue the institution owing to its indebtedness (see p. 311).
42. TCU's Anne Burnett Marion School of Medicine, established in 2015, is actually TCU's second medical school. The first ceased operations in 1917 (see p. 312).
43. The two parking garages increased TCU's building footprint by 750,270 square feet—that's more than was added between 1914 and 1995 (see p. 316).

CHAPTER 1

In the Beginning . . . Thorp Spring (1873–1895)

Singer and songwriter Carole King once famously asked, "So far away, doesn't anybody stay in one place anymore?" Well, that might also apply to TCU and its forebearers, or at least during the institution's first forty years or so. Dr. Colby Hall, who wrote the definitive story of TCU's first seventy-five years, posits an excellent case can be made that Add-Ran University (TCU's forebearer) was birthed in Fort Worth in 1869. However, our story begins in September 1873 in Thorp Spring, eponymously named for "old Man Thorp," who held certificates for nearly all the land in that region. Thorp was convinced a school would attract people to the area, and so he successfully encouraged brothers Addison and Randolph Clark to move their school away from the temptations inherent to wild and wooly Fort Worth. The school was chartered in April 1874 as Add-Ran Male and Female College. It was not named in honor of founders Addison and Randolph, but of Add-Ran, Addison's first born, who died and was buried in Fort Worth. An initial thirteen students were soon joined by 104 late enrollees. Classes were conducted in a preexisting building for the first four years, followed by a move into the "Main," with its first section erected in 1877. The original building stood until well into the twentieth century, employed as a storage facility after Add-Ran's move to Waco. The Main was enlarged several times, including a substantial redo necessitated by a fire. As Colby Hall stated, "The completed structure was indeed a magnificent one for the time." Students lived with teachers or

OPPOSITE
The original building from the 1870s. Courtesy of Mary Couts Burnett Library.

ADD-RAN DORMITORY

THORP SPRING

HERE J. A. CLARK
AND HIS TWO SONS,
ADDISON AND RANDOLPH
BEGAN A PRIVATE SCHOOL

CHARTERED IN 1873 UNDER THE
NAME OF ADD-RAN CHRISTIAN
COLLEGE • REMOVED TO WACO ON
DECEMBER 25, 1895 • REESTABLISHED
AT FORT WORTH IN 1909 AS TEXAS
CHRISTIAN UNIVERSITY

Erected by the State of Texas
1936

an approved family during the institution's first few years. Beginning in 1883, female students were required to board in the dorm, with male students following a few years later.

While little remains of the original Main, which was demolished in 1946, two vestiges from Thorp Spring may be found on TCU's present campus. The first is the thirteen thousand-pound cornerstone of the Main, which was moved in the summer of 1992 to the base of the Clark Brothers statue of Addison and Randolph Clark (discussed in Chapter 7), which is situated between the Mary Couts Burnett Library and Winton-Scott Hall. The second is the ceremonial TCU mace, which is carried into commencements by the chief marshal. It was fashioned by woodworker Robert Kramer in 1999 from a red oak beam rescued from the Thorp Spring Main.

Add Ran-Jarvis.

ABOVE
Students and faculty in front of the Main Building at Thorp Spring, c. 1878. Courtesy of Mary Couts Burnett Library.

LEFT
The Main Building at Thorp Spring after reconstruction following a fire in the spring of 1905. Courtesy of Mary Couts Burnett Library.

T. C. U. AT WACO

CHAPTER 2

A Brief Stop—and a Catastrophic Fire— in Waco (1895–1910)

T horp Spring provided a bucolic setting for Add-Ran's early years, but financial difficulties precipitated relocation to just north of Waco, on fifteen acres formerly occupied by the Waco Female College, a Methodist school founded in 1857. A single large building had been erected on the grounds, which was assumed by the First National Bank and then sold to the trustees of Add-Ran. The first payment was facilitated by the sale of Addison and Randolph Clark's homes as well as that of 320 acres of Collin County land belonging to Randolph's wife. The Thorp Spring-to-Waco move occurred Christmas Day, 1895.

As described by Colby Hall, the building, like its predecessor in Thorp Spring, became known as the Main, and "was, indeed, a magnificent structure, with ample rooms for Dining, Library, Chapel, Gymnasium and Parlors, as well as recitation and living rooms, all in one large building." It was constructed of solid brick, with the lower walls some eighteen to twenty-four inches thick, and was among the largest college or university buildings in the southwest. It was reported that Baylor University, the state's oldest institution of higher learning, had nothing to rival the Main. Brick walls stood between all rooms but, unfortunately, the floors, stairways, and roof were wooden. The Main underwent several rounds of remodeling, including the addition of a fourth floor. In its final form the first floor was dedicated to classroom space

OPPOSITE
The Waco campus with the Girls' Home, Townsend Memorial Hall, and the Main Building pictured from left to right, c. 1903. Courtesy of Mary Couts Burnett Library.

for the business college, the library of roughly six thousand volumes, two modern laboratories, and the business office. Classrooms, a chapel, and faculty offices encompassed the second floor. The two upper floors were given over to housing for male students in addition to "well-appointed parlors" where various literary societies met.

The Main was joined by three buildings through the years. They were a "Girls' Home" (a dormitory for female students), Townsend Memorial Hall (which provided additional classroom space), and a service building that provided central heating to the campus. Concrete sidewalks connected the buildings.

Renamed Texas Christian University at the start of the 1902–1903 academic year, the institution's trajectory was seismically altered by a conflagration that swept through the Main on March 22, 1910. It originated in the southwest corner of the building, with flames as high as two hundred feet, and the losses included most of the library holdings, a pipe organ, and nine upright pianos. Fortunately, no loss of life was incurred, and faculty, staff, and students were able to remove at least a fraction of their personal possessions in addition to some textbooks and other university property. Classes resumed in short order for the 367 students, utilizing various makeshift locations that included the homes of some faculty.

TCU survived the fire, but as we already know, this set into motion events that returned the institution to the very city—Fort Worth—where Addison and Randolph Clark began teaching over forty years previously. After the fire, a bidding war of sorts ensued between Fort Worth and Waco. Waco, imagining themselves as the "Athens of Texas," made an offer, but it did not come close to matching Fort Worth's, which was $200,000 plus fifty acres of land several miles from town. The city also provided assurance of connections to utilities and extension of a streetcar line to campus. TCU accepted the offer and leased a series of two-story buildings on the corner of Weatherford and Commerce Streets for its first year in Fort Worth, before moving to its current campus.

ABOVE

Aftermath of the March 22, 1910, fire that destroyed the Main and changed TCU's destiny. Courtesy of Mary Couts Burnett Library.

OPPOSITE

Aerial view of the west campus with the BLUU in the foreground and downtown Fort Worth in the background. Photograph by James Anger. Courtesy of TCU Marketing and Communication.

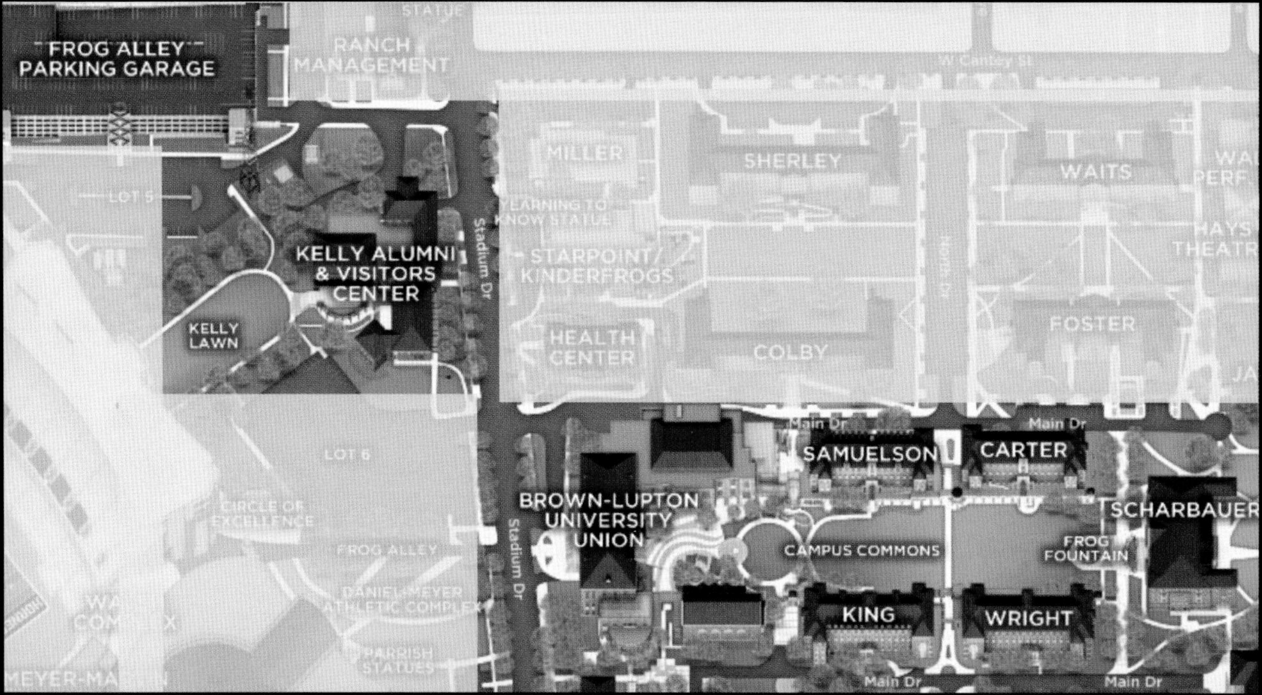
FROG ALLEY PARKING GARAGE
STATUE
RANCH MANAGEMENT
W Cantey St
MILLER
SHERLEY
WAITS
LOT 5
YEARNING TO KNOW STATUE
STARPOINT/ KINDERFROGS
KELLY ALUMNI & VISITORS CENTER
Stadium Dr
KELLY LAWN
HEALTH CENTER
COLBY
FOSTER
Main Dr
Main Dr
SAMUELSON
CARTER
LOT 6
BROWN-LUPTON UNIVERSITY UNION
Stadium Dr
SCHARBAUER
CIRCLE OF EXCELLENCE
CAMPUS COMMONS
FROG FOUNTAIN
FROG ALLEY
DANIEL-MEYER ATHLETIC COMPLEX
KING
WRIGHT
PARRISH STATUES
Main Dr
Main Dr

CHAPTER 3

The Kelly Center and the Campus Commons

Dee J. Kelly Alumni and Visitors Center

Dedicated and opened in November 1996, the Dee J. Kelly Alumni and Visitors Center provides the starting point for our tour. You may elect to park in the close-by Frog Alley parking garage, located immediately to the northeast of Amon G. Carter Stadium. Free visitor parking is available. As you leave the garage to the east you'll notice a 323-foot-tall tower to your right, which provides the signal to TCU's student-run FM radio station KTCU (The Choice). Erected in 1979, it is the tallest point on campus. From there it's a short walk south down Stadium Drive to the Dee J. Kelly Alumni and Visitors Center, which offers a central gathering place for campus visitors and the close-to one hundred thousand TCU alumni worldwide. The Kelly Center is a busy place indeed, hosting over one thousand meetings annually. When opened in 1996, the single-story building checked in at twenty-two thousand square feet and represented a welcome upgrade relative to the former home of Alumni Affairs (now Alumni Relations), a modest house on Princeton Street. In addition to space constraints, the previous location presented significant parking challenges to visitors. The Kelly Center's design was melded from four of the top alumni centers in the country, creating a nice flow. Complete with a receptionist's desk, the spacious

OPPOSITE
Map showing the campus structures discussed in this chapter.

lobby provided easy access to the various rooms in the building, including offices for the Frog Club and the Alumni Association. Other rooms of note included the Scharbauer Library (named for Kerry Wallace Scharbauer and Trustee Emeritus and former Board Chair Clarence Scharbauer), the Tucker-Scully Dining Room (named in honor of the Scully and Tucker families by Jean and Emeritus Chancellor Bill Tucker), the Parrish Conference Room (named for Sue and Bill Parrish), the Monroe Conference Room (named for Betty and J. A. J. Monroe), the Moncrief Conference Suites (named in honor of W. A. "Monty" Moncrief), the Ray Gallery (named for Betty and Trustee Emeritus Jerry Ray), and the Justin Board Room (named for Jane and trustee John Justin Jr.), meeting place for TCU's Board of Trustees. Larger gatherings are enabled by the dividable Cox Banquet Hall (named for John L. and Maurine Cox) that accommodates three hundred people for plated dinners, more for other types of events. Among other things, the Kelly Center provides prime views of Amon G. Carter Stadium, including from the John & Jean Roach Terrace (named for Trustee Emeritus John Roach and his wife Jean), a terraced area to the building's rear that is highlighted by the Blackmon/Mooring Fountain.

The $6.2 million center was funded by gifts and pledges from thirty-five donors. The largest of these were a pair of $1.75 million commitments from the Burnett Foundation and the Sid W. Richardson Foundation, both of whom requested the alumni center bear the name of Dee J. Kelly. Additional naming gifts came from John L. and Marine Cox, John '41 and Jane '43 Chilton Justin, the William A. and Elizabeth B. Moncrief Foundation, and Clarence '73 and Kerry '73 Wallace Scharbauer. In addition, over seventeen thousand contributions of $100 were made toward a building maintenance fund. These individuals are recognized by the engraved bricks on the John and Jean Roach Terrace. The Kelly Center represented one of the largest advancement efforts of TCU's five-year, $100 million "Next Frontier Campaign."

A founding partner of the Kelly, Hart & Hallman Law Firm, Dee Kelly '50 (1929–2015) was arguably Fort Worth's most influential attorney during the lion's share of his career. His loyalty to TCU ran deep, as he served on the Board of Trustees from 1971 to 2007. He also served as co-chair of the Next Frontier Campaign mentioned above. At the time of his death, Chancellor Victor Boschini stated: "He was an amazing driving force behind many improvements we see today on our campus." And at the time of the center's dedication, then Chancellor Bill Tucker said: "Dee Kelly has been a leading Trustee and unfailing supporter of the University for years. What better way to honor a distinguished alumnus who has stood behind and beside his alma mater as Dee has."

Designed by Hahnfeld Hoffer Stanford, the Kelly Center was doubled in size in 2018. The $12.5 million project was kickstarted by a $4 million gift from the Dee J. Kelly Foundation and the Kelly family, including Trustee Dee Kelly, Jr., Cindy Barnes, and Craig Kelly. Two other lead gifts were received from The Burnett Foundation and Anita and J. Kelly Cox. There were an additional one hundred gifts to the project. In addition to facelifts to the extant offices, conference rooms, and the Justin Boardroom, a second story was added, providing much-needed offices and storage space for Alumni Relations. The second-story Alumni Relations Terrace now offers a spectacular view of campus. The addition of a catering kitchen provides much-needed flexibility, given the many events held in the Kelly Center. The whole building has a high "wow" factor, and that is certainly apparent as you enter the updated Kritser Lobby and Atrium. Its towering display cases house various TCU-related memorabilia, including treasured pieces from the building's namesake. From the rotunda above to the honed black granite tile flooring below, this atrium sets the stage for visitors and staff alike.

You can exit the Kelly Center through the east-facing front door where you entered and make your way southward down Stadium Drive to the street crossing in front of the Brown-Lupton University Union (BLUU).

ABOVE
Dee J. Kelly at the Kelly Center, 2013.
Photograph by Amy Peterson. Courtesy of
TCU Marketing and Communication.

RIGHT

Dee J. Kelly Alumni and Visitors Center, 2018. Photograph by Leo Wesson for the Linbeck Group, LLC. Courtesy of TCU Marketing and Communication.

The Campus Commons

Certainly no portion of TCU's main campus has undergone a greater twenty-year metamorphosis than has the acreage now collectively known as the Campus Commons. With a gentle ascent in elevation from west to east, the Commons has Scharbauer Hall and Frog Fountain perched on its easternmost apex. The central green space, often populated by students engaged in study or leisurely activities, is flanked by four residence halls (Kellye Wright Samuelson and Amon G. Carter to the north; Teresa and Luther King and Mary and Robert J. Wright to the south), and culminates to the west in the Brown-Lupton University Union, commonly referred to as "the BLUU" (pronounced like the color). Among other things, the Campus Commons has become the site of campus gatherings such as concerts, commencement receptions, and the annual Christmas tree lighting (which for years took place in front of Sadler Hall). While at the cost of some stately live oaks, all of this replaces a rather nondescript parking lot and the old student union, described below, that conjoined Reed Hall. In TCU's early days in Fort Worth, this space was populated by maintenance shacks and sheds with dirt-road access through a wild and weedy field. A dairy once occupied a portion of this space; its cows supplied milk to the school's boarding facility. The dairy ceased operation before 1930; the wooden maintenance buildings were removed by the late '40s. How far we've come since then!

Brown-Lupton University Union (BLUU)

Let's begin at the BLUU. At a cost of $49.3 million, the three-story, 145,700-square-foot Brown-Lupton University Union was dedicated September 2, 2008. The union's striking front face is highlighted by the five-story King Tower, which has the capacity for illumination in five colors, including purple of course! Named for Roberta and Trustee Roger King '63, the clock tower is perched above an impressive two-story arch that beckons visitors into the Rose Entry Plaza and Courtyard, named in honor of donors Lisa and Emeritus Trustee Matt Rose. This grand arch serves as your

ABOVE
East façade of the BLUU, 2019. Photograph by Jeffrey McWhorter. Courtesy of TCU Marketing and Communication.

entrance into the BLUU itself or, through it, to the massive green space of the Campus Commons. It is but one of many features that renders the BLUU so visually impressive. The University Union was designed on the premise that students desire quality, convenience, and choices . . . and all abound in the BLUU. For example, there are 311 inside doors and 13 doors leading to the outside. Now that's convenience for you. How about food and drink you ask? Well, you can stop in Union Grounds, a coffee shop on the ground floor to your left as you enter the building. In addition to coffee and other beverages, you can grab a made-to-order sandwich. Replacing the Corner Store that originally occupied this spot, Union Grounds was renovated in 2013 to provide more seating. Not your cup of tea (or coffee) you say? Then you can venture onward to the ever-popular Chick-fil-A, which in 2014 replaced "1873 Sports Grill and Cafe," the short-order restaurant present when the BLUU opened. Want more variety? Then it's up one floor to the all-you-can-eat, six hundred-seat Market Square with its seven food stations (including a salad bar, separate area for vegan and vegetarians, pizza, and meat-carving stations). Market Square accepts cash, but students utilize various meal plans.

But the BLUU is about much more than convenience and sustenance. There are lounges, meeting rooms of various sizes, the campus post office, and a spirit shop (which you passed as you entered the building). The third floor is given over to the Chancellor's Dining Room and the Chambers, the meeting place for the Student Government Association. A 450-seat, dividable ballroom is also situated on the third floor on the building's north side. On the south side, the ground and second floors are occupied by Leadership and Student Development and include an entire wing dedicated to organizations. These range from special interest and religious groups to fraternities and sororities. The location serves to keep the groups' activities centered on campus. Situated on the southeast corner is the Brachman Auditorium, named in honor of Trustee Solomon Brachman, his wife Etta, and their family. The auditorium has flexible seating, ranging from 352-seat theatre style to rounds for more intimate gatherings. A well-appointed foyer runs the length of the auditorium and provides both its entrance as well as the perfect venue for pre- and post-event receptions. It is named in honor of Christina '83 and Mark Johnson, whose service on the board of trustees includes the chairmanship. For the musically inclined there is an electronic keyboard at the east end of the foyer, inviting you to tickle its ivories. It is a modern complement to the grand piano that sits outside the foyer to the third-floor ballroom on the BLUU's north side. Immediately outside is the Johnson Amphitheatre, named in honor of Christina '83 and Mark Johnson, whose service on the board of trustees includes the chairmanship. Finally, you may wish to spend some time on the ground floor in the southeast corner at the Schmidt Heritage Center, named in memory of Elizabeth L. and James B. Schmidt Jr. and made possible by a gift from Trustee Ken Huffman '66. The center's panels will guide you through TCU's history, with trinkets and historical items recounting TCU's past from both humorous and poignant perspectives.

ABOVE
Portrait of Tom J. "Coca-Cola" Brown located in the BLUU. Photograph by James Anger. Courtesy of TCU Marketing and Communication.

ABOVE
Portrait of Charles Lupton located in the BLUU. Photograph by James Anger. Courtesy of TCU Marketing and Communication.

The names Brown and Lupton are both worthy of mention. Tom J. "Coca-Cola" Brown was a member of the TCU Board of Trustees from 1940 to 1950 and also vice president of the Fort Worth Coca-Cola Bottling Company. His great interest in TCU student life, especially that of the athlete, was made manifest in the construction of several additional buildings that bear his name, including a residential community and the student health center, both later stops on our tour. In 1941, Brown made a pledge of $100,000, the largest commitment by any one individual to the building campaign initiated with the Sadler administration. Following World War II, he pledged another $300,000. Then, in partnership with his friend, Charles A. Lupton, he established the T. J. Brown & C. A. Lupton Foundation. A daughter of C. A. Lupton, Gloria Lupton Tennison, served on the TCU Board of Trustees until the time of her death in 1991. Portraits of Tom Brown and Charles Lupton are located on the third floor of the BLUU.

As you exit the BLUU to the east, you will happen upon a bench replete with a bronzed statue of TCU's mascot SuperFrog, who is flashing the famous frog hand sign as he greets passersby. Cast in 2012 by San Antonio artist Doug Roper, the bench was funded by the Student Government Association. Similar, but of course superior to the University of Texas's "Hook 'em Horns" and Baylor University's "bear claw," TCU's signature hand gesture is reputed to have arisen in 1980 on the way to a cheer camp in Tennessee. Interestingly enough, the first such hand sign in the old Southwest Conference, "Gig 'em, Aggies," arose before the 1930 TCU/Texas A&M football to signify frog hunting.

As you gaze across the Campus Commons, you'll no doubt note the graceful Fortson Promenade (named for Emeritus Trustee Kay and Ben Fortson '57) leading eastward. An elevated view reveals the pavers are fashioned to form the image of a horned frog. Collectively, the Fortson Promenade complements perfectly the Allman Amphitheatre (named for Trustee Allie Beth McMurtry Allman '62) and a water feature named Gayle's Pond (honoring Emeritus Trustee Roger Ramsey's wife Gayle).

ABOVE
The SuperFrog statue outside the BLUU with SuperFrog preparing to celebrate commencement, 2016. Photograph by Amy Peterson. Courtesy of TCU Marketing and Communication.

Brown-Lupton Student Center ("the Main")

The BLUU replaced the Brown-Lupton Student Center, which was conjoined to Reed Hall. This on-campus place for students to congregate socially came late to TCU. In the early Fort Worth years when the unbroken land still stretched out into fields and valleys surrounding the TCU hill, daylong picnics and excursions to the Trinity River north and west of the campus were on every weekend agenda. Large groups would hike several miles to and from favorite sites. Some students learned to swim in the Trinity back before there was a gym and a swimming pool. After social mores relaxed in the early '30s to allow dating and dancing, the students still found no adequate and convenient space to exercise their recently granted privileges. But TCU students, as students everywhere will, found places for social interaction. One of the most popular sites during the '30s and '40s was the drugstore at the corner of Bowie and University: its soda fountain was always bustling with the student population from across the street.

The first designated "student lounge" area on the campus was in the basement of the old Administration Building (now Reed Hall). Heralded in TCU's student newspaper the *Skiff* as "a dream come true," this lounge was opened and "presented" to the student body in April 1948. The lounge had a seating capacity of sixty-five, a soda fountain that cost $1,600, a cigarette machine that would "save many a long trip to the drugstore," and a coin-operated jukebox for dancing. It was to operate until 10:30 p.m., and a statement attributed to then President Sadler made it clear that "privileges of the lounge will be shared by both sexes."

Provision of more space was slow in coming, however, and student unrest over the matter grew. Finally, in 1952, Dr. Sadler announced that a "friend" of the university had significantly increased the possibility of securing funding for a new structure to accommodate all student activities. The friend was Glen Woodson who, as manager of the T. J. Brown and C. A. Lupton Foundation, brought the need to the attention of his directors. The result was the Brown-Lupton Student Center. Completed in 1955, the building underwent significant renovation and expansion in 1967 and 1991, again with generous funding from the Brown-Lupton Foundation. The student center was the design of Preston Geren and bears the architectural stamp of the mid-century building era at TCU. Buff brick, cast stone, and polished granite recall

the Winton-Scott Hall and foreshadowed the similar styling of the Rickel Building erected some twenty years later.

Known colloquially as the Main, the student center housed the main kitchen and cafeteria, several smaller food service areas, the university bookstore, offices and meeting rooms for the Student House of Representatives, a large common study-lounge area, study rooms, the Chancellor's Dining Room, and a ballroom with a seating capacity of seven-hundred-plus. In addition, a number of other rooms were available for university-related functions. The largest of these, the Woodson Room, was named in honor of TCU Trustee Glen Woodson.

Perhaps to the nutritional historian, the food options through the Main's years provide a glimpse into the culinary evolution of the college student's palate. Namely, the simple one-choice lunch cafeteria offering of the Main's first decades morphed into a smorgasbord in later years. In addition to this diversification in the cafeteria itself, ancillary venues came on board that provided more variety, including an à la carte soup-and-sandwich in the basement (named the Pit), to-go Frog Bytes, the all-you-can-eat (or should that be "all-you-could-have-eaten"?) salad bar named Eden's Green (which was actually located in conjoined Reed Hall), a Pizza Hut (added in 1989 but closed several years later), and a sushi bar, opened in 2006, which ironically enough was the same year the board of trustees voted to demolish rather than subject the Main to yet another round of renovations. And the walls came tumbling down in 2008, with functions nicely subsumed into the BLUU.

Residence Halls on the Campus Commons: (Samuelson, Carter, King, Wright)

After sitting a spell, and maybe even taking a selfie with SuperFrog, you can enjoy a walk up the open area of the Campus Commons on either its grassy center section or the covered walkways that demarcate Kellye Wright Samuelson and Amon G. Carter Residence Halls to the north or Teresa and Luther King and Mary and Robert J. Wright Residence Halls to the south. Samuelson and Carter Halls first welcomed students in the fall of 2007, while King and Wright Halls came on line the following semester. Samuelson, closest to the BLUU, was also home to TCU's Counseling

ABOVE
King Residence Hall on the
Campus Commons, 2016.
Photograph by Glen Ellman.
Courtesy of Glen Ellman.

and Mental Health Center (now named Substance Use and Recovery Services) until their move to Jarvis Hall. At approximately fifty thousand square feet each, King and Wright are home to approximately 314 students total. Samuelson and Carter accommodate the same number. All are coed and were built for sophomores. In the past few years TCU's enrollment growth has turned Samuelson and Carter Halls into first-year student housing. Each pair of residence halls has community space between them. On the north side of the Campus Commons, the Carter Technology Center has a bank of computers and printers for students, and it serves as a common meeting place for student programs. On the south side, the Wright Media Center features a large-screen TV and pool table. Carter Hall also has a large community space, open 24-7 to all residential and nonresidential students, that formerly served as an IT tech center. Collectively these residence halls represent a concerted effort, first articulated in 2003, to render TCU an even more residential institution, in particular one with a significantly

ABOVE

Frog Fountain with Scharbauer Hall and Wright
Residence Hall in the background, 2017. Photograph
by Jeffrey McWhorter. Courtesy of TCU Marketing
and Communication.

higher proportion of students of upper-class standing living on campus. The construction was completed by Austin Commercial, and KSQ Architects provided the four buildings' designs.

All four residence halls contain a mixture of floor plans, ranging from one-bedroom to four-bedroom suites, all with a shared living room and in-suite bathroom. Living rooms are a feature of some of the doubles as well as all of the triples and quads. And of course all contain a micro-fridge. A free laundry room, a baking kitchen, study lounges, and a free print station also grace each. Students have increasingly found that these amenities, plus proximity to classes and the BLUU, render on-campus housing exceedingly attractive.

And now a bit about the individuals for whom these four residence halls were named. Mary and Robert J. Wright Hall honors Trustee (1993–2013) Robert "Bob" Wright '50 and his wife Mary. Mrs. Wright was the founder and president of Medical Space Design, Inc., a Dallas interior design firm specializing in hospitals, churches, banks, and offices. She subsequently created a separate division, MSD Air, transferring the firm's skills to the refurbishment of jet aircraft. She began her career as a fashion model in New York and Miami, appearing on the covers of national magazines such as Glamour, Vogue, and Charm. Her portrait is proudly displayed in the Joan Rogers Conference Room in the Mary Wright Admissions Center, a later stop on our tour. Mr. Wright founded Medical City Dallas and was influential in shaping national health care and public policies in his capacity as president of Medical Group Management Association. The Wrights received the Horizon Award from TCU in 1996, and Mr. Wright was named Valuable Alumnus the same year. Kellye Wright Samuelson Hall honors the memory of the Wrights' late daughter. A later stop on our tour will be Tom Brown/Pete Wright Residential Complex, named for Mr. Wright's uncle Pete. More on him later.

Teresa and Luther King Hall was named in honor of the 2011 recipients of the Royal Purple Award. A graduate of the University of North Texas, Teresa King is a long-standing civic leader, among other things serving on the executive board of the Fort Worth Symphony, the Van Cliburn Board, and the Princeton University

ABOVE
Portrait of Mary and Robert J. Wright located in Wright Residence Hall. Photograph by James Anger. Courtesy of TCU Marketing and Communication.

Department of Art and Archaeology Advisory Council. Luther King ('62, MBA '66) has served on the boards of numerous privately held companies and philanthropic organizations. He is president and founder of Luther King Capital Management Corporation, a firm with offices in Fort Worth, Dallas, Austin, and San Antonio that provides investment advisory services to high-net-worth individuals and a variety of organizations. He received an honorary doctorate from TCU in 2021, recognizing his service on TCU's Board of Trustees beginning in 1992 and including a six-year stint as board chair. In 2006 the Kings established the Luther and Teresa King Family Foundation. Its mission is to support various worthy causes, which have included establishing a series of endowed scholarships for TCU students as well as construction projects such as the residence hall that bears their name. The Kings' support of academics has been recognized by the naming of the Luther King Capital Management Center for Financial Studies in the Neeley School of Business for Mr. King and the endowment of the Teresa Ann Carter King Dean of the College of Fine Arts in Mrs. King's honor. The legendary Amon G. Carter will be discussed later when we tour another, more public edifice bearing his name.

Frog Fountain

One of TCU's most iconic structures is Frog Fountain, which you'll pass on your way to our next stop. Originally situated in front of the Brown-Lupton Student Center, it was designed by Texas artist Buck Winn in 1969 and was installed by the Fort Worth architectural firm of Joseph R. Pelich Associates. The $69,000 construction of Frog Fountain was supported by a $25,000 gift from Dr. and Mrs. H. Houghton Phillips Sr., of San Antonio. Lotus flowers have widespread historical, cultural, and spiritual significance, including that of symbolizing education. In this case the four lotus flowers represent the passing of knowledge between the four classes—first year through senior—of the student body. Frog Fountain took a one-and-a-half-year hiatus in 2006 and 2007 during the construction of the east end of the Campus Commons. It was relocated slightly to its present position directly in front of Scharbauer Hall. Version 2.0 enjoys wraparound seating, a larger pool, and LED lighting (of course with purple!). As well, the lotus flowers underwent a thorough cleaning and the pumps were upgraded. The reinstallation of Frog Fountain coincided with the March 2008 dedication of the Frog Plaza, upon which it sits. The Plaza, designed and built by Newman, Jackson, Bieberstein, Inc., was made possible by the generosity of the Roach family, including Jean W. Roach '64, John. V. Roach, '61 and '65, Trustee Amy Roach '89, Lori Roach Davis '95, and Craig Davis '95. John Roach was chairman of the board of trustees from 1990 until 2005. His accomplishments will be discussed in the next chapter in conjunction with the Honors College that bears his name. Similarly, Jean Roach's name will come up again when Kinderfrogs is covered. In recent years Frog Fountain and Plaza have become a solemn place the TCU community gathers to reflect on the passing of one of its own, usually a faculty, staff, or member of the student body.

ABOVE
Frog Fountain at dusk with the BLUU
in the background, 2014. Photograph
by Michael Clements. Courtesy of TCU
Marketing and Communication.

Scharbauer Hall

With an April 10, 2010, dedication, the opening of Clarence and Kerry Scharbauer (pronounce skar-burr) Hall went a long way toward satisfying an acute need for space for the AddRan College of Liberal Arts and the Honors College. Some of you will recognize Scharbauer Hall as standing on the site of the Brown-Lupton Student Center, which was demolished in 2008. Named for Clarence Scharbauer III and Kerry Wallace Scharbauer, this four-story structure was built at the cost of $25 million by the Linbeck Group and designed by New York-based Cannon Design in association with Hahnfeld Hoffer Stanford. Both its interior and exterior invoke the sort of Ivy

ABOVE
View of Scharbauer Hall with Frog Fountain in the foreground and the steeple of Robert Carr Chapel in the background, 2019. Photograph by Jeffrey McWhorter. Courtesy of TCU Marketing and Communication.

League feel so appropriate to the domicile of AddRan, the college most central to fulfilling TCU's mission of grounding all students, irrespective of major, in the liberal arts. While the patio adjoining the west entrance certainly supplies a grand overlook to the Campus Commons, the east-entrance foyer sets a truly academic tenor, complete with a statue of *Madonna and Child*, a striking recapitulation of Michelangelo Buonarroti's masterpiece, that greets visitors. And while an elevator and other stairs in the building provide alternative routes to the second floor, the open, east-facing staircase, accented by mahogany-stained railings, provides immediate and regal access to the AddRan College dean's office. The mood is completed by the second-floor life-sized recreation of Donatello's statue *Saint John the Baptist*.

Scharbauer Hall features a sixty-eight-seat debate chamber, which is modeled after Great Britain's House of Commons. A library is also located on the first floor and is stocked with TCU faculty-authored books. The John V. Roach Honors College occupied the south portion of the first floor until its 2023 move to Sadler Hall. With its move, a portion of the first floor was given over to the Office of Sponsored Programs as well as the Graduate Studies Office. (More on the college in the discussion of Milton Daniel Residence Hall.) In addition to the AddRan Dean's Office, the second floor has a series of meeting rooms, classrooms, and a writing lab, as well as serving as home to the Departments of Geography and Political Science. The Departments of Philosophy, Modern Languages, and Spanish and Hispanic Studies occupy the third floor, with the fourth floor given over to the Departments of Economics, Criminal Justice, Sociology and Anthropology.

AddRan holds the distinction of being TCU's oldest college, welcoming every TCU undergraduate student for 150 years and counting. Boasting thirty-eight programs of study, thirteen departments, and teaching eight languages, AddRan plays a central role in TCU's core curriculum. As stated by Dean Sonja S. Watson: "Liberal arts is the front porch of the university. AddRan really is the heart of TCU." AddRan College also included mathematics and the sciences for many years before an academic reorganization in 2000, during which the College of Science & Engineering was created.

Midland born and raised Clarence Scharbauer III '73 served as chairman of TCU's Board of Trustees from 2011 to 2017 after joining the board in 1990. He was a trustee and past president of the Abell-Hanger Foundation and of the Midland College Foundation. TCU honored him in 1998 as its Most Valuable Alumnus. His TCU-related accomplishments include chairing the committee that oversaw the 2010–2012 renovation of Amon G. Carter Stadium, of which the Scharbauers were project founders. The multigenerational support of the Scharbauer family extends to the Midland Memorial Hospital, as evidenced by the 2013 dedication of the seven-story Scharbauer Tower. Kerry Wallace Scharbauer '73 is an active civic leader in Midland. She was recognized in 2018 as the annual CASA West Texas Champion for Children at the Power of One Luncheon and Children's Style Show. At TCU, in addition to the building that bears their name, the Scharbauer family has supported numerous other building projects, academic initiatives, and the athletics program.

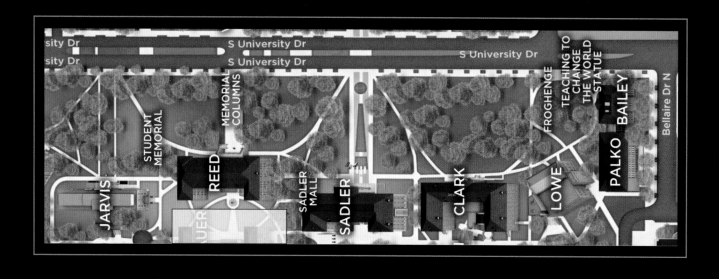

CHAPTER 4

The Original Fort Worth Campus

OPPOSITE
Map showing the campus structures discussed in this chapter.

L eaving the east entrance of Scharbauer, you'll encounter "Ol' Rip," named in a 2012 contest by senior engineering major Kyle Morales, and yet another visual reminder of TCU's mascot. The original horned frog Ol' Rip purportedly survived thirty-one years in a time capsule in the Eastland County Courthouse, a feat reminding those present at the capsule's 1897 opening of Rip Van Winkle. Created by sculptor Joe Spear, the bronze sculpture recapitulates the artist's original "horny toad" in Santa Fe, California. Speaking of horns, Ol' Rip underwent a post-casting "surgery" to have his horns dulled for fear the originally sharp edges and points could constitute a liability issue. Rest assured, Ol' Rip still looks appropriately fierce.

Jarvis Hall

You may enter Jarvis either through its west entrance to the northeast of Scharbauer Hall or skirt around to the front entrance, which faces University Drive. Built in 1911, Jarvis's front exterior has remained largely unchanged over its 120-plus-year history. Waller & Field, leading Fort Worth architects of the early twentieth century, designed the building to serve as a women's residence hall in the Classical Revival style, featuring a flat roof fronted on the east by a central pedimented portico supported by

ABOVE
Jarvis Hall looking north, 1920s.
Courtesy of Mary Couts Burnett
Library.

OPPOSITE
Jarvis Hall with swing in the
foreground, 2022. Photograph
by Phil Hartman.

four massive Ionic columns. The building is faced in the buff-yellow brick trimmed with cast stone that, with a few notable exceptions, distinguishes TCU buildings. In 1955, renovation removed the second- and third-story wooden galleries that were suspended between the central columns and the east wall of the building, and aluminum window frames replaced the earlier wooden ones.

Jarvis is one of the few surviving buildings of the pre-World War I campus. From 1911 to 2008, but for two brief periods, it housed female students. These were from September 1942 to January 1944, when men attending the World War II flight instruction programs being taught on the campus were housed in Jarvis, while the women were moved into the newly built Foster Dormitory. Then, between 1950 and 1953, overcrowding dictated that Jarvis space be again temporarily assigned to male residents.

In its days as a residence hall, you could enter the front door and be greeted by a small parlor. More spacious and elegantly appointed in its youth, it was the school's sole accommodation for social affairs until 1942, when a larger, more modern room

was provided by the new women's residence hall, Foster Hall. In addition to the festive teas and faculty receptions regularly hosted here, the Jarvis parlor provided women residents a place to entertain their friends and beaus—under the watchful eye of the hall matron. It was also used for more somber occasions, such as the funeral service in 1923 for one of Joan Swaim's grandfathers, Frank L. Harris, the university's first steward of a cafeteria-style dining hall. The bulk of the building was given over to eighty rooms designed for double occupancy. A 1955 renovation included the installation of central air-conditioning, new bathroom fixtures throughout, additional storage and study space, as well as modern kitchen facilities.

Jarvis was closed for nine months in December 2007 to allow for a second round of extensive remodeling for the purpose of transforming it from a residence hall to an academic building. When reopened, the third floor was given over to the School of Music, with acoustically enhanced practice rooms and faculty offices. The first and second floors became occupied by Career Services, Religious & Spiritual Life (formerly Campus Ministries), International Student Services, International Resources, Community Involvement, Quality Enhancement, and, until 2023, Graduate Studies and Research. The Counseling and Wellness Center as well as Substance Use and Recovery Services (formerly Alcohol and Drug Education) now occupy the second floor. Well-appointed conference rooms are now situated on each floor. The front entrance remains a distinguishing feature of the building, but Jarvis's west entrance is now more aesthetically pleasing with a retro-style porch recapitulating the building's original look. Its glassed doors lead visitors into an atrium with an exposed staircase. Situated on Jarvis's front wall, a bronze plaque provides additional information about this original campus building. Also in front, hanging from a large live oak, is a swing, which was installed in the 1971–1972 school year . . . it's not coin operated, so feel free to try it out if you're so inclined.

Jarvis is not only old in years, but its name also is venerable. Called simply the "Girls' Home" when built, it was soon named by vote of the Board of Trustees in honor of Major and Mrs. J. J. Jarvis, devoted and lifelong supporters of the university. Major Jarvis was a Fort Worth lawyer, businessman, and entrepreneur, whose interest in education was early evidenced by his advocacy of free public schools, an enterprise that met fierce opposition in the Fort Worth of the late 1870s and 1880s. When the infant forerunner of TCU had been relocated in Thorp Spring, Major and Mrs. Jarvis gave generously of their money and time to secure its mission. When Add-Ran

College was chartered in 1889 as Add-Ran University (today spelled AddRan) under the control of the Christian Churches of Texas, Major Jarvis was elected the first president of the board. He was responsible for expanding facilities provided by the one building at Thorp Spring, and one of the additions, "a four-story stone with seven good rooms," was known as "Jarvis Building."

Ida Van Zandt Jarvis, sister of General K. M. Van Zandt, without whose biography the history of Fort Worth cannot be told, was herself not only active but indeed influential in the affairs of TCU. An account written by Add-Ran alumna Frankie Miller Mason represents her as sympathetic to students, and one delightful story has her with white-flagged "truce" umbrella in hand confronting the president of the college, Addison Clark himself, on behalf of a large portion of the student body whose expulsion seemed imminent, all because of what she considered to be a slight infraction of the rules. The controversy was sparked by the discovery that a young male student had walked a young lady from the Thorp Spring campus to her home in the little town one evening, a strictly forbidden practice in 1882. In his defense, a large number of classmates owned up that they, too, had at one time or another violated that rule as well as others, whereupon Dr. Clark informed them all that they could consider themselves dismissed from the school. Mrs. Jarvis, viewing the punishment as too severe for the crime, made such a case that the president soon saw the absurdity in his rigid discipline, reportedly broke into laughter, and ended in not only pardoning the offenders, but also awarding them special privileges for a brief time.

By her own statement in an interview with Frankie Mason in 1935, it was Ida who authored the 1889 charter making Add-Ran College a university. In an 1895 catalogue, she was listed as supervisor of the Girls' Home at Thorp Spring. In 1915, she was successful in having established the university's School of Home Economics, believing that every young woman should be taught how to sew and to cook. In 1931, she was the first woman elected to the board of trustees and served in that capacity until her death in 1937. Interestingly and appropriately, her place was filled by another woman, Sadie Beckham, who had since 1919 been the Jarvis Hall matron, supervisor of women, and later, dean of women. It was Mrs. Sadie who, as legend has it, each evening at seven, stood on the front steps of Jarvis ringing her cowbell to summon her charges into the fold for the night. In her time, young ladies living on the campus were not permitted out "after hours," nor to "date," nor to dawdle, and certainly not to dance. Major and Mrs. Jarvis's eldest son, Van Zandt Jarvis, would continue his par-

ABOVE (TOP)
Major J. J. Jarvis. Courtesy of Mary Couts Burnett Library.

ABOVE
Ida Van Zandt Jarvis. Courtesy of Mary Couts Burnett Library.

ents' support of the university, serving on the board of trustees for thirty-nine years, thirteen as the president. Two children of the Jarvises' other son, Daniel, were both graduates and long-time staff members at TCU, Dan as a professor of geology and Ann Day Jarvis McDermott as special collections librarian.

Native American Monument, Student Memorial, Memorial Columns/Veterans Plaza

As you make your way from Jarvis southward to Reed Hall, pause for a moment between the buildings and imagine the honeysuckle arbor that once covered the short walk from the south portico of Jarvis to the north Reed entrance. In a less multitudinous time, the arbor, with its sweet-smelling blossoms, served as the backdrop for outdoor graduation exercises held for many years on the lawns just east of the walk. There was rumor, too, that couples enjoying early socials called promenades (remember, no dancing in those days!) would find its dark foliage a protection from ever-vigilant chaperones. The arbor was removed in 1948 because, according to one TCU *Skiff* report, its "vines were beginning to die," and it had become "a trash catcher." A planned replacement never came to fruition.

On October 1, 2018, a monument was dedicated on this site to the Native American tribes who lived in this region of Texas, including on TCU's property, for so many years before their forced displacement. Cast in granite, the monument reads in part: "We respectfully acknowledge all Native American peoples who have lived on this land since time immemorial. TCU especially acknowledges and pays respect to the Wichita and Affiliated Tribes upon whose historical homeland our university is located."

You may also wish to stop at the Student Memorial, located a bit closer to University Drive relative to the Native American Monument. The memorial was proposed and funded by TCU Student Government in 2013 to provide a quiet place for reflection and to honor TCU students and alumni who are no longer with us. It features a single flute or "lily pad" patterned after the four on Frog Fountain. In this case, the flute symbolizes the role even a single person plays in the TCU community. The concept borrows on the Oklahoma City Bombing memorial with a single empty chair. Fittingly, the Student Memorial's plaque bears the inscription: "*Mem'ries sweet, comrades true.*"

From the Student Memorial, turn southward along the sidewalk until you are in front of Reed Hall and the walk toward University Drive. Along these paths—the oldest on the campus—you can pause and ponder a past still perceptible to those who have been here before and still accessible even to the first-time visitor. Here, the shrubs and trees are older, the concrete cooler, and even though it runs close by, the buzz of busy University Drive seems less intrusive than elsewhere on this west side of the campus. Those who return with memories from the years before 1949 will look in vain for a small, concrete vine-covered bandstand, an early landmark that stood on the lawn to the north of the esplanade. Once a band did play on it, while girls and their beaus walked around the campus grounds during the danceless "proms," and once pageants were staged and cheerleaders cheered from its platform. Slowly falling into disuse and crumbling into disrepair, it was removed when this side of the campus was graded and University Drive widened.

An early tradition held that each graduating class, on parting, would present a gift to the university in appreciation and commemoration of their time within its halls of learning. For several years, donated monies purchased portions of sidewalk paving for the campus. To note such gifts, the class would have a plaque, with members' names engraved, set into the stretch of walk for which they had paid. Over the years, needed campus improvements have left little evidence of the commemoratives, which included a masonry gateway from a Cantey Street entrance to the campus, a flagpole and a sundial situated across the walk opposite the bandstand, and a decorative stone flower bench. Given in memory of English professor Walter E. Bryson, the bench stood just east of the flagpole.

Measuring twenty-one feet tall and twenty-seven feet wide, the Memorial Arch that originally stood near where the freestanding Memorial Columns are today was itself a gift from the Class of 1923, presented in honor of the students and alumni who paid the supreme price in World War I. The original memorial was a flat-bricked arch supported by brick piers and limestone Ionic columns. The span forming the arch was embellished with an entablature containing relief panels of an eagle and cartouches. The arch was the design of Clyde Woodruff of the architectural firm of Van Slyke & Woodruff. By 1949, when University Drive was widened and the arch was relocated and reconstructed into the present columns, there had been another war, and more dead heroes, so the new memorial was dedicated to them all.

In 2005, spearheaded by then Texas Secretary of State and TCU Trustee Roger

ABOVE
Memorial plaza facing Reed Hall, 2010.
Courtesy of TCU Marketing and
Communication.

Williams '73, who keynoted the November 12 dedication, over $100,000 was raised to expand this quiet portion of campus dedicated to those who made the ultimate sacrifice for our country. Architect Michael J. Bennett '78 designed Veterans Plaza, which incorporates the bronze plaques, a gift from the class of 1923. The columns are made of Indiana limestone; the expanse between the columns is of Carthage stone. The names of the dead from World Wars I (dedicated in 1923) and World War II (dedicated in 1949) are inscribed on bronze plaques on the east front of the memorial, and the names of the 1923 seniors are listed on a similar bronze tablet on the west side. The plaza also honors the sacrifices and accomplishment of alumni and students who served in conflicts in Korea, Vietnam, the Gulf Wars, and operations in Afghanistan and Iraq. The plaza encompasses the existing memorial pillars and includes garden areas and walkways that span from the east side of Reed Hall to a fountain northwest of the Mary Couts Burnett Library on the east side of University Drive. On the west side of the monument is a grove of trees. It is intended to symbolize the TCU community, one in which individuals depend upon and complement one another. The absence of trees on the plaza's west side symbolizes those veterans who were lost in war, with the space where the trees would have stood containing plaques bearing the names of the fallen.

You can now retrace your steps up to Reed Hall.

Reed Hall

Reed Hall is Jarvis Hall's companion in history. It was at the northeast corner of this building that the first cornerstone on the Fort Worth campus was laid in 1911. Called simply the Administration Building until 1960, when Sadler Hall was built to house primary administrative units, it has since been named in honor of Dave C. Reed, Austin businessman, church leader, and university supporter who served on the TCU Board of Trustees from 1920 until his death in the crash of his private plane in Virginia in 1948. An honorary Doctor of Laws degree awarded Dave Reed in 1944 cited the TCU benefactor for his many contributions to the life of the university and referred to him as "a specialist in the finest of all arts—the art of living." Earlier, a two-story home on nearby Princeton Street that housed girl residents and later ministerial students had been named Reed Cottage. The "cottage" gave way long ago to an expanding

campus community, but the old Ad Building endures to recognize the generosity of its namesake.

Throughout its long history, the Administration Building—Reed Hall—has provided space for classrooms and faculty offices; nearly every academic program on the campus began instruction in this building. It has also been, at various times, home to university presidents and vice presidents, and once housed the library, the business and registrar offices, the post office, the university bookstore, the kitchen and dining room, the student lounge, and, for thirty-eight years, the only room large enough for campus assembly of any size—the old auditorium. Named Townsend Hall, after its smaller predecessor on the Waco campus which was so named in honor of the S. E. Townsend family of Midland, the auditorium was variously used for chapel and church services, theatrical productions, graduation services, and student programs and presentations of all types.

Unlike Jarvis, Reed Hall has undergone extensive alterations—so many, in fact, that only long memory and old pictures can say how it once was. Its original façade was a larger replica of Jarvis, with six Ionic columns supporting a shallow gable roof that projected over the central entrance veranda. Cross-paned double wooden doors bore brass doorplates enhanced with reliefs of the university's official mascot, the Horned Frog.

In the 1960 renovation design of architect Joseph Pelich, the original classical architecture was transformed into neo-Georgian; the six columns were removed; the formerly flat roof was restructured into a hip-style overall, and the wide front steps were replaced by stairs mounting on each side to a red-tiled terrace, railed with wrought metal and cast stone. Three sets of double aluminum-and-glass doors replace the wooden entrance, and the brass frog plates gave way to aluminum also. But the past, as pasts do, still persists and can be discovered, when you know where to look for it. If you stand on the sidewalk just near either corner of the front steps and let your eye follow up high along the drainpipe, you can see where the bricks of now join the bricks of then. Despite the passage of almost sixty years the newer is not quite as seasoned and yellowed by time as the older, smoother brick. Real old-timers will recall that ivy once covered the walls, even to the roof. Many on the faculty from the latter half of the twentieth century will recall the Faculty Center, which occupied the west central extension on the second floor of Reed. Formerly the galleried balcony

of the old auditorium, it was floored and remodeled into a large lounge area in 1955. Carpeted and handsomely furnished with comfortable seating, drapes, and decorative objects, it found service as a faculty club and luncheon room. It was also used by the Faculty Senate, for ROTC officer induction ceremonies, special lectures, afternoon teas, and, occasionally, for wedding receptions. The 1955 renovations provided office space for the administrative staff of AddRan College of Arts and Sciences and for the humanities faculties of English, history, geography, and modern languages. AddRan College is the oldest of TCU's academic units, retaining a portion of the institution's initial name of Add-Ran Male and Female College. For many years Reed Hall was structurally joined on the west to the Brown-Lupton Student Center, but it now stands alone with the latter's 2008 demolition.

ABOVE
The south entrance to the Administration Building (now Reed Hall) with Jarvis Hall to the north, 1918. Courtesy of Mary Couts Burnett Library.

Reed entered its second century of existence with a sixteen-month remodeling project, reopening in the fall of 2010, and imbued with airy stairways, high-tech classrooms, study lounges, and seminar rooms designed to foster student interaction. The makeover was predicated, in part, on the opening of Clarence and Kerry Scharbauer Hall, to which the dean's office and several departments in AddRan College of Liberal Arts were relocated. The main entrance remains on the east side facing University, but a one-story portico supported by four columns now greets west-entering visitors. The new features have made Reed a quieter, more energy-efficient environment for teaching and scholarship. Reed is now home to the departments of history and English as well as the Center for Texas Studies, the William L. Adams Center for Writing, and the Center for International Studies: TCU Abroad. A bronze plaque is situated in front of Reed, providing more information about the building's history.

In their one hundred-plus years, the old walls of Reed have witnessed much of the university's history. In 1918, it survived an airplane collision at its northeast parapet. The young pilot, who was buzzing his girlfriend in Jarvis Hall, was thrown from the single-engine machine and landed, unhurt, on the honeysuckle arbor below. In addition to the vast numbers of matriculates who have walked its halls, it has also been visited by celebrities, including American poets Carl Sandburg, Robert Frost, and Vachel Lindsay, and once played host to the orator William Jennings Bryan and renowned pianist Ignace J. Paderewski.

And, perhaps not quite as famous, there was the cow who, with the help of pranksters, somehow found its way into President Waits's office and spent the night there. One story has it that, although the unfortunate creature was quickly removed upon discovery the next morning and the area thoroughly cleaned, a distinct "essence de bovine" persisted in the southeast corner on the first floor for many days. A later, and longer, residence was established in the early 1950s by an old stray dog that was adopted by the student populace and clandestinely allowed to sleep in the basement student lounge. So highly regarded was the "Old White Cawlie Dawg" that he won every student election for several years as a write-in candidate until he, as the cow before him, faced inevitable expulsion. In the early 1990s, the "Reed Hall Flasher" visited the building on several occasions before he was chased down and turned over to Campus Police by Dr. Bob Frye, an award-winning professor of English, who employed the athletic prowess that once made him a star college basketball player.

OPPOSITE
Reed Hall. Photograph by Rodger Mallison. Courtesy of TCU Marketing and Communication.

You can next proceed southward from Reed Hall to Sadler Hall. In so doing you'll pass the Sadler Mall, an outdoor courtyard situated between the two buildings. The mall features not only tables designed for relaxed conversation and study but also one of the more imposing of the TCU Horned Frog statues on campus. The Texas horned lizard, *Phrynosoma cornutum*, was adopted as TCU's mascot in 1896 when the school was in Waco. The six-foot, rust-brown campus landmark was commissioned by the 1984 Student House of Representatives. Styled and cast in metal by artist Seppo Aarnos, it has become one of the campus's favorite landmarks and was once subject to superstition; namely, for decades, thousands of nervous test takers rubbed its nose for good luck. It remains a popular venue for graduation photos. Something about the cocky tilt of its head captures the fancy of residents and visitors alike. The *Huffington Post* once included the mascot artwork among "the most loved statues on College campuses." Amusingly enough, some months before it was installed, then-Chancellor William E. Tucker, '56 MDiv, and former football coach Jim Wacker were concerned that pranksters might attempt to ride the statue (or even worse), so they implored Aarnos to make the horns a menacing deterrent.

Sadler Hall

From 1960 until 2020, the stately building that is M. E. Sadler Hall housed the chief administrative and business units of the university. Designed by Preston M. Geren and completed in September 1960 at a cost of $1.2 million, it is the second structure to occupy this site. In 1912, a men's dormitory was erected here as the fourth building on TCU's Fort Worth campus; it was named Clark Hall in honor of the school's founders. By 1959, the older building was in such a deteriorated condition that it was deemed unsalvageable and was demolished to provide space for the new administration building. The old Administration Building was renovated into the classroom and office facility now known as Reed Hall.

Built during the administration of Chancellor MacGruder Ellis Sadler, the present four-story structure was named Sadler Hall by the board of trustees in recognition of the long and successful service of the man chosen in 1941 to guide the university's fortunes. Having distinguished himself as a student leader at Atlantic Christian College,

ABOVE
Built in 1912 to serve as a men's residence
hall, Clark Hall stood on the site now occupied
by Sadler Hall. Courtesy of Mary Couts
Burnett Library.

Vanderbilt, and Yale, where he was awarded the BD and PhD degrees, he was first the dean of Lynchburg College, then minister of the Central Christian Church in Austin, Texas. At the time of his appointment as president of Texas Christian University (the title of the chief executive officer was changed to chancellor in 1959), eight buildings stood on the campus. Upon his retirement in 1965, twenty-one new buildings had been erected and five existing structures had been renovated and/or enlarged. The quarter-century Sadler era would be noted for this previously unequalled campus expansion, as well as for strong and steady guidance. Upon his death in 1966, his friend, protégé, and successor, Dr. James M. Moudy, gave this valediction: "A mighty oak has fallen and a thousand seeds have scattered."

The design of Sadler Hall combines some of the elements of the early campus architecture with later construction characteristics. The color scheme of buff brick and red-toned roofing is continued, as is the use of tall columns—this time with Corinthian capitals—that support a gabled portico over a wide, stepped entrance veranda. For many years a traditional campus Christmas program—since moved to the Campus Commons—took place before these portals, with students, staff, faculty, and administrators joining in the singing of carols and the lighting of a giant evergreen.

In the central foyer of Sadler Hall, a gallery displays a large oil painting of Dr. Sadler as well as a bronze bust—a remarkable likeness of the educator, sculpted by Electra Waggoner Biggs. It was commissioned and presented to the university by friends of the late chancellor. Pictures depicting buildings and scenes of TCU past and present, provided in 1991 by Chancellor Emeritus William E. Tucker and his wife Jean, are also on view in the gallery. A bronze outline of the university seal is set in the terrazzo floor, a gift of the Classes of 1961 and 1962. The foyer is dedicated to Marion Day Mullins, who earned several degrees from TCU and was an honorary member of the board of trustees from 1977 until her death in 1988.

ABOVE
Chancellor M. E. Sadler surveying the construction
of the building that would bear his name, 1959–1960.
Courtesy of Mary Couts Burnett Library.

OPPOSITE
Sadler Hall, 2018. Photograph by Jeffrey McWhorter.
Courtesy of TCU Marketing and Communication.

For many years the first and ground floors of Sadler Hall accommodated the business, admissions, and registrar's offices, the student affairs complex, student financial aid, printing and mailing facilities, and the post office. The upper two floors housed the offices of the chancellor, vice chancellors, development staffs, public relations, extended education, news service, and the Robert J. and Mary Wright Boardroom. The building underwent a major renovation in 2011, one year after Reed Hall. The objective was to bring Sadler up to the standards of other campus buildings, new and old, during a flurry of activities that led some to describe the institution as "Texas Construction University." Among other things, all windows were replaced, rendering the building more energy efficient. Printing and mailing, the Office of Admission, and portions of Student Developmental Services progressively vacated over the preceding decade, allowing for expansion of the remaining units. The second floor underwent a complete makeover, being completely gutted save for the four exterior walls and columns holding up the floor. The floors were also renumbered, with the former ground floor renamed the first floor. Among other things, this meant faculty and staff were no longer summoned (occasionally on pins and needles) to "the third floor of Sadler" to meet with upper administrators. Somehow, at least to one author (PH), the "fourth floor of Sadler" doesn't have the same ring. Nor does "the third floor of The Harrison," the current location of TCU's upper administration. A second major remodeling effort occurred during 2021 and 2022—with each floor reduced to its core structural elements—paving the way for Sadler's 2023 inhabitation by the John V. Roach Honors College and two departments (Women & Gender Studies and Critical Race and Ethic Studies) of AddRan College of Liberal Arts.

As you leave by the front entrance of Sadler Hall, cast your eyes eastward toward University Drive and beyond, to take in the panorama that includes the Intellectual Commons, which stretches from Sadler to the Spencer and Marlene Hays Business Commons, home to the Neeley School of Business. Your eyes will be drawn to the walkway bearing three flagpoles proudly flying the US, Texas state, and TCU flags, the tallest checking in at seventy feet. At the direction of the Chancellor's Office, the TCU flag is periodically lowered to half-mast to memorialize the passing of individuals, primarily faculty, staff, and students, who played key roles in TCU's present or past. A nine-thousand-pound university seal resides at the base, serving as the flag plaza's centerpiece. Donated in 1997 by Chancellor William E. Tucker and his wife Jean, the seal is a tribute to Jean Tucker's late father A. V. Jones and contains the uni-

versity motto, name, and emblem sandblasted into its surface. The flagpoles were re-moved, rebuilt, and re-installed in 2019, fittingly enough by Dallas-based Betsy Ross Flag Girl, Inc.

A caveat must be entered now into the text as we suggest you stay on the formally laid-out walks during the remainder of your time on this southwesterly portion of the campus. Pictures and old-time memory recall the tennis courts that once were here in days when campus was almost completely devoid of trees, and each warm Texas day of the years since their removal has witnessed made-up games of volleyball, touch football, lacrosse, and, more recently, frisbee-throwing. In the late '40s and most of the '50s, this turf belonged to the Cowboy, and for years it was rumored that it still be-longed to his ghost. Cowboy Monroe, onetime groundskeeper, was by far the crustiest critter to roam this range. Armed with a hefty garden hose and a whistle, his bowed legs stuck into ancient boots and his wizened face topped with an oversized cowboy hat, he was the enforcer of territorial ground rules and wouldn't hesitate to fire a well-aimed water volley from his hose toward anyone—student, professor, or administra-tor—who dared to step onto his grass. Of course his ghost makes exceptions for stu-dents who play football, toss the frisbee, or study, as well as for the occasional class that meets on the grounds bordering University Drive. The current TCU grounds crew are highly competent, equally prideful of their work, but most definitely less protective than Cowboy once was.

Clark Hall

The name of this residence hall, long male-only but currently coed, is a legacy, appropriately handed down to mark and hold a place of honor for the Clark name in the university's story. When Sadler was built on the original Clark Hall site, the name was passed south to the new building, which itself supplanted a former residence hall called Goode, in honor of the primary donor to its construction cost, Mrs. M. A. Goode of Bartlett, Texas. The original Clark Hall of 1912 was so-named as a "memorial" to the two brothers, Addison and Randolph Clark, founders of the university. Both brothers were living at the time of the announcement of the proposed honor, and permission to use their name was granted after modest hesitation. Chalmers McPherson, endowment secretary, expressed the sentiment behind the proposition: "It is better, by far, to place flowers at the feet of the living than to strew them on the grave of the dead. . . . In harmony with this thought it occurred to some . . . to begin plans for a memorial to the brethren . . . Clark . . . while they were still among us." Within a week of this pronouncement, Addison was dead.

The present Clark Hall recognizes not just the brothers but their progenitors and descendants, as well. Joseph Addison Clark Sr., and his wife, Hettie D'Spain Clark, took an active part in the founding of Add-Ran College in 1873 at Thorp Spring. A sister, Ida Clark Nesbit, and a younger brother, Tommy, also shared the family interest in the new school. Particularly important to TCU history is Joseph Lynn Clark, Randolph's son, who wrote the book entitled *Thank God We Made It!*, which documents his predecessors' dedication to the "unwearying dream," recounting the family's efforts and accomplishments in the field of education. Professor Clark's papers, including letters and family documents, are in the Special Collections of the Mary Couts Burnett Library on the campus.

Before 1948, Clark and Goode were the only permanent structures that housed men. But old Clark and old Goode were more than just student housing units. Goode was built initially as a home to ministerial students and, very early in the school's Fort Worth history, provided living quarters for TCU staff and faculty members and their families. Prior to 1952, all science departments of the university, at one time or

ABOVE (LEFT)
Randolph Clark, c. 1910. Courtesy of Mary Couts Burnett Library.

ABOVE
Addison Clark, c. 1913. Courtesy of Mary Couts Burnett Library.

LEFT
Joseph Addison Clark, c. 1850. Courtesy of Mary Couts Burnett Library.

another, were located in the dark, dank basements of either Goode, Clark, or the old gymnasium to the south. It will be remembered, too, that old Clark Hall was turned over to the Navy V-12 training unit between 1943 and 1945. Other quarters were found for the war-diminished civilian male student population "for the duration."

The present Clark Hall was built in 1958, and with its "E" shape provides as much room as the former Clark and Goode Halls combined. For many years rooms were designed for double occupancy, and each was furnished with bunk beds and built-in desks and drawers. The architectural style of Clark follows that of other campus residence halls of that time period with its Georgian façade, the buff brick, red-tiled roof, and entrance veranda. Clark was gutted and underwent a complete makeover in 2008. The cinderblock walls were replaced with drywall and each room now has its own thermostat. Features include an attractive new back entrance, front stairs to the basement with free laundry facilities and a game room, a new lobby with marble flooring and front desk, a new front door, and new windows throughout. The 2008 renovation also brought amenities such as new furniture and flat-screen televisions. Hallways were painted plum, and doors have a mahogany look and feel. Rooms are now a mixture of sizes and styles, with some sharing suite-style bathrooms. Early in its use, freshmen and sophomore men were assigned rooms in Clark, but the residence hall currently houses about 220 first-year men and women.

Erma Lowe Hall

Directly south of Clark Hall is the building that is home to the School for Classical and Contemporary Dance in the College of Fine Arts. Long ago known as "the little gym" and more recently as the Ballet Building, the structure was named in 2011 to honor Erma Lowe's distinguished record as a dedicated volunteer, philanthropist, and TCU trustee. The wife of Ralph Lowe, for whom TCU's Energy Institute is named, Mrs. Lowe received the Honorary Alumni Award in 1979.

As you might suspect, the building was not originally designed for dance. It was, in fact, built in 1921 as a gymnasium, which was the center for all physical education activities until 1973, when the Rickel Health and Physical Education Building usurped these activities. Called in its youth "a magnificent edifice…that bids fair to develop into one of the most complete plants in the South, in point of both space and equipment,"

the old gym at times was praised but, as with many older buildings that suffer from benign neglect, had its critics.

The multilevel structure was the original design of official TCU architects Van Slyke & Woodruff, the same firm that fashioned the Memorial Arch. The "little gym," as it came to be called after a larger barnlike field house was built in 1926, was constructed of the buff "TCU brick" and featured industrial steel sash windows and a flat roof with curved parapets on each side. The high basement contained classrooms and offices; the swimming pool, men's and women's locker rooms, and more offices occupied the entrance level; a basketball court with a spectator balcony was on the third floor, as were two handball courts; the topmost floor eventually housed a weight room.

In addition to the physical training curriculum, TCU's athletic programs were directed from these halls prior to the construction of the Daniel-Meyer Coliseum (now Ed and Rae Schollmaier Arena) in 1961. It was from a central office on the gym's main floor that legendary football coach "Dutch" Meyer dreamed the plans and plotted the plays that would make him and his Horned Frogs famous in the '30s and '40s. It was on the third-floor hardwood court that TCU basketball teams first competed in Southwest Conference games, and it was from another office in this same building that basketball coach Buster Brannon drew his x-and-o schemes that brought Southwest Conference championships to TCU in the early '50s.

By 1973, all physical education and athletic programs had moved to new quarters, and a program within the fine arts curriculum that had been growing since its inception in 1949 was looking for more room. The gym's pool, basketball court, and weight room were transformed into the present large studios for the instruction of ballet and modern dance. One handball court became a costume room, the other a storeroom, and although the old locker rooms continued as dressing rooms, the men's accommodations became the women's, and vice versa.

The ballet program was initiated in 1949, when David Preston, a professional dancer, joined the fine arts faculty. TCU was one of the first two major universities to offer the bachelor's degree in ballet. Given quarters in one room that measured nineteen by nineteen feet in the then-new Fine Arts Building, the experimental course's first class numbered fifty-two. By 1952, the program had achieved international recognition, its enrollment had increased to 150, and, having entirely outgrown its small studio, the program moved to "Building 10," a temporary barracks located on the east campus

that more than tripled studio space. Mr. Preston was succeeded by another professional of international acclaim, Fernando Schaffenburg, who not only carried on the dance school's tradition of excellence but also was responsible for initiating a community company, the Fort Worth Ballet. Schaffenburg invited Jerry Bywaters Cochran to join the faculty and the BFA in Modern Dance was established in 1975. In 1989, Ellen Page Shelton became chair of the Department of Ballet & Modern Dance, and later the director when the department became the School for Classical and Contemporary Dance.

The building underwent a substantial renovation in 2010 and 2011, during which the dancers were temporarily relocated to several buildings on campus. Renovations were made possible by the support from the Lowe Foundation, created in 1988 by the building's namesake and her daughter, TCU Trustee Mary Ralph Lowe. The foundation also established the Ralph and Erma Lowe Chair of Texas History, the first of its kind in the state. Architects at Bennett Benner Pettit (formerly Gideon Toal) worked closely with Director Shelton to reconfigure and then renovate the "little gym." The central staircase was removed and they agreed on a somewhat industrial "New York loft" look with open ceiling, exposed duct work, and columns. Much of the interior is concrete and the three new lobbies in Erma Lowe Hall's north tower incorporate original exterior walls with brick designs both embedded and in relief. The renovation reorganized the interior spaces to enhance teaching and learning. The three spacious studios remain, the largest of which became a convertible 160-seat theatre with technical capacities and public access and amenities. Other newly formed spaces include a more-developed Pilates studio and somatics lab now known as the Shelton Studio, costume and production shops, a twenty-six-station Mac lab, a student lounge with kitchen, more office space, and an elevator. Although the original door facing University Drive is still present, the main entrance was relocated to the west side of the building.

In 2012, TCU was presented with the Preservation Project Award from Historic Fort Worth, a nonprofit organization committed to preserving the historic character of Fort Worth. Sarah Trac, executive director of Historic Fort Worth, stated: "TCU invested in this historic building instead of tearing it down. It was a win for the program and a win for the campus community." Situated in front of Erma Lowe is a historic marker in the form of a bronze plaque that provides additional information about this historically rich building that joined the campus landscape early on.

TCU Megalith and "Teaching to Change the World" Statue

As you leave the east side of Erma Lowe, two outdoor structures deserve your attention. The first, whose name puts a horned-frog spin on Stonehenge, is formally known as the TCU Megalith, or more colloquially as "Froghenge." It is situated in the shade of sprawling live oaks as you train your eye toward University Drive. Designed and funded in 2005 by Dr. R. Nowell Donovan, provost and holder of the Charles B. Moncrief Chair of Geology, Froghenge is modelled on the megaliths (literally big

ABOVE
Froghenge, TCU's megalith, 2022. Photograph by James Anger. Courtesy of TCU Marketing and Communication.

stones) found in his native British Isles. Consisting of eleven stones quarried from Oklahoma and Idaho, the stone circle is 40.5 feet in diameter and includes three outlying monoliths placed at 120-degree angles. A single recumbent stone (the Stone of the Teacher) represents the university, and the monoliths point to Robert Carr Chapel (the Stone of the Search for Meaning), the Bailey Building (the Stone that passes the torch), and Erma Lowe Hall (the Stone of Happiness). As was envisioned by now Provost Emeritus Donovan, Froghenge has developed into a popular location for outdoor class sessions. According to recent legend, while within the circle, no one is allowed to tell untruths (unless as part of a theatrical production), and also anyone who loses their temper in debate must leave it. Oh, if only these maxims extended beyond Froghenge to today's world of politics!

The second structure is a ninety-six-inch tall bronze statue, situated directly in front of the Bailey Building, that is fittingly entitled "Teaching to Change the World." Weighing in at more than 1,200 pounds, the statue of a little girl, blissfully posed atop a globe, is intended to inspire education students and other passersby. Added to the campus in 2008, it serves as a perfect symbolic prelude to the buildings that house the College of Education. Mounted on a stone platform, the sculpture was made possible through the generosity of Malcolm Louden '67, in honor of his parents, H. Malcolm Louden and Olive Gooding Louden. It was crafted by Dallas artist Angela Mia de la Vega.

It's now time to get educated about the domicile of the College of Education.

The Mabee Complex (the Bailey Building and Palko Hall)

The J. E. and L. E. Mabee Foundation Education Complex consists of the Bailey Building, one of TCU's original Fort Worth campus buildings, and Betsy and Steve Palko Hall. The foundation makes grants for capital expenditures to charitable nonprofits and to private colleges and universities as well as for the purchase of major medical equipment in Texas and five other states. The Mabee Complex was dedicated in 2007 coincident with the completion of Palko Hall and a major renovation to the conjoined Bailey Building. The grand, north-facing steps of the Bailey Building signal your entrance into the College of Education (known until 2007 as the School of Education).

Although the legend above the columned entrance proclaims it The Bailey Building, it was built as the home for Brite College of the Bible. The fifth structure to be built on the Fort Worth campus, the Bailey Building is situated at the southernmost boundary of the 1914 campus. Its walls were the first in the school's history to house a single academic program; specifically, for the instruction of the "preacher boys," as Dean Colby Hall so warmly called them. For thirty-nine years it was utilized thus. Brite College, now Brite Divinity School, moved in 1954 to the religion center on the east campus, which we will walk a bit later.

At the suggestion of then-President F. D. Kershner, Fort Worth architects Sanguinet and Staats patterned their design of the 1914 building after the College of the Bible in Lexington, Kentucky. Buff-yellow brick and cast stone were again primary materials, and a flat roof and Tuscan columns that still support the pedimented portico harmonized with the early campus architecture. There was, however, slightly more ornamentation on the structure than on the other four buildings. This can be seen in the rusticated masonry on the ground floor, the decorative cornices, and the sculpted stone emblem on the portico's pediment.

In 1958, after the religion programs had moved to new quarters, the old Brite College building was renovated under the direction of architect Preston Geren. A hipped, red-tiled roof replaced the former flat one; the second story entrance was restructured to ground level, aluminum windows supplanted wooden ones, and air-conditioning was added throughout. At that time, it was renamed the Bailey Building, receiving its name by way of the generosity of the family of Mary Ann and Robert Bailey, West Texas pioneers who lived in Fort Worth for many years. Always friends and supporters of TCU, the Baileys' interest carried over to their children and grandchildren. A daughter, Nora Bailey Gee of San Angelo, was responsible for planning the memorial to her parents and gave substantially toward its construction. A portrait of Mrs. Gee is on view in the second-floor lounge.

TCU's education program has grown from its inception in 1909 as a small department within the AddRan College of Arts and Sciences to the status of a separate college, offering classes in elementary and secondary education, as well as physical education and special education. Since its establishment in 1924, it has earned accreditation by the Texas Education Agency and the National Council of Accreditation of Teacher Education. Approval by the national council means that certificates granted by the school are recognized in many states other than Texas.

ABOVE
Brite College of the Bible before it
became the Bailey Building, 1928.
Photograph by Sue Harvey. Courtesy
of Mary Couts Burnett Library.

Coupled with enrollment growth and the inevitable erosion through the passage of time of Bailey's beauty and functionality, Dean Sam Deitz made a presentation to the board of trustees advocating for improvements to the facility, leading Mrs. Anne Jones to make an unsolicited first gift of $500,000 to expand Education's facilities. By 2006 over $11.5 million had been raised, exceeding the target by $1.3 million, and including a lead gift from Betsy, Nick, Alexis, and Steffen "Steve" Palko. Dr. Steve Palko was the former vice chairman and then president of XTO Energy, Inc. and held a strong

interest in education. His involvement with the college included serving as the founding chair of its board of visitors. This subsequently impacted his decision to pursue a doctoral degree in the college, which in turn led to a faculty position for some years.

Palko Hall is 24,600 square feet and, along with a glass atrium seamlessly connecting it to the Bailey Building, resulted in nearly tripling (to 36,135 square feet) the footprint of the college. The building has ten classrooms, a 150-seat lecture hall, four conference halls, and thirty faculty/staff offices. A large patio and second entrance face Bellaire Drive to the south, providing a location for quiet study and conversation. In addition to it harmonious merger with Palko Hall, the Bailey Building was restored to its original splendor during the 2006–2007 construction. This included reverting the front entrance to recapitulate its original look, one with an exterior façade featuring a large staircase leading up to the columned front entryway. The construction was carried out by the Beck Group, with Omniplan the architectural firm. As Chancellor Victor J. Boschini stated at the complex's reopening in September 2007: "TCU has always had a wonderful school of education and we will finally have a facility to match."

Some of you might recall that temporary buildings once stood on the ground now occupied by Palko Hall. Among others, these structures' denizens included the faculty and staff of the Ranch Management Program, which relocated to the Rockefeller Building on the northwest portion of campus. And some years later, faculty in TCU's fledging Department of Engineering were housed here prior to the opening of the Tucker Technology Center on the east campus. Both stops come a bit later on our tour.

Let's now explore the southern portion of the west campus.

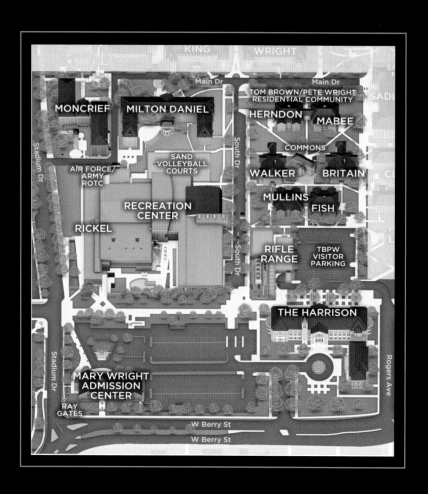

CHAPTER 5

The South Portion of the West Campus

We are now ready to make a loop encompassing a swath of land that includes residence halls, the University Recreation Center (formerly the Rickel Building), the Mary Wright Admission Center, and lastly the Harrison, the relatively new home to TCU's central administration. As with all segments of our tour, you are free to pick and choose, or even to skip ahead entirely to suit your wanderlust. And as with the rest of the tour, you will encounter an impressive mix of old and new, with the mortar barely set in some buildings, while others remain only as photos and etched in our memories.

OPPOSITE
Map showing the campus structures discussed in this chapter.

TCU Rifle Range

Leaving Bailey or Palko, you can meander westward to the TCU Rifle Range, skirting one of the few parking lots remaining in the campus's interior. Home to the highly competitive women's rifle team, which captured NCAA national titles in 2010, 2012, and 2019 and also includes winners of four air rifle national titles, the range boasts twelve firing targets with movable target carriers. You may enter the lobby area and view some of the championship trophies along with additional national awards garnered by the team. The Rifle Range is flanked to the southwest by one of TCU's three high-efficiency chiller plants that pump cold air to campus buildings. For years this was the site of a maintenance annex, formerly a practice gym until Daniel-Meyer Coliseum (now Schollmaier Arena) was built in 1961.

University Recreation Center/ Rickel Academic Wing

From the rifle range it's a hop, skip, and jump across South Drive to the University Recreation Center, which includes the Rickel Academic Wing facing Stadium Drive. The Rickel Academic Wing was christened the Cyrus K. and Ann C. Rickel Building for Health, Physical Education, and Recreation during its September 1972 dedication and before a substantive 2001 expansion. Joseph R. Pelich Associates was responsible for the architectural planning of the original 140,000-square-foot building. "TCU brick" faced the lower portion of the original building, while cast stone-clad pillars supported overhanging crushed stone panels, which offer protection for the walkway that partially surrounds the building on three sides. The dark rose granite of the wide entrance veranda and the vertical entrance pillasters provide design relief and interest. These features have been retained with the 2001 expansion.

Prior to the completion of the Rickel Center, all physical education classes and recreational sports used facilities of the "little gym," the original gymnasium built in 1921 and later renovated (and subsequently renamed Erma Lowe Hall) to accommodate the School of Fine Arts' ballet and modern dance programs. In the 1960s, enrollment increases and a national emphasis on physical fitness and sports participation raised awareness that TCU's physical education facilities were seriously lacking. By 1967, formal recommendations suggested new space be designed to train health and physical education majors and to meet requirements of "a development and adaptive program . . . for the general welfare and well-being of the TCU community." Architectural plans and preliminary estimates of building equipment placed the cost of such a structure at $3 million.

Hearing of the university's need, the Cyrus K. and Ann C. Rickel Foundation of Fort Worth made a challenge gift of $1 million. Rickel was a Fort Worth industrialist who built a small welding supply firm, Big Three Industrial Gas and Equipment Company, into a national corporation. Two years later, after university officials considered reduction of the original proposal because of lack of funding, Rickel made another commitment that insured the construction would proceed as planned. Neither Cyrus Rickel nor his wife, Ann, who died in 1964, ever sought credit for their philanthropy, but after strong urging by TCU Trustees, Rickel gave his permission for their names to be associated with the structure. "Cy" Rickel was a member of the board of trustees from 1968 to 1972. He also received the Alumni Association's "Royal Purple" award in 1970. Other major contributors to the building were the Amon G. Carter Foundation, Earl E. Combest, Bess N. Fish, the George and Mary Josephine Hamman Foundation, the Kresge Foundation, the J. E. and L. E. Mabee Foundation, and the United States Steel Foundation.

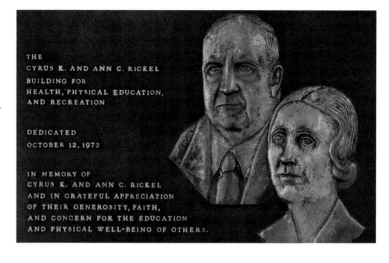

At the cost of $30 million, the 2001–2003 expansion added 202,000 square feet, simultaneously tripling the building's size and rendering TCU's recreational sports facilities second-to-none, particularly when considering the size of the institution's student body relative to other Big 12 Conference rivals. Austin Commercial served as the builder, with Cannon Design and Hahnfeld Hoffer Stanford the architects. The project received an award in 2004 from the Canadian- and US-based *Athletic Business* magazine. They cited its inviting atmosphere and distinctive copper roof perched above the east entrance, through which you can enter and take a look around. The building also gained its somewhat verbose name, the University Recreation Center/ Rickel Academic Wing, although a few still refer to the building as "The Rickel."

Among other things, the increased footprint allowed for substantial expansion in the areas of fitness, nutrition, health, and testing. The recreational portion of the building includes a large gymnasium with bleachers where the Lady Frog volleyball team regularly rocked the house until their 2020 move to Schollmaier Arena. On the south is a natatorium with a six-lane, twenty-five-yard lap pool and a twenty-two-foot deep diving well, which collectively serve as home to both the men's and women's NCAA swimming and diving teams. Bleachers accommodate more than one hundred spectators for viewing competitions. Both pools also have underwater observation windows in the lower level, primarily as an aid to instruction. The east portion of the building includes a nine-thousand-square-foot weight room, a three-thousand-square-foot cardio area, a thirty-foot climbing wall, racquetball courts (one of which converts to a squash court), and a hardwood gym with three basketball courts.

ABOVE

Bronze plaque honoring Cyrus K. and Ann C. Rickel located in the Rickel Wing of the TCU Recreation Sports Building. Photograph by James Anger. Courtesy of TCU Marketing and Communication.

PAGES 98-99

TCU Recreation Sports Building with the reflection of Milton Daniel Residence Hall on the windows, 2013. Photograph by Jeffrey McWhorter. Courtesy of TCU Marketing and Communication.

ABOVE

The weight room in the TCU Recreation Sports Building, 2019. Photograph by Jeffrey McWhorter. Courtesy of TCU Marketing and Communication.

Rollin' N Bowlin', a smoothie bar, sells a variety of healthy and semi-healthy foods and drinks. Comfortable seating for lounging and studying is available for student, faculty, and staff usage. Joggers on the one-eighth-mile elevated track can peer down and observe those in the weight room and on three of the building's five basketball courts. The basement features various game tables as well as locker rooms, some for rank-and-file faculty, staff, and students, while others are dedicated to student-athletes. A southeast building exit provides access to an outdoor pool and patio, frequented by sunbathing college students and young kiddos alike. With a dozen classrooms, the Stadium Drive-facing Rickel Academic Wing is home to the Department of Kinesiology, the TRIO Programs, Army ROTC, and Air Force ROTC Detachment 845, which has crosstown agreements with several area schools, including Texas Wesleyan, Dallas Baptist University, and Tarrant County College.

The grounds immediately to the north and east of the Rickel have undergone changes as well. For many years, nine tennis courts stood behind the original Rickel

ABOVE
Beach volleyball team practice with
Milton Daniel and Moncrief Residence
Halls in the near background, 2019.
Photograph by Jeffrey McWhorter.
Courtesy of TCU Marketing and
Communication.

Building. And in the early nineties, two outdoor beach volleyball courts were added to the building's north side. In 2016 the latter underwent a substantial upgrade, rendering them suitable for TCU's nationally ranked NCAA-level women's beach volleyball team. In addition, a 4,100-square-foot complex was added to the University Recreation Center, providing separate locker rooms for indoor volleyball and beach volleyball, a shared team lounge, a common recruiting room, a formal entrance supporting both programs, and a viewing location for beach volleyball competition.

As you exit the northeast door you can look across the sand volleyball courts and see the backs of two upcoming stops, Milton Daniel and Moncrief Residence Halls. It is possible to shorten your tour a bit by heading directly to the Mary Wright Admission Center and the Harrison, but the few extra steps afford nice views of both residence halls.

Tom Brown/Pete Wright (TBPW) Residential Community

As you exit the University Recreation Center, proceed along the sidewalk northward toward the Campus Commons. To your right is the Tom Brown/Pete Wright Residential Community, which replaced the two residence halls originally occupying these grounds, both housing male students for many years. Tom Brown Hall, completed in 1947, was named in honor of Tom "Coca-Cola" Brown. An enthusiastic follower of TCU's athletic fortunes, Brown was informed of the new building's name at a surprise ceremony during half time of the 1948 spring training football game. Coach Dutch Meyer and Athletic Director Howard Grubbs presented the bottling company executive with a plaque on which was mounted a picture of the $325,000 building. Brown was praised for his longtime interest and loyal support of student groups. The residence hall initially had three "non-communicating" sections and housed 130 men, including varsity athletes who lived in the west wing. This was, in fact, the first designated residence area for TCU athletes. Tom Brown was discussed earlier in this book in conjunction with the BLUU.

Pete Wright Dormitory, built in 1955, was located immediately south of Tom Brown and, although structural problems and lack of occupancy demand were evident as early as 1974, it served in this capacity until 1988. Afterwards it briefly housed a portion of TCU's Advancement team as well as the campus telephone switchboard, but the decision was ultimately made to demolish both Tom Brown and Pete Wright Residence Halls. Like Tom Brown, "Mr. Pete" is deserving of our attention. Loy Calvin Wright—letterman, alumnus, athletic director, treasurer of the university, business manager, trustee—was apparently a rare species with no known enemies. Tall, angular, calm, and soothing, Mr. Pete was associated with the university for over sixty-eight years. At the age of twenty-one, Wright entered TCU's preparatory department in 1904, when the school was still in Waco, receiving his high school diploma there in 1906. He graduated from the university's baccalaureate program in 1910, having distinguished himself especially as a tackle on the early Frog football teams. Returning to TCU in 1922 for a ten-year stint as athletic director, he was subsequently appointed business manager and treasurer. As such Mr. Pete wisely managed TCU's business affairs for twenty-three years, retiring in 1955. He was elected to the board of trustees in 1957 and served until his death in 1972. Mr. Pete's personal sacrifices to bolster

the institution during financial crises warrant special mention, as he worked one year without benefit of salary and, along with his president, E. M. Waits, took to *"walking the streets to meet the TCU payroll."* Wright's honors include the 1955 dedication to him in the annual, *The Horned Frog,* the Valuable Alumnus Award in 1959, and 1967 induction into the TCU Ex-Lettermen's Hall of Fame.

The apartments that constitute Tom Brown/Pete Wright Residential Community have significance in at least two regards. First, they represent the first phase of a ten-year concerted plan (which has subsequently stretched to twenty-plus years) to reshape residential living on TCU's campus. Second, this was TCU's first substantive effort to provide students a living environment beyond the traditional "two-to-a-room with communal restrooms" dormitory experience. The $23 million project began with the $100,000-plus demolition of first Pete Wright and then Tom Brown Halls, followed by the erection of six apartment-style residence halls that were put into service in 1999 and 2000. The project's architectural firm was Lotti, Kirshan & Short with construction by Linbeck Associates. Each of the six residence halls has quad apartments that feature private bedrooms, two bathrooms, a kitchen, and a living room. Two hundred and ninety-two upper-class students call these on-campus apartments their homes. In addition to these six residence halls, the TBPW Commons Building has several living-room-style lobby areas, an outdoor patio with a wood-burning fireplace, and a walkout balcony. The building is adorned with a copper roof and a clock tower. In 2014, twelve of the apartments—two in each building—were remodeled to update the kitchens and living rooms.

The six buildings are: Harold D. & Imogene Herndon, B. M. and Frances Britain, Bess N. Fish, Marion Day Mullins, Granville and Erline Walker, and J. E. & L. E. Mabee Residence Halls. Dr. Harold D. Herndon and his wife supported TCU in numerous ways, including establishing professorships in music and geology. The couple also funded the Harold D. and Imogene Herndon Middle Income Scholarship. Dr. Herndon served on the TCU Board of Trustees from 1956 to 1975 and as an honorary trustee until his death in 1998. B. M. Britain '24 and his wife Frances supported TCU throughout their lifetimes by, among other things, establishing seven charitable trusts benefitting the university. Named in their honor, the B. M. & Frances Britain Society recognizes individuals who have made gifts to TCU in their wills. Bess Fish served as a TCU Trustee from 1972 to 1978. Marion Day Mullins was a charter member of TCU's Library Association. Dr. Granville Walker '35, '37 received an Honorary

Doctor of Divinity in 1947 and the distinguished alumni award in 1959. He was the senior minister at University Christian Church from 1943 to 1973. The Granville and Erline Walker Professorship in Brite Divinity School was established in honor of the Walkers. Mabee Hall is named in honor of J. E. and L. E. Mabee, whose charitable foundation has made grants totaling over $1.2 billion for capital expenditures and for the purchase of major medical equipment in Texas and five other states. The J. E. and L. E. Mabee Foundation Education Complex, discussed in the previous chapter, also bears the foundation's name.

Milton Daniel Residence Hall

Milton Daniel Hall is located west relative to the Tom Brown/Pete Wright Residential Complex. Built according to the familiar design of Joseph Pelich, it was completed in 1957, as was its near mirror image to the north, Colby Hall. Both Milton Daniel and Colby initially housed the eight fraternities and eight sororities introduced to the campus for the first time in 1956. In 1973, after the Greek chapters had settled into new quarters on the Worth Hills campus, Milton Daniel became home to the male athletes, remaining thus until Moncrief Hall was opened in September 1988. With a capacity of three hundred, Milton Daniel now houses students in the John V. Roach Honors College.

Milton Enoch Daniel, for whom the hall is named, was a 1912 graduate of TCU and, much like his colleagues in that era, was a lifelong supporter of his alma mater. Daniel captained the football team in 1911 and served as registrar in 1911 and 1912. He briefly returned to the school as football coach, director of athletics, and instructor in the short-lived law school in 1916, before entering the military and serving in World War I. As his friend and fellow student Pete Wright was to do, he helped hundreds of deserving students finance their education. It was reported that Daniel kept "thousands of dollars on deposit" at the university to be used for this purpose. Throughout Daniel's tenure on the board of trustees (1927–1958), his influence was felt in many programs, but he was especially supportive of building campaigns, athletics, and ranch management. He had served as chairman of the board for five years when he died in 1958, leaving to TCU a gift that was at the time second in value only to that of Mary Couts Burnett. Earnings from the approximately $7 million estate were assigned to TCU for the general development of the university and with no specific designations as to their use.

Milton Daniel Hall, with its somewhat derisively applied moniker "Milton Hilton," had grown long in the tooth by the end of the last millennium. It was known for its dark, musty, dungeon-like atmosphere generated by the decades-long wear and tear imposed by rambunctious male residents. Now "Milton Ritz Carlton" might be a more appropriate pseudonym after a $10 million renovation in 2010 completely transformed the building. The splendor is apparent even as you approach Milton Daniel, with its graceful tiered approach walkways and two-story, arched entrance. Upon entry you are greeted by a wood-panelled great hall with marble flooring. An open staircase off the lobby descends to a basement lounge with a piano, mini-theatre and game room. From there it's possible to step outside to a tiered patio surrounded by a retaining wall, perfect for studying or socializing. Double and triple rooms take up the majority of the basement, first, and second floors, with singles and doubles on the third floor reserved for students with upper-class standing. The second-floor lounge features a pool table, while the third floor has larger common areas and a main lounge with a faux fireplace and an arched bay window. Each room has hardwood flooring and comes equipped with its own thermostat. Rooms have standard TCU furnishing, including a microfridge, sink, and extra-long twin beds.

The John V. Roach Honors College had a humble beginning in 1962, the brainchild of Chancellor James M. Moudy and Professor of Religion Paul Wassenich, who served as the program's director for its first six years. The central mission of Honors was originally defined as "the stimulation and encouragement of academic activity at the highest level," and this is still the case. It acquired college status in 2009 with a $2.5 million gift from Paul and Judy Andrews honoring their friend and mentor John V. Roach, '61, MBA '65. John Roach (1938–2022) was a longtime Fort Worth civic and business leader and former chair of the TCU Board of Trustees. He made significant contributions to mathematics, science, and computer science education in the United

ABOVE
John and Jean Roach. Courtesy of John V. Roach Honors College.

PAGES 108-109
Milton Daniel Residence Hall, 2010. Photograph by Carolyn Cruz. Courtesy of TCU Marketing and Communication.

States, including TCU in his efforts. For example, Roach helped launch the national Tandy Technology Scholars Program, which rewards teachers and students who are leaders in those disciplines. He was a marketing visionary widely credited with transforming the computer from novelty to a ubiquitous household feature. This feat was accomplished with the late-1970's introduction of the Tandy TRS-80 personal computer made by the Tandy Corporation, a company he joined in 1967, ascending to the position of CEO in 1981. Incidentally, the TRS is an acronym for Tandy-Radio Shack, paying homage to Tandy Corporation and the Radio Shack stores that sold Tandy products.

Moncrief Hall

Immediately to the west of Milton Daniel is Moncrief Hall, which joined campus as the eighteenth residence hall in 1988. Heralded as the new athletic dorm, the building was designed by Albert Komatsu and originally housed 224 men and women. It was intended primarily for student athletes; however, since the 1991 NCAA sanctions against "athletic dorms," Moncrief Hall's tenure for this purpose was brief, ending in 1995. It is now coed, with 265 first-year students living there.

The architectural plan of Moncrief is somewhat different from previously built residence halls in that its shape is roughly that of a squared "Z," and it is four stories high, rather than the three that was previously the norm. The two wings are separated by the crossbar of the "Z." Also in contrast to other residence halls on the campus at the time, Moncrief had seven small lounges instead of one or two large ones. Three of these were furnished as study areas; four were TV/recreation rooms. One large room, the Bess N. Fish Lounge, was named for a major contributor to the university and an honorary member of the board of trustees and was reserved for special occasions. Located on a fourth-floor corner, it has a sweeping view of the athletic complex to the west. Perhaps most significantly in the 1990s, all rooms were arranged as suites. This is still the case after its 2010 renovation by the Beck Group, as the capacity ranges from two to four to a room. For some, the bathroom connects as an adjoining room, while in others the bathrooms are located on the same floor, separated by gender.

As its name would imply, the residence hall was financed primarily by families of W. A. Moncrief (1895–1986) and his son W. A. "Tex" Moncrief Jr. (1920–2021).

ABOVE
Moncrief Residence Hall, 2013.
Courtesy of TCU Marketing and
Communication.

LEFT
W. A. "Tex" and Deborah Moncrief
with Chancellor William Tucker.
Courtesy of Mary Couts Burnett Library.

Moncrief Hall is a manifestation of the family's interest in TCU athletics, as evidenced by the 2003 naming of Amon G. Carter's playing field in their honor. "Tex" Moncrief confessed at the dedication ceremonies of the $5.6 million structure that he was a "dyed-in-the-wool Horned Frog fan," showing his "purple pride" by finalizing his speech with a booming "Let's go Horned Froggies!" The Moncriefs have long been generous supporters of university programs in addition to athletics. Three academic chairs have been endowed: the W. A. Moncrief Jr. Chair of Physics, the Charles B. Moncrief Chair of Geology, and the W. A. "Tex" Moncrief Founding Chair of Engineering. The geology chair was given in honor of "Tex" and Deborah Moncrief's son, Charlie (1949–2021), who was a member of the TCU Board of Trustees from 1984 to 1992. His wife, Kit Tennison Moncrief, is currently vice chair of the board of trustees.

Mary Wright Admission Center

Continue past Moncrief to Stadium Drive, then turn left and proceed southward past the Rickel Academic Wing until you encounter a wide pedestrian walkway, which until recent years constituted the eastern portion of Bellaire Drive North. For many years the blocks bounded by Stadium Drive, Bellaire Drive North, Rogers Street, and West Berry Avenue were residential, increasingly given over to rental housing. Now, with but one exception, the houses are in the history books and this land has been integrated into the campus . . . some as parking lots, some populated with buildings. Continuing past the walkway and angling slightly to your right, you shortly reach an important "front porch to the University"; namely, the Mary Wright Admission Center. As its name indicates, the center houses TCU's admissions staff, responsible for the recruitment, admission, and enrollment of all first-year, transfer, and international students. The ambience of its north-facing main entrance is enhanced by tasteful landscaping and a bubbling water feature. The view from Berry Street is also pleasing to the eye. An editorial comment is warranted here: the hard-working admissions staff, led by Dean of Admission Heath Einstein, do a superb job of recruiting prospective students to TCU. The institution's ability to attract somewhere around 20,000 applications for a first-year class of roughly 2,500 undergraduate students is based on many factors, but admissions' ability to "tell the story" ranks close to if not on top of the list.

In the increasingly competitive nature of college admissions, it became evident by the end of the last millennium that a showcase building was needed to put TCU's best foot forward to prospective students and their families. This was in part because the Office of Admission had significantly outgrown its allotted space, having spread over three of Sadler Hall's four floors. The Mary Wright Admission Center answered the call nicely, among other things allowing consolidation to a single, highly accessible location for the first time in many years.

Your entrance to the building positions you in a showcase rotunda with a TCU-themed chandelier and a raised, windowed ceiling that glows purple at night. With its mixture of leather, stone, and technology, the décor is designed to market to prospective students and their families by exposing them to amenities such as gourmet coffee at a java station, touch-screen kiosks chock full of TCU information, a Steinway piano playing Beethoven softly in the background, and images parading across the rotunda. Visitors can also view memorabilia, both academic and athletic in nature, including a replica of the 1938 Heisman Trophy won by Davey O'Brien '39 of the national champion Horned Frogs. The strategy behind the admissions office experience is to stimulate all five senses: from *visually* experiencing infographics and items in the display cases and all over the lobby; to *smelling* and *tasting* coffee, tea, or hot chocolate; to *listening* to background music; and to *touching* interactive screens. In addition, two receptionists welcome guests and receive phone calls . . . a far cry from the automated approach employed by most division-one schools. The fourteen thousand-square-foot building not only includes small interview rooms and staff offices but also features the one hundred-seat Raymond A. Brown Admission Classroom, named for TCU's Dean of Admission at the time of its August 2010 dedication, and the more intimate Joan Rogers Conference Room, honoring trustee and former admission staff member Joan Rogers. The parking surrounding the building is also a big improvement, as previously prospective students and their families were not infrequently forced to wander from lot to lot before finding a parking spot, and only then navigate their way to Sadler Hall. In this regard, 109 is an important number, as it was the allotment of close-by parking spaces reserved for campus visitors. Daily campus tours often depart from the latticed patio next to the building.

ABOVE
Portrait of Mary Wright located in the Wright Admission Center. Photograph by James Anger. Courtesy of TCU Marketing and Communication.

OPPOSITE
Interior of the Wright Admission Center. Photograph by Rodger Mallison. Courtesy of TCU Marketing and Communication.

Construction was facilitated by a donation from Mary and Trustee Robert J. Wright, benefactors spoken of in discussing the residence halls on the Campus Commons. The building's name honors the many accomplishments of Mary Wright, which were summarized in Chapter 3. With Cannon Design and Hahnfeld Hoffer Stanford as architects and construction by Linbeck, the Mary Wright Admissions Building took only seven months to build.

Sight unseen but important nonetheless are the seventy-three wells situated beneath the building. They comprise a critical component of the geothermal system used to provide climate control. Heat is transferred in a continuous loop underground instead of more conventional but less efficient air transfer. The $200,000 price tag has translated to an annual reduction in heating and cooling bills of roughly 20 percent.

The Harrison Building

From the Mary Wright Admission Center it's a short walk eastward to reach "the Harrison," home to TCU's central administration. The name recognizes the transformative philanthropy of Brenda and Mike Harrison '64. In 2019 the couple committed $10 million to establish an endowed scholarship fund, the Brenda and Mike Harrison '64 Endowed Scholarship Program, for students from middle-income families, thus addressing one of TCU's highest priorities. Brenda Harrison, a Texas Tech graduate, practiced speech pathology in two independent school districts in West Texas. She has served her community through her church, Juliette Fowler Communities, Samaritan Counseling Center, and as cofounder of Midland Inspires, a women's organization supporting community improvement in Midland County. Mike Harrison served on the TCU National Alumni Board and the Permian Basin Regional Council. He was also elected as a Reeves County Judge. The Harrisons own the Anderson Ranch and Dixie Cattle Company in the Pecos, Texas, area. The couple truly bleeds purple, as Mr. Harrison's father (for whom the Nell A. and W. Oliver Harrison Building is named) and brother both graduated from TCU, as did two of their four children.

Providing a striking south border to TCU's campus, the Harrison was dedicated November 5, 2021, and served to unite almost all the university's administrative programs under one roof, with the majority having relocated from Sadler Hall. The eighty-six-thousand square-foot building consists of two wings: a main, three-story portion that runs east-west, and a two-story wing on the east that extends from north to south. Taking thirty months to complete, the exterior consists of "TCU" blended-blond brick complemented by over 8,200 cast-stone details, all of which required extensive exterior steel to support. A large arched central opening flanked by an impressive tower contribute to the building's grandeur. The Harrison is accented by two-story carved bay windows on the east and west ends of the three-story wing, with a west-facing second-story balcony present on the two-story wing. The grounds in front of the building are immaculately landscaped, with a circular fountain at the center of the drive-through, allowing ready access to the front door for vehicular drop-offs. Hahnfeld Hoffer Stanford and Cannon Design served as architects, with Vaughn Construction the builders of the $57-million-dollar structure.

In addition to a grand lobby, the first floor houses the BNSF Railway Center for Career and Professional Development, Scholarships and Financial Aid, the Dean of Students Office, a portion of Information Technology, the Office of Institutional Equity, and the Office of Diversity and Inclusion. The second floor is home to Financial Administration, Student Affairs, a portion of University Advancement, and Marketing & Communication. It includes a "town square" for lunching and other communal activities. The Provost's Office, Chancellor's Office, and a portion of University Advancement occupy the third floor, which also includes the Wright Board Room. It is definitely worth your time to walk through the large lobby, where you can admire a portrait of the Harrisons and also look at "TCU: Among the Firsts," a pictorial exhibit paying tribute to pioneers from diverse backgrounds who have contributed to the university's success. One of those is Allene Parks Jones '63, who in 1962 was one of the first three Black undergraduate students to enroll at TCU. She returned six years later as the university's first Black professor, specializing in clinical psychiatric nursing and teaching for nearly thirty years.

ABOVE
Portrait of Brenda and Mike Harrison located in The Harrison. Photograph by James Anger. Courtesy of TCU Marketing and Communication.

LEFT
The Harrison Building. Courtesy
of TCU Facilities Services.

CHAPTER 6

University Drive and West Berry Street

::

The West Side of University Drive

Our tour will now take us slightly off campus, but it will be well worth the relatively few extra steps. Leaving the Harrison through its north-facing door, walk past Palko Hall and the Bailey Building until reaching the west sidewalk on University Drive, at which point you can venture south (right) until you arrive at the northwest corner of University Drive and West Berry Street. You've just passed by a thriving collection of businesses that sprang up over the past twenty-plus years, beginning with Einstein Bros. Bagels in 1997, followed almost immediately by Smoothie King, a New Orleans-based juice bar. They are currently joined by Stop N Go Gyros and Potbelly's Sandwiches. They inhabit a facility built in 1947 that housed Marvin Electronics until 1996. With a look congruous with many campus buildings, the northwest corner of West Berry and University is currently occupied by a Chase Bank branch, which opened in 2017 and replaced a corner gas station.

You may now wish to glance back at University Drive, one of the two north-south arteries that bisect campus. From 1911 until 1923, the now-busy four-lane thoroughfare was a dirt-and-gravel extension of Forest Park Boulevard, down the middle of which came the streetcar from Fort Worth, three miles to the north. The southern

OPPOSITE
The drugstore on the "TCU Strip," 1920s. Courtesy of Mary Couts Burnett Library.

boundary of the campus, marked by the original Brite College building (now the Bailey Building), was literally the end of the line. Only prairie lay farther south and west, and until the early '20s, the eastern horizon was unobstructed as well. The sale of large tracts of land to real estate developers and a subsequent residential housing boom brought paved streets, businesses, churches, and public schools to the area. The strip of shops on the east side of University Drive across from the Bailey Building, which we'll soon visit, was built during this time. It was long known as the "drag," or more recently the "TCU Strip." The Strip included a drugstore at the corner of Bowie and University, a popular student hangout in the '30s through the '60s.

West Berry Street

You can cross University Drive at the University/West Berry intersection and proceed directly into the TCU Campus Store, where you may elect to do a bit of shopping, including for TCU-branded clothing. But before you enter, take a look down West Berry Street to the east, for it is a highly evolved road. Little more than a dirt lane when TCU relocated to Fort Worth in 1910, West Berry Street enjoyed such growth that by the 1940s it was a bustling commercial district convenient to students and local residents alike, in part owing to its easy pedestrian access and ample median parking. The city then widened the street and extended it to Hulen Street to the west, resulting in significant increases in traffic with corresponding decreases in parking and pedestrian traffic. Consequently, by the mid-1990s, while some businesses, particularly fast-food restaurants, continued to thrive, West Berry Street had undergone significant decline as the nation had largely moved from shopping in individual stores to large malls. This prompted the development of the Berry Street Initiative, a cooperative effort of the city of Fort Worth, local citizens, and a concerted effort from TCU, led by Don Mills, vice chancellor of Student Affairs, and Chancellor Bill Tucker. The result has been a phased and sustained effort to convert the stretch of West Berry between Forest Park Boulevard and University Drive into an urban village. Made possible by a series of federal grants in excess of $9 million, improvements include wider sidewalks, pedestrian crosswalks, landscape planting boxes, and benches. In conjunction with this initiative, TCU purchased several properties that line West Berry Street, including the current site of the Campus Store.

The TCU Campus Store

The university store and its forebearers have an interesting history. While certainly not as impactful as the devastating blaze that brought TCU to Fort Worth, a building-enveloping fire makes for an interesting chapter in the story. For many years, the bookstore was a part of the Brown-Lupton Student Center ("the Main"), but in 1997 it moved into a seventeen-thousand-square-foot building, formerly a Tom Thumb Food Center, immediately east of its current location and facing Berry Street. Managed by Barnes & Noble, the TCU Bookstore underwent a second renovation of the fifty-six-year-old building in late 2005 to early 2006, only to sustain a devastating amount of

ABOVE
The TCU Campus Store with the TCU Strip in the background, 2017. Photograph by Matthew Allen. Courtesy of Follett Higher Education Group.

damage due to a fire on March 26, 2006. The decision was quickly made to build an entirely new structure and, as the title in the TCU *Skiff* succinctly stated on January 15, 2008, "*$7.5 million, two years, one fire later, (the) bookstore is back.*" Again managed by Barnes & Noble, the current building had double the square footage of the old, and it contained an expanded café, mezzanine with a study area, and an outdoor patio. The new building incorporated principles of an urban village by placing the facility near the street for easy pedestrian access, with parking in the rear. Management passed to the Follet Higher Education Group and the store was renamed the TCU Campus Store, reflecting the reality that books account for a decreasing percentage of sales. Follet renovated the building in 2021, among other things adding dressing rooms.

The suggested route for our tour does not proceed to the following five buildings, but of course you are welcome to stroll down West Berry Avenue should you so choose. In that case, you'll pass by the Allan Saxe Garden, situated behind the Campus Store at Berry Street and Cockrell Avenue, named for Dr. Allan Saxe, an author, lecturer, philanthropist, and emeritus professor of political science at the University of Texas at Arlington.

Fort Worth Contemporary Arts Gallery

Located on the northwest corner of West Berry Street and Greene Avenue, the Gallery is maintained by TCU's School of Art. The two-thousand-square-foot venue provides the opportunity for students, faculty, staff, and alumni to engage with the community, with exhibits by national and international artists. The Gallery is open Wednesday through Saturday from 12:00 p.m. to 5:00 p.m. and by appointment.

The GrandMarc

Opened in 2006, the GrandMarc at Westberry Place occupies the entirety of the block bounded by Greene Avenue, West Bowie Street, Waits Avenue, and West Berry Street. The apartment-style building was designed to serve the housing needs of some TCU students. It is the result of a partnership between TCU and the Dallas-based

developer/property manager Phoenix Property Company, with the Robert A.M. Stern firm the architects of record. The architecture of the GrandMarc adopted the pedestrian-friendly principles of an urban village by moving the facility façade to the sidewalk and hiding parking in a garage between the two major sections of the building. The six stories facing Berry have a Spanish-style look, complementing a number of other buildings along Berry. The five stories facing TCU on Bowie Street feature the buff brick so ubiquitous to campus. There are 244 units of between one and four bedrooms. Common areas include a movie room, a pool & spa, and a gym. The six hundred-space interior parking lot is available to residents as well as to customers who frequent the thirty-thousand-square-foot ground floor, which is given over to various retailers.

Those who have frequented campus for decades can recall the transition of this block once dominated by single-family residences to one with progressively fewer residences—and those were primarily student rentals—to its pre-GrandMarc look of a whole-block parking lot save for one small structure facing onto Greene Avenue. That increasingly decrepit building served as the home for various restaurants, including the Austin-based franchise Schlotzsky's. Beginning in 1986, you could go there to get a mighty fine pizza pie served up by Richard Perotti and his son Richard Jr. Perotti's now anchors the ground floor of the GrandMarc, along with TCU Printing and Copying, Fruitealicious (making smoothies and bubble tea), 9Round (a kickboxing workout facility), BBQ Chicken (Korean), Insomnia Cookies, Salata (a salad restaurant), Fat Shack, and Truist Bank. Some will recall the quality cuisine served up at Café Brazil, which occupied the southwest corner of the building from 2011 to 2019. Others might remember the "Pizza Hut on stilts," located one block to the west, present in the 1970s through the 1990s.

One block east of the GrandMarc is the ever-popular Kings Liquor store, which has been a package store for the general public, including TCU students, faculty, and staff, for over fifty years. A bit more to the east is Kubes Jewelers, a presence on Berry Street for almost seventy-five years. Your arrival at Kubes will be signaled by the large Post Clock located near the front entrance, which was a gift to the community from the Kubes family.

Human Resources

TCU's Human Resources had led a somewhat itinerate existence through the years, including a stint on the site now occupied by the Harrison. However, HR appears to have landed a permanent home in 2018, when it moved into a completely renovated twenty-six-thousand-plus-square-foot structure originally built in 1950. Located on the southwest corner of Merida Avenue and West Berry Street five blocks east of University Drive, the building was for many years the place of worship for West Berry Church of Christ (more recently University Church of Christ). The building has been cleverly repurposed, with the former sanctuary now serving as a large common work space flanked by private offices.

Institute of Behavioral Research

Located on the northwest corner of Sandage Avenue and West Berry one block to the east of the HR building is a nondescript structure that houses a powerhouse institute. Some older alums may recognize the location as the former home of Colonial Cafeteria, where decades of TCU students congregated for some off-campus dining that was plentiful and (mostly) tasty. The facility is now home to the Institute of Behavioral Research (IBR), a private, not-for-profit entity. IBR is currently a part of the College of Science & Engineering. Established in 1962 by the late Professor Emeritus Saul B. Sells, IBR works in close collaboration with the Department of Psychology. Its mission is to evaluate and improve health services that address drug abuse as well as related mental health and social problems. The institute has fulfilled its mission through the successful acquisition of large research grants, primarily from the National Institutes of Health.

Hyatt Place TCU

OPPOSITE
Hyatt Place Fort Worth/TCU, 2021. Photograph by Greg Frnka. Courtesy of GPF Architects, LLC.

PAGE 130
Rooftop of TCU Hyatt with campus in the background. Photograph by Rodger Mallison. Courtesy of TCU Marketing and Communication.

One block east of the IBR building and anchoring the southeast corner of campus is the Hyatt Place TCU. Opened in February 2021 on the block bounded by Sandage Avenue, West Bowie Street, McCart Avenue, and West Berry Street, this six-story hotel offers amenities that include the "Lot 12" rooftop bar (so named because the building occupies the former site of TCU's parking lot 12) with panoramic views of the TCU campus and downtown Fort Worth, a 3,500-square-foot ballroom, Topgolf Swing Suites with seventy-eight virtual courses, and a private event space. And by the way, you can rent a room there, too. Alumnus and hotel owner John F. Davis III, president of Campus Hotel Venture, was instrumental in developing this partnership between his company and TCU. In December 2021 the hotel was named the best new property by Hyatt Hotels Corporation. One former occupant of this site was the Back Porch, famous among students in the 1970s for its salad bar and homemade ice cream. Customers could receive their salads gratis by correctly guessing their weight.

The Strip

It's now time to venture back to campus. As you mosey along the east side of University Drive, you'll encounter a thriving collection of shops that underwent a substantial metamorphosis over the past thirty years or so. The future of the TCU drag appeared fragile in the late 1980s and 1990s, as perhaps best epitomized by the TCU Theatre at its south end. This historic structure lay fallow for more than ten years before serving transiently as the home to Stage West, and even more fleetingly as a performance hall dubbed "The Frog." Thankfully, the strip is now thriving, with a diverse and still-evolving array of businesses. No account of this now-bustling stretch of real estate would be complete without mention of three venerable establishments. The first, the TCU Drugstore, was a favorite between-class hangout that served sandwiches and fountain drinks beginning in the 1930s, in the location now occupied by Flash. The second, Jon's Grille, was owned and operated by Jon Meyerson for eighteen years and served up as fine a burger and "killer" club sandwich as you'd find anywhere. The third, Record Town, also anchored the strip, in this case for over fifty years. Alas, all are now gone, although Dutch's, named by co-owner Louis Lambert '81 for legendary TCU coach Dutch Meyer, has been a most worthy successor to Jon's Grille. Dutch's has expanded through the years to have a full-service bar, burrito bar, and outdoor seating both behind and on top of the restaurant. Among other accomplishments, Dutch's won the *Fort Worth Star-Telegram*'s 64-restaurant, March Madness-style burger war some years back. Speaking of burgers, famed chef Jon Bonnell has opened a burger and BBQ restaurant (Jon's Grille) just around the corner on West Berry Street. From north to south the current storefronts consist of Flash the University Store, Dutch's, Buffalo Bros Pizza, Wings & Subs (a part of chef Jon Bonnell's Restaurant Group), The Pub, Jimmy Johns, Shipping and Mail, Ampersand (a coffee shop), Pizza Snob, and McAlister's Deli. In addition, some of you may recall that the now-thriving strip was populated at various times over the past forty years by Sampley's, TCU Cleaners, The Tanning Salon, the Greek House, Donuts 'N More, Salsa Limon, Sol de Luna, and Necessities, to name just a few. You may wish to window shop, grab a bite to eat, or wet your whistle at one of the fine establishments that populate the strip. Having done so, you are now situated to cross Bowie Street and walk the east campus.

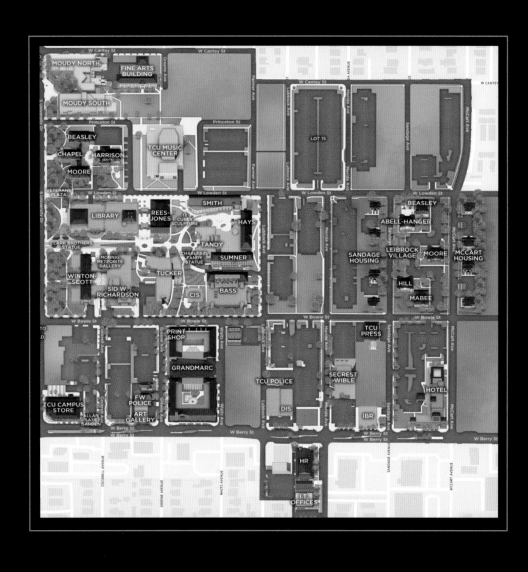

CHAPTER 7

The East Campus

Winton-Scott Hall

Please allow both authors a spot of reminiscing as you enter the front of Winton-Scott Hall, which is situated on the southeast corner of University Drive and West Bowie Street. For one of us (JHS), this was the building where her father spent a significant portion of his career as a biologist, chair of the Department of Biology, and head of TCU's Pre-health Professions Program (now Institute). His was indeed an impactful career by any measure. For the second (PH), the fifth floor of the building served as his professional residence for over thirty years before moving to the Tucker Technology Center to finish out his TCU career. Thousands of mem'ries, mostly sweet, and certainly comrades true!

The completion of the Winton-Scott Hall in 1952 brought instruction in all the sciences together under one roof for the first time in over thirty years. When the school opened its fall semester of 1911 on the new Fort Worth campus, the laboratory sciences were taught in the only building used then for instruction, the Administration Building (now Reed Hall). As each discipline grew, space was provided for the enlarged science programs in the basements of extant buildings. Soon, and for long, the old Clark dormitory was home to the combined biology/geology department; Goode Hall housed chemistry; and the physics department was located in the gymnasium, now the Ballet Building. The chemistry department made one more move to temporary buildings on the east campus before settling in to Winton-Scott.

OPPOSITE
Map showing the campus structures discussed in this chapter.

Heralded in the *Skiff* as "one of the outstanding little science buildings in the United States," with facilities unsurpassed in the Southwest, the five-story structure was the design of architects Wyatt C. Hedrick, Preston M. Geren, and Joseph R. Pelich. Its basic style follows that of other post-World War II campus buildings with buff brick and cast-stone trim, red-tiled hipped roof, and a plain classical aspect. Aluminum was extensively used for decorative interest, as seen in the window spandrels, the grilles above the high cornice, and the cast aluminum central door grilles that carry representative symbols of the four major sciences the building initially housed: an amoeba for biology at upper left, the sun for physics at lower left, a geologic cross-section at upper right, and the apparatus of chemistry at lower right. The central entrance is set in relief by a dark polished granite facing, the first use of this material on campus buildings. Four exterior sculptures—one each of cast aluminum on the west front wings, and one each of cast stone over the north and south entrance porticoes—are also symbolic of the use for which the building was intended.

Winton-Scott Hall is the only academic building on the campus named in honor of the faculty who actively contributed, through teaching and research, to the programs housed within its walls. Professor Will M. Winton and his protégé, Gayle Scott, were both geologists who had significant influence not only within the science curriculum at TCU, but also within their chosen profession. Professor Winton began his long tenure in 1913, as chairman of the biology/geology department. He never completed his doctorate at Rice Institute (now Rice University), but his research in the field of geology won him national recognition as a fellow in the American Academy of Science. National acclaim, as well as local renown as respected teacher and colleague, led the university in 1951 to bestow on him the honorary doctor of science degree. Professor Winton was responsible for initiating two medical science programs at TCU, including the pre-medical program (now Pre-Health Professions Institute), which has long boasted an acceptance rate to medical schools twice the national average. Winton chaired the pre-medical program from 1918 to 1950, two years before his 1952 retirement.

Gayle Scott was one of Professor Winton's first students, receiving his bachelor's degree in 1917 and his master's in 1920. After serving as an officer in the First World War, Dr. Scott pursued his studies in geology at the University of Grenoble, France, where he received his doctorate in 1925. A specialist in cretaceous geology, he compared cretaceous sediments of Texas with those of western Europe in his doctoral

ABOVE
Winton-Scott Hall in the latter stages of construction, 1953. Courtesy of Mary Couts Burnett Library.

thesis, causing a mild controversy at the time; his hypotheses were later found to be correct. As Winton had before him, Scott became professionally involved at the national level as a publishing researcher and active participant in geologic societies. Married to the TCU president's daughter, Mary Elizabeth Waits, "Scotty," as he was affectionately known, had an active interest in many aspects of the TCU world, but none more active than his participation in its athletic programs. He chaired the faculty athletic committee from 1937 until 1948 and was president of the Southwest Conference Athletic Association. At the age of fifty-three and at the peak of his career, his life was cut tragically short by an inoperable brain tumor.

Perhaps no building on campus better epitomizes TCU's twenty-first-century commitment to upgrading research and teaching facilities, some of which had fallen into a state of benign disrepair, than Winton-Scott, which was actively avoided by Office of Admission tour guides leading prospective students and their families. This is decidedly no longer the case. One and a half million dollars' worth of renovations occurred between 2001 and 2003, including a complete makeover of the fifth floor to yield state-of-the-art research laboratories and offices. This was a part of a three-year, $30 million project to renovate academic buildings, the first in a series that transpired on campus. A second wave of extensive renovations occurred during the summer of 2015, upgrading teaching labs, research labs, departmental offices, and faculty offices. Among other improvements, a series of rooms just inside the west entrance were re-purposed into two study rooms and a community-style study lounge. In addition to facilities, the first fifteen years or so of the current millennium were also marked by a comprehensive and systematic upgrade in research and teaching equipment. The first two decades of the new millennium were indeed the glory years in academics as well as on the gridiron!

Winton-Scott Hall currently houses the departments of biology and psychology, with mathematics and military science having relocated in 2000 and 2008, respectively. Worth a visit is the extensive marine shell collection displayed in lighted museum cases on the fourth-floor corridor. A gift of Mrs. Ruth F. Mudd, the collection is maintained by the Department of Biology.

Sid W. Richardson
Physical Sciences Building

Access to the Sid W. Richardson Physical Sciences Building, or Sid Rich as it is colloquially known, may be made by exiting either the north or the south entrances of Winton-Scott and walking east to the ramped walkways leading to the courtyard separating the two buildings. Alternatively, third- and fourth-floor passageways will take you from one building to the other. Choosing the interior route guarantees more adventure . . . it is easy, even for campus veterans, to become lost in the labyrinthine halls and stairways of Sid Rich. The building is legendary in this regard, as stated in a fairly recent tongue-in-cheek article in the student publication TCU 360: "Infamous for confusing un-suspecting students, the Sid W. Richardson Building chews up first-year students and spits them right back out." Despite this admonition, it's worth some exploration. And you'll find its denizens to be friendly enough, even the chemists and physicists!

In many ways, the Sid W. Richardson was the most ambitious building to be added to the campus up to that point the time. Its construction, begun in 1968, was to complete a $7.6 million science research complex that included the conjoining of a remodeled Winton-Scott Hall. The plan was for the latter to quarter the life sciences and for the new building to house the physical sciences, as well as a computer center that had been established in 1961 and was originally located in Dan Rogers Hall. When the complex was completed, the space for instruction and research in the sciences at the university was more than tripled. At 149,842 square feet spread over five floors, Sid Rich remains the university's largest academic facility.

The basement level is home to a portion of Information Technology, although the bulk has relocated to a facility on Pond Street. Also present are research and teaching labs for the Department of Physics and Astronomy as well as four of TCU's largest lecture halls, two with capacities of roughly one hundred and the other two seating roughly two hundred people each. Each is built with amphitheatre armchair seating. One of us (PH) lectured regularly throughout his career in Lecture Halls 1 through 4, as they are unimaginatively named, and estimates he spent a total of slightly over 4,000 hours (equivalent to 170 full days!) disseminating word of microbiology and genetics. Hopefully some of it sank in! The Departments of Geological Sciences and Environmental Sciences are on the second level; the Department of Physics and

Astronomy occupies the bulk of the third floor; and the Department of Chemistry and Biochemistry is found on the fourth. A fifth floor, the so-called "penthouse" level, was envisioned by Dr. Leigh Secrest as offices for the TCU Research Foundation, of which he was the founding president. For years it was occupied by the offices of University Relations, Publications, and Editorial Services. A significant portion is now given over to the Koehler Center for Instruction, Innovation & Engagement. As described in their mission statement, "The Koehler Center is dedicated to facilitating ongoing, reflective discourse regarding instruction and learning, including engaging with faculty, instructional staff, departments/units, and administration." Long an important faculty resource, the Koehler Center played a central role in TCU's rapid pivot to remote learning, mandated by the COVID pandemic. The center's name honors Dr. William H. Koehler, who spent much of his thirty-five years at TCU in administration, most notably serving for twenty-four years as the institution's chief academic officer. Provost Koehler was a fierce advocate for the teacher-scholar model, insisting faculty strive for excellence in both their instructional and scholarly activities. He also took a keen interest in athletics and is credited by those in the know with laying the groundwork leading to TCU's resurgence, particularly on the gridiron, which is discussed in Chapter 9. The topmost floor also accommodates a large meeting room, which was once used by the TCU Board of Trustees and by the Faculty Senate. Amusingly, back in those days, the building's residents were tipped off to upcoming board meetings by a fresh coat of paint that appeared in the Sid Rich elevator car.

The design of the Richardson building, conceived by renowned architect Paul M. Rudolph, was to some a drastic, unnecessary departure from traditional TCU style. To others, it was a work of art, a forward-looking, welcome break from the monotonous squared classical look of the past. Aware of the controversy, Rudolph, speaking at the cornerstone-laying ceremony, commented that the building looked to the traditional architecture of TCU and also to the future. He continued, "I know of no other university that has tried to house its best scientists in what is, hopefully, a work of art." According to Rudolph, each element of the building would be "clearly articulated." There would be no attempt to hide such interior necessities as columns and stairs. Ironically, by the early 1990s, the open stairwell was in violation of fire codes. The university was directed to enclose all stairs, thus violating the aesthetic intent of the architect. Like Winton-Scott Hall, Sid W. Richardson has undergone several rounds of substantial renovations over the past twenty years.

The Monnig Meteorite Gallery is a must-stop on your tour. Located in the second-level entrance lobby just off the courtyard between Sid Rich and Winton-Scott, the gallery was dedicated February 1, 2003, ironically enough just hours after the space shuttle *Columbia* disintegrated upon re-entry, killing all seven crew members. The gallery is the public face of the Monnig Meteorite Collection, the largest of its kind in the southwest. TCU was bequeathed the collection by Fort Worth businessman Oscar Monnig (1902–1999), as a natural outgrowth of his friendship and professional relationship with Dr. Art Ehlmann (1928–2017), emeritus professor of geology. Dr. Ehlmann served as the curator of the collection until these responsibilities were taken up by Dr. Rhiannon Mayne, the Oscar and Juanita Monnig Endowed Chair of Meteoritics and Planetary Science. The gallery was closed owing to the COVID pandemic at the time of this book's writing, so you might check before your campus walk to see if it has reopened. Where else can you literally touch a piece of Mars and gaze upon hundreds of meteorites, including one found in 1492, the year Columbus sailed this way? Also displayed in this area of the building, in cases along the north and south halls, are rocks, minerals, geodes, and fossils.

The name of the science complex honors the foundation that granted the greater portion of its construction funds. Speaking at the cornerstone ceremony in 1968, Perry R. Bass said that the grant fulfilled a promise made by his uncle, the late Sid Richardson (1891–1959), to do "something significant" for TCU. Richardson's fortune came through enterprises in oil, cattle, and land in early twentieth-century Texas. His interests extended over a wide range, and his philanthropy is nowhere more evident than in the foundation's generous support of education. A bronze bust of the philanthropist, sculpted by Electra Waggoner Biggs, stands in the north entrance lobby. Other significant contributors to the more than $7 million cost of the science center were the Amon G. Carter Foundation of Fort Worth, the Moody Foundation of Galveston, and the United States Department of Health, Education, and Welfare.

William E. and Jean Jones Tucker Technology Center

After exiting the Sid Richardson Building on its south side, turn left and walk about fifty yards eastward along the Bowie Street sidewalk, passing a loading dock between Sid Rich and our next stop, the William E. and Jean Jones Tucker Technology Center. William E. "Bill" Tucker (1932-2022) served on the faculty of Brite Divinity School from 1966 to 1976, the last five years as dean. He returned to TCU in 1979 as chancellor, dispatching his duties with grace, dignity, humor, energy, and enthusiasm until his 1998 retirement. Under his leadership, the campus gained five buildings, doubled the size of its library, and launched an engineering program. The university's endowment increased substantially (from a mere $53 million to over $750 million) during his tenure as chancellor. You could safely argue that this spurred TCU's explosive growth, both in reputation and the square footage of its physical plant, over the ensuing twenty-five years. In addition to her many duties as the wife of a chancellor, Jean Jones Tucker '56 was a Fort Worth community leader. Apropos for a building

ABOVE
Chancellor William E. and
Jean Jones Tucker, 1993.
Courtesy of Jan Scully.

that houses Departments of Computer Science, Engineering, and Mathematics, a student-built robot delivered the shears for Mrs. Tucker to cut the dedication ribbon at the September 12, 2002, dedication. Five photographs of the Tuckers on their West Texas ranch hang on the left wall of the first floor as you walk from south to north through the building.

At a cost of $25 million, the Tucker Technology Center has a modern look befitting the departments housed there, but the use of buff TCU brick allows a seamless blend with other campus buildings. Tucker takes an inverted L shape, with the leg facing north toward campus. The east and north walls both describe shallow curves and are made largely of glass, which contributes both to a distinctive exterior and an abundance of natural sunlight. Included are seven traditional classrooms, four seminar rooms, nine teaching labs, a machine shop, and the dean's office for the College of Science and Engineering. The dean's office serves as the administrative home to the college's eleven departments and five institutes, which are located primarily in Tucker, Sid Rich, and Winton-Scott. The College of Science and Engineering is TCU's second largest, as measured by either the number of majors (second to the Neeley School of Business) or credit hours generated (second to AddRan College of Liberal Arts). Jazzman's Café was present briefly in the basement before giving way to an additional computer lab. The building underwent substantial renovation in the summer of 2018, which included the addition of faculty office space, creation of a fourth dedicated laboratory for engineering majors conducting their senior design projects, and relocation of department chairs and administrative assistants closer to their respective departments. A large atrium encompassing the building's four floors is situated at the juncture of the leg and arm of the L-shaped building. Its basement level is put to frequent use as a study site, with students seated on chairs and couches or scrawling formulas on dry-erase boards. If possible, arrange your visit to coincide with the college's Michael and Sally McCracken Annual Student Research Symposium, held each April and named for longtime biologist Mike McCracken and his wife, the former serving as dean (first of AddRan and then of Science and Engineering) with distinction for a remarkable twenty-seven of his thirty-seven years at TCU (see www.srs.tcu.edu). Attending the

SRS provides the opportunity to converse with the hundreds of science and engineering graduate and undergraduate students who will eagerly share their research findings in poster-board presentations.

You can now retrace your path, exiting the Tucker Technology Center on its south side toward Bowie Street.

Center for Instructional Services

Looking to the east is a modest single-story building facing onto West Bowie Street. As its name suggests, the Center for Instructional Services (CIS) provides technical support to the campus's teaching facilities, a weighty responsibility indeed in this day and age.

In days past, a number of wooden structures stood on the grounds occupied by the Tucker Technology Center and the Center for Instructional Services, including one housing the TCU Counseling Center. This building, an old army barracks, was moved to the campus sometime in 1946 or 1947, along with sixteen others the university purchased from army camps at Brownwood and Abilene following World War II. Due to the large numbers of veterans re-entering college, TCU experienced a sharp rise in enrollment and needed extra space for classrooms and dormitories. Four of the wooden structures were placed behind the "little gym" (now Erma Lowe Hall) on the west campus to house male students; the remaining thirteen were located in this general area of campus. In the early 1950s, as permanent quarters became available for the programs housed in the barracks, most of the locally dubbed "Splinter Village" had been removed. Also existing only as past memories are the metal structures once occupied by the Department of Sociology, an academic unit currently in the AddRan College of the Liberal Arts, and the Institute of Behavioral Research. Finally, the Department of Biology maintained a greenhouse in this area from the 1940s through the 1990s.

Paulette Burns Contemplative Garden

Heading north into campus with the CIS building to your right, you may wish to spend a few quiet moments in the open area between Tucker Technology Center and the Annie Richardson Bass Building. You are now in the Paulette Burns Contemplative Garden, dedicated April 27, 2018, in memory of a remarkable individual who was known for her platinum white hair and cheerful persona. As dean of Harris College of Nursing and Health Sciences, Dr. Burns's legacy is that of growing programs and changing lives. The number of students enrolled in Harris College programs almost doubled during her eight-year tenure as dean. As stated in the inscription on a plaque

LEFT
The Paulette Burns Contemplative Garden with the Bass Building in the background, 2022. Photograph by Phil Hartman.

BELOW
Dean Paulette Burns, 2011. Courtesy of Dean Chris Watts, Harris College.

marking the garden: "The concentric shapes of grass in this space represent the ripples of influence Dean Burns left with students, faculty and staff members." The tranquility of the garden is enhanced by a striking wind tree, donated by Provost Nowell Donovan and his wife, Jeanne.

Annie Richardson Bass Building

The Annie Richardson Bass Building follows the earlier Sid W. Richardson Building in architectural style with its curved "corners" and open stairwells, as well as the materials used in its construction. It comes as no surprise, then, that Preston Geren, who served as an associate to Paul Rudolph in the design of the Richardson Building,

ABOVE
Annie Richardson Bass. Courtesy
of *Fort Worth Star-Telegram*.

OPPOSITE
Annie Richardson Bass Building,
2010. Courtesy of TCU Marketing
and Communication.

was principal architect for the Bass Building. A common chord is also struck in the names of the two buildings. Annie Richardson Bass was Sid Richardson's sister and the wife of locally prominent physician, E. Perry Bass. Their son, Perry R. Bass, had long been director of the Richardson Foundation. Mrs. Bass was an active educational and civic leader. Although the Sid W. Richardson Foundation was the principal source of funds for the structure, other significant support was secured from the Karl and Esther Hoblitzelle Fund of the Southwestern Medical Foundation of Dallas, the J. E. and L. E. Mabee Foundation of Tulsa, the US Department of Health, Education, and Welfare, and Anne Burnett Tandy. Mrs. Tandy provided funding for the nursing college's learning resource center in honor of Fort Worth surgeon W. Burgess Sealy.

The Bass Building houses the dean's office for the Harris College of Nursing and Health Sciences, which includes the academic programs known as TCU Nursing and the School of Nurse Anesthesia, as well as the Departments of Social Work and Nutritional Sciences, the latter administratively residing in the College of Science and Engineering. TCU Nursing began as a privately run school founded in 1912 by Fort Worth physician Charles Houston Harris. It became Dr. Harris's dream to establish a college with a baccalaureate program in nursing. In 1946, thirty-four years after its inception, the nursing school became the Harris College of Nursing affiliated with Texas Christian University. Lucy Harris (no relation to Dr. Harris) was employed as first organizer and dean of the college and served in that capacity from 1946 until her retirement in 1967. In 2000, coincident with a global reorganization of TCU colleges, schools, and programs, the college was renamed, first as the College of Health and Human Sciences and then as Harris College of Nursing and Health Sciences, reflecting the synergy gained by the inclusion of other units whose shared mission is to train quality and compassionate health-care providers. Two other departments in the college, Communication Sciences and Disorders and Kinesiology, are located in the Miller Speech and Hearing Clinic and the Rickel Academic Wing of the University Recreation Center, respectively.

With funding provided in part by the Sid W. Richardson Foundation, the Bass Building was expanded beginning in 2013 to include an additional 36,500 square feet. The existing 52,000 square feet also underwent a major renovation. The Cannon Design firm served as the design architect, with Hahnfeld Hoffer Stanford the architect of record. The Linbeck Group carried out the construction. Completed and dedicated in 2015, the expansion cost $16 million with an additional $12 million

Atrium of the Bass Building. Note the EKG tracing along
the wooden slats to the right, 2017. Photograph by Erin
Little. Courtesy of TCU Marketing and Communication.

for renovation of the existing space, which was completed December 2014. At the time, Provost Nowell Donovan dubbed the building "Paulette's Palace," a compliment to Dean Paulette Burns, who successfully convinced the upper administration that the college needed additional facilities. The addition expanded the number of faculty and staff offices; added classrooms and lecture halls with state-of-the-art technology and equipment; updated the Harris College Health Professions Learning Center; and expanded the basic-care clinics with four state-of-the-art examination rooms and high-fidelity simulation labs. The kitchens in Nutritional Sciences also received a much-needed makeover.

As you enter the west side of the building you will be immediately struck by the large, open-area study atrium that spans the building's length, creatively exposing the north exterior wall of the original building and the south-facing portion of the addition. The atrium is bisected by a staircase integrating the new with the old. Train your eye on the former and you'll notice a series of metal strips, about three inches wide, that span the wall roughly thirty feet off the ground. From east to west they represent the tracing of an EKG, a fitting accoutrement given the building's inhabitants. As you exit to the east, you might pop around the corner to take a peek at the large living-dining room flanked by small, pleasantly landscaped patios. This is the comfortably furnished "Bass Living Room," which is used extensively by the Department of Nutritional Sciences.

Spencer and Marlene Hays Business Commons:
Charles D. Tandy Hall, Tom and Marilyn Sumner Hall, Spencer Hays Hall, Kim and Bill Shaddock Auditorium, and Steve and Sarah Smith Entrepreneurs Hall

Immediately north of the Bass Building, the M. J. Neeley School of Business is housed in the Spencer and Marlene Hayes Business Commons, which was dedicated January 31, 2020. A short walk up Lubbock Avenue from the Bass Building positions you at the Commons' main entrance, allowing access to a complex that integrates the five buildings constituting the Neeley School's physical plant: namely, Charles D. Tandy Hall, Steve and Sarah Smith Entrepreneurs Hall, Tom and Marilyn Sumner Hall, Spencer Hays Hall, and Kim and Bill Shaddock Auditorium. All are seamlessly interconnected.

ABOVE
Dan D. Rogers. Courtesy of Mary Couts Burnett Library.

In addition to classrooms, faculty and staff offices, meeting rooms and restrooms, Hays Commons has the following layout: first floor: Kinder Café, the Luther King Capital Management Center for Financial Studies, the workroom for the William C. Conner Educational Investment Fund, and the Behavioral Lab; second floor: banquet room, TCU Neeley Executive Education, Executive MBA, graduate programs, MBA lounge, Neeley Student Success Services, Center for Real Estate, Sales and Customer Insights Center, Kim and Bill Shaddock Auditorium, Undergraduate Programs; third floor: academic departments, Center for Supply Chain Innovation, Entrepreneurship and Innovation, Master of Accounting Program; fourth floor: dean's suite and board room.

Gone is Dan Rogers Hall, which was built in 1957 and was conjoined with Tandy Hall. It would be difficult to find a truer, more loyal and stalwart supporter of TCU than Dan Rogers, who throughout his adult life never wavered in his enthusiasm for his alma mater. A member of the Class of 1909, he was a band member, cheerleader, and class officer. Upon graduation, he was instrumental in organizing the alumni association and served as its first president in 1913. An avid sports fan, Rogers promoted the building of the first stadium on the Fort Worth campus, old Clark Field, whose wooden bleachers and steel stands were erected on land just west of where Hays Commons now stands. Dan D. Rogers was a member of the university's board of trustees for thirty-seven years, serving on numerous building committees and on the Board Athletic Committee. The memory of this TCU graduate, who was a respected leader in the church, business, and civic communities of Dallas, inspired the fund-raising campaign to build the hall that would honor his name. Dan D. Rogers Hall was completed in the summer of 1957 at a cost of $825,000, most of which came from contributions of Dallas businessmen and industrialists who were colleagues and friends of Rogers. Facing onto Lubbock, it was demolished immediately prior to the 2018-2020 construction that yielded Tom and Marilyn Sumner Hall, Spencer Hays Hall, and Kim and Bill Shaddock Auditorium.

At slightly over forty-six thousand square feet, Charles Tandy Hall was completed in 1989, with Kirk, Voich, and Gist the architects of record. Despite a very different look, the architects achieved a harmonious blend integrating Tandy and Rogers Halls, one that has been preserved in the now Tandy-to-Hays transition. Upon entering Tandy, one is immediately met with an expanse of glass, chrome, and brown brick-tile. The crisp, clean lines of the building and its appointments recall the business world

and strongly resemble a bank. An open stairway with glass panels and chrome trim mounts through the center of the atrium to upper floors, where more glass doorways lead to wood-paneled office suites furnished with wood, black leather, and chrome. Modern office equipment hums; cushioned carpets absorb extraneous sound. An appropriately situated edifice commemorating Charles Tandy stands southwest of the exit from Tandy Hall. The $300,000 statue, developed by artist Jim Reno, was a gift from the Burnett-Tandy Foundation, which Anne Burnett Tandy established after her husband's death in 1978. It was situated on the north side of the Tarrant County Courthouse for twenty-eight years until its 2008 relocation to campus.

For a solid thirty years, the name of Tandy was known worldwide as a leader in the electronics and computer industries. After graduation from TCU in 1940, a year at Harvard Business School, and a brief stint in the navy, Charles David Tandy set about acquiring the small businesses that would eventually grow into the giant Tandy Corporation. He first started a chain of successful leathercraft stores throughout the United States. Then, in 1963, Tandy negotiated acquisition of a Boston electronics firm, Radio Shack Corporation, which would become internationally known with annual profits estimated at $2 billion. When Tandy died in 1978, an endowment from his estate and that of his widow, Anne Burnett, established the Anne Burnett Tandy and

Charles Tandy Foundation. Both Tandys served on the board of trustees at one point in time or another. A major gift from the foundation provided the funding necessary to begin planning TCU's new business facility.

Completed in 2003, the Steve and Sarah Smith Entrepreneurs Hall added over forty-five thousand square feet to the Neeley footprint. Construction was by the Linbeck Group with Ellerbe, Becket & Hahnfeld Associates, the architects of record. Costing $15.5 million, this modernistic three-story building has thirteen classrooms and twenty-two team meeting rooms. It houses a major portion of the Neeley School's MBA program as well as the Ryffel Center for Entrepreneurial Studies. Smith Hall has an open feel, with an atrium spanning its east-to-west length that affords a view of the upper two floors. Smith Hall was made possible through a gift from TCU parents Steve Smith and Sarah Hales. Sarah served on TCU's Board of Trustees from 2001 through 2009. Steve, an entrepreneur, attended the University of Texas at Austin and the University of Texas at El Paso. He cofounded Excel Telecommunications in 1989 and has maintained a diverse spectrum of business operations and investments.

With the dawn of the new millennium it has become clear that while the 2003 addition of Smith Entrepreneurs Hall was much needed, the Neeley School's increased enrollment and ascendant national reputation necessitated a substantive expansion to its physical plant. An advancement campaign was formally launched in 2014 under the direction of Dr. O. Homer Erekson, the John V. Roach Dean of the Neeley School of Business from 2008 through 2019 and a 1974 TCU graduate with majors in economics and political science. In addition to his other responsibilities, Dean Erekson was instrumental in all aspects of the advancement, building planning, and construction phases of the project. The result became what is now collectively known as the Spencer and Marlene Hays Business Commons, encompassing $75 million in new construction. Hahnfeld, Hoffer & Stanford was the architectural firm of record and Cannon Design served as the contractor. The addition of Hays Hall, Shaddock Auditorium, and Sumner Hall added a much-needed 132,954 square feet (minus the 37,253 lost from removal of Dan Rogers Hall).

Two significant gifts were particularly instrumental in fueling the Neeley School's expansion initiative. The first, to the tune of $30 million, was from Spencer Hays '59 and his wife Marlene. The same couple's generosity had previously made possible the Marlene and Spencer Hays Theatre and Marlene Moss Hays Hall, later stops on our

ABOVE
Sarah Hales and Steve Smith. Courtesy of TCU Marketing and Communication.

RIGHT
Portrait of Spencer and Marlene Hays located in the Hays Business Commons. Photograph by Phil Hartman.

FAR RIGHT
Portrait of Tom and Marilyn Sumner located in Sumner Hall. Photograph by James Anger. Courtesy of TCU Marketing and Communication.

tour. Spencer Hays, who served on TCU's Board of Trustees from 1987 to 2003, was CEO of the Tom James Company, the world's largest manufacturer and direct seller of custom clothing. He was also the executive chairman of the Southwestern Company, where he began selling books door to door during his student days. The Hays received the medal of Commander of the Legion of Honor, France's highest award, given in recognition of their substantial gift of art to the Musée d'Orsay. Their portrait is featured prominently in the east entrance to Hays Hall, the primary entrance into the commons. The second gift, in the amount of $5.5 million, was made by Tom Sumner '67, MBA '68, CEO and chairman of Houston-based Allpoints Service Corporation, and his wife Marilyn '68. Mr. Sumner has founded six successful companies and served on both the National Alumni Board and the board of trustees. In addition to her degree from TCU, Marilyn DeMoss Sumner earned an MS from the University of Houston. She cofounded an education consulting company, Insights for Leaders, which provides advice to school districts in the Houston area. A portrait of the Sumners is located on the ground floor off the hall's south entrance.

Upon entering the complex from Lubbock, which is now closed to motorized traffic between West Lowden Street and West Bowie Street, you will almost immediately

ABOVE
The Hays Business Commons as viewed from the northeast, 2022. Photograph by Phil Hartman.

encounter the Dan D. Rogers Rotunda that honors the legacy of Dan D. Rogers. Present is a Neeley time capsule as well as various displays testifying to the excellence inherent in the Neeley School. There are also plaques enumerating the almost two dozen endowed professors and other endowed faculty positions in the Neeley School. As well, the names and affiliations of the Neeley Board of Advisers and the Neeley Dean's Council are given here. Spencer Hays Hall includes a state-of-the-art large classroom, several other classrooms, team rooms, and more casual space for student study and gathering. The dean's office occupies the top floor with a view of downtown Fort Worth, providing a visual connection to the location of many businesses in what is now the twelfth largest city in the United States. Running parallel to the Bass Building to the south of Hays Hall, Sumner Hall houses both undergraduate and graduate student services, faculty offices, and conference rooms. To the north, the 201-seat

Shaddock Auditorium, named in honor of Dallasites Kim and Bill Shaddock, is highlighted by environmentally conscious terrazzo floors and staircases. Bill Shaddock '73 is president and partner of the Shaddock Development Company as well as owner and CEO of Capital Title of Texas, the largest independent title company in the United States. Kim McDonald Shaddock has long utilized her university education in social work and sociology as a special education teacher in the Dallas Independent School District.

As you exit the commons to the west, take a moment to admire three exterior trappings of Hays Commons. You will first encounter a landscaped area situated between Smith Hall, Hays Hall, and Tandy Hall. This is the Roach Family Plaza, a calm outdoor gathering space highlighted by a water feature. Second, donated by Frost Bank, the "15 Cubes" statue has adorned the green space slightly to the west of Smith Hall and Tandy Hall since its creation in 2003. Márton Váró, best known for sculpting the iconic angels that adorn downtown Bass Hall, cast this work of art as a symbol of the entrepreneurial spirit and its inherent risk taking. Third, located on the passageway between Spencer Hays Hall and the Shaddock Auditorium, you will find two bas-relief panels, for Management and for Production, which were retained from the outer walls of Dan Rogers Hall and moved to their current location.

ABOVE
Bill and Kim Shaddock (sixth and seventh from the left) at the dedication of the Kim and Bill Shaddock Auditorium. Courtesy of TCU University Advancement.

The Neeley School

ABOVE
M. J. Neeley, 1970s. Courtesy of
Mary Couts Burnett Library.

As early as 1884 TCU had courses in business. Called then the Commercial School, its curriculum included "complete accounting," commercial arithmetic, and commercial law. Except for a brief period between 1886 and 1890, business studies have since been offered under various organizational names: the School of Business from 1896 to 1901; the College of Business from 1901 to 1922; and the Department of Business Administration from 1922 until 1938, when it again became the School of Business. In 1967, it was named the M. J. Neeley School of Business.

In 1947, M. J. Neeley was elected to the university's board of trustees, thereby entering upon an extremely active tenure that lasted twenty-five years. In that time, he served on many committees that set policy and determined direction for the school and was directly involved in the fund-raising, planning, and construction of no less than seven major buildings, including the one that first housed the M. J. Neeley School of Business, Rogers Hall. In 1972, Neeley retired as chairman of the board but continued as an honorary trustee until his 1996 passing. In recognition of this extraordinary man's personal service and his generous financial contributions, the school in 1967 bestowed upon him the honorary doctor of letters.

The Neeley School, TCU's largest college using number of majors as a metric, currently offers the following degrees: BBA, master of accounting, MBA (full-time, professional, executive, energy, and health care options), MS (supply chain management and business analytics options). Neeley is currently ranked as the ninth best undergraduate business school in the US, and its graduate programs enjoy similarly stellar national rankings, including the EMBA program ranked as the best in the state of Texas and thirteenth best in the world.

Rees-Jones Hall

After departing the Hays Commons and venturing west you will almost immediately encounter Rees-Jones Hall, which holds the distinction as TCU's first truly interdisciplinary academic building. Specifically, while no academic buildings technically belong to one college or another, they all have more-or-less discipline-specific ties to

ABOVE
Rees-Jones Hall, 2015. Courtesy of
TCU Marketing and Communication.

one, or sometimes, two colleges. Not so with Rees-Jones, as Provost Nowell Donovan so appropriately articulated during the November 2014 building dedication: "The building belongs to nobody. This building belongs to everybody. We are creating a space where our young Einsteins and young Picassos can get together and appreciate each other's disciplines."

The three-floor, sixty-two-thousand-square-foot Rees-Jones Hall has Cannon Design as its design architect and Hahnfeld Hoffer Stanford as the architect of record, and was built by Linbeck. The $27.2 million price tag was substantially defrayed by a $20 million gift from the Rees-Jones Foundation, the majority of which went to endow

the Karyn Purvis Institute of Child Development, described below. The foundation was formed by Jan and Trevor Rees-Jones, a TCU Trustee. Rees-Jones was the CEO of Chief Oil and Gas, a company instrumental in the development of the Barnett Shale. Rees-Jones Hall houses academic classrooms, faculty offices, interdisciplinary space, study areas, and several academic units. Currently these include two departments in AddRan College of Liberal Arts (Women and Gender Studies, and Critical Race and Ethnic Studies), the Idea Factory, the Karyn Purvis Institute for Child Development (KPICD), and the Ralph Lowe Energy Institute. Founded in 2007 and located on the first floor, the Ralph Lowe Energy Institute serves as a nexus to connect students and seasoned professionals to discover, discuss, and innovate sustainable solutions to all things energy. The institute is part of the Neeley School of Business but retains strong ties to the College of Science and Engineering. In 2021, through the generous financial support of board of trustees member Mary Ralph Lowe, the institute acquired the Ralph Lowe name, honoring her late father for his longtime leadership in the energy industry. Also located on the first floor, the TCU Idea factory was the 2010 brainchild of chemistry professor Dr. Eric Simanek, the Robert A. Welch Chair of Chemistry. It provides an environment and the resources where an idea can be advanced to a prototype and potentially beyond. The Idea Factory is now part of the Neeley School of Business. Housed on the third floor, the Karyn Purvis Institute of

Child Development (KPICD) grew out of the work of psychologist Dr. David Cross and his doctoral student, the late Dr. Karyn Purvis, for whom the institute was named in 2016. With the tagline "learning to change the world … for children," the institute's mission is to help children suffering the effects of early trauma, abuse, or neglect. Drs. Purvis and Cross developed a groundbreaking and transformative approach, which they named Trust-Based Relational Intervention (TBRI®), for interacting with "children from hard places," as Dr. Purvis so lovingly described them. With over twenty full-time faculty and staff, KPICD offers an undergraduate major and minor and a graduate degree. It also conducts cutting-edge research and worldwide training sessions to disseminate the principles of TBRI®. The gift by The Rees-Jones Foundation for the building was motivated in large part by Jan and Trevor Rees-Jones's fervent desire to make the world a better place for children. Their foundation partners with nonprofits in North Texas and around the world to help defend the welfare of children suffering from abuse or neglect.

In addition to the academic units housed in Rees-Jones Hall, there are three physical "stars of the building," so to speak. The first is the Incubator Lab, which occupies the south portion of the third floor. Well worth a walk or elevator ride, the Incubator Lab's high ceilings, large windows, and open feel have made it ideal for meetings, group discussions, and brainstorming sessions. The same attributes also lend the building its distinctive exterior look, particularly when viewed from the south. The second feature is the classrooms present on all three floors. Purposely designed larger than most TCU classrooms, each possesses loads of technology, dry-erase boards on all four walls, and easily movable furniture. As a result, the Rees-Jones Hall classrooms are coveted teaching locations, as the venue allows faculty to engage in active-learning teaching modalities that resonate with the students of today. Without belaboring the point, the traditional "sage on the stage" pedagogical approach—in which the professor drones on, often unwittingly inundating students like a metaphorical fire hydrant—is on life support and has been increasingly abandoned. Requisite to this instructional transformation are classrooms providing an inherent nimbleness, allowing faculty to serve more as a "guide on the side," facilitating interactive learning. This classroom design is coveted by more than TCU faculty; one of us (PH) recalls the provost of the University of North Texas Health Science Center as being particularly taken with Rees-Jones Hall after visiting … so much so that he returned with a cadre of planners hoping to recapitulate these features in building planned for their Health

Science Center. The third feature worth a specific mention is the atrium, which features a large portrait of Jan and Trevor Rees-Jones as well as the maxim "Knowledge is Power" expressed in twelve languages. The atrium exposes two floors, revealing a stairwell, study carrels, conference rooms, and murals devoted to subjects such as world population growth and global water distribution.

A walk up the Intellectual Commons:
Senior Bricks, L'entre-deux anneaux, "We Can, Together," and Clark Brothers Statue

The next building on our tour is Mary Couts Burnett Library. You can enter the library on its west side directly from Rees-Jones Hall through the walkways on the second floor or on the ground floor by crossing a courtyard, replete with tables and chairs for students who prefer outside study. Alternatively, you may elect to proceed up the walkway that is bounded by the Tucker Technology Center, Sid W. Richardson and Winton-Scott to the south, and Rees-Jones and Mary Couts Burnett Library to the north. This swath of campus is referred to as the Intellectual Commons, although of course intellectual endeavors are by no means limited to the confines of these buildings.

You will now encounter four outdoor campus features of note along your walk toward University Drive. To observe the first, stop roughly even with the ramp leading down from the Winton-Scott–Sid Richardson courtyard and gaze down. There you will find engraved bricks bearing the names of graduating seniors, each of whom contributed fifty dollars toward the university's scholarship fund, a tradition begun 2001. The second is the L'entre-deux anneaux ("between two rings") sculpture, situated beneath the south-facing columned portico of Mary Couts Burnett Library. A commemorative plaque and the statue, designed by Bernard Ney, were presented to TCU on March 14, 2002, by the Honorable Ariette Conzenius Paccoud, Luxembourg's ambassador to the United States. Next is the art installation "We Can, Together," which was unveiled in spring 2021. Created by Dan Jian, assistant professor of art and the twelve students in her Drawing II class, the two-sided mural portrays how identity and history differentially informed the works of two artists, Henry Matisse,

a white man, and Romare Bearden, a Black man. The mural was installed ahead of Reconciliation Week, the 2020 series of events celebrating TCU's multiyear Race and Reconciliation efforts to investigate and document TCU's relationship with slavery, racism, and the Confederacy.

Finally, you'll encounter the Clark Brothers statue, once known as Founders Statue. It was fashioned in 1992 by sculptor Carol Thorton '48 with assistance from students Paul Lucke and Chip Armstrong. The brothers Addison and Randolph Clark are portrayed walking across campus as the youthful thirty- and thirty-one-year olds

they were when founding what is now Texas Christian University. Standing eight feet tall and weighing roughly one thousand pounds, its base contains the original 1873 Thorp Spring cornerstone, which had been recently relocated to campus. Clark Brothers statue had its genesis in conversations between Chancellor William "Bill" Tucker and Provost William "Bill" Koehler. Paid for by Chancellor Tucker and his wife Jean, the statue was bronzed in Santa Fe.

Mary Couts Burnett Library

After taking in Clark Brothers statue, you can turn right to behold the grand façade of Mary Couts Burnett Library. Perhaps no other academic unit on campus has undergone as many metamorphoses as has this, the building most central to any university's core mission of knowledge acquisition, storage, and dissemination.

A brief history lesson is now in order. On the morning after the devastating fire in Waco that destroyed the main building and the school's library housed within, librarian Nell Andrew held aloft the *Waco Semi-Weekly Tribune* that had just been delivered and exclaimed: "With this paper we shall begin the rebuilding of the TCU Library." Instead of Waco, of course, the rebuilding would take place in Fort Worth. From 1911 until 1925, the library was provided space on the second floor of the Administration Building (now Reed Hall) in a main reading room just twenty-four by thirty-six feet and a stack area of the same dimensions just below, on the first or "basement" level. Increased acquisitions and student enrollment soon led to a need for additional space. In 1923, when the need seemed most critical, TCU became the recipient of a $3 million estate gift (valued at over $51 million in 2022 dollars) that would undergird the school's financial foundation for years to come—the Mary Couts Burnett Trust. Of course this is speculation, but it's reasonable to postulate that TCU would have not survived the Depression without her gift. Even with it, payment of salaries were delayed several times and faculty took a series of across-the-board pay cuts totalling 43 percent between 1930 and 1934. A stipulation of the bequest was that $150,000 be set aside immediately for the construction of a building and, at the suggestion of then President E. M. Waits, the building to be erected was the Mary Couts Burnett Library.

Born in 1856, Mary Couts was one of five daughters of Colonel James Robertson Couts, a prominent banker and rancher of Parker County. Her father was an admirer of Addison Clark and had made gifts to the pioneer institution during the Thorp Spring days. Mary Couts became the second wife of S. Burk Burnett, a wealthy Fort Worth cattleman. The one child born to the couple, S. Burk Burnett Jr., died as a young man. An often told but unconfirmed account of the circumstances leading to her gift is as follows. By 1920, the relationship between husband and wife had grown tense. Burnett claimed in court that his wife was suffering from "hallucinations" and won a sanity judgment against her. He was then successful in having her committed to limited asylum in a private Weatherford home, until she engineered her own release on the very day, in 1923, of Burk Burnett's death. With the good counsel of her physician, Dr. Charles Harris (who later founded the Harris College of Nursing), she set about to free herself from the charge of insanity. She would also have to fight in court for her "widow's half" of the Burnett estate. Not long after having won the battle for the Burnett estate, seemingly out of the blue, she made her December 1923 bequest to the university. Before that time, Mrs. Burnett had shown no apparent interest in either the school or, indeed, the world of academe. Her choice of TCU as the recipient of her estate was purportedly guided by her physician, Dr. Harris, and perhaps by recollection of her father's support of AddRan College.

By the fall of 1924, the library building was well underway, but Mrs. Burnett was not to see it in its final splendor. She died just before its completion in December of that year. It is told, however, that prior to her death she was driven by the building in its finishing stages and was able to see and perhaps derive pleasure from the all-but-complete structure that would bear her name. The only known portrait of Mary Couts Burnett as well as a commemorative plaque that acknowledges her story hangs on a wall at the top of the "Knowledge is Power" steps on the library's east side.

The library was the first building to be located on university property bordering the east side of University Drive. Prior to the library's construction in 1925, this undeveloped hardscrabble land had been used primarily as an athletic field. The small football stadium, Clark Field, a cinder track, and a baseball diamond were located there. The rest of the land was covered with the ever-present Johnson grass and a few wildflowers, among which scudded the little horned frog. After the football field was relocated in 1930, and until the Winton-Scott Hall was built in 1952, the library stood solitary on this side of the campus.

The core of the original building is the Gearhart Reading Room. Previously known as the Cecil and Ida Green Reading Room, it served as the original reference room and the only public reading area in 1925. The sturdy oak tables and chairs that still reside in the room date from that time. The upper portion the north side of the reading room provides glimpses of the 1950s era bookstacks. This room has long served as the building's anchor, and it still allows students to study in a space that harkens back to the era of the building's namesake. It will remain a beloved spot on campus for many years to come . . . as well as one of memories of day's past, for this grand room has been

ABOVE
Mary Couts Burnett, c. 1886. Courtesy of Mary Couts Burnett Library.

ABOVE
Mary Couts Burnett Library, c. 1929.
Courtesy of Mary Couts Burnett Library.

witness to a spectrum of human activity from serious study to gala receptions to budding college romances. As a librarian previously on the staff, one of us (JS) attributes her choice of profession to the fact that her parents, Professor of Biology Willis Hewatt and Elizabeth Harris, were wed here in a ceremony conducted by the college president. Music was provided by a faculty ensemble, and the reception was prepared by the college cafeteria staff, headed by the bride's mother, Mrs. Georgia Harris.

Little remains to view of the exterior of the initial library building, for three subsequent enlargements, in 1958, 1982, and 2013, surrounded and subsumed the original building and grounds. To the architects' credit, however, 1925 seems comfortably sandwiched between and is compatible with the more recent expansions. The most recent renovation gives silent testimony to the original 1920s-era building through its grand west side façade and garden feature, coupled with the historical images and exhibits on the east side. The design of the original Mary Couts Burnett Library was that of the local architectural firm of W. G. Clarkson and Company. The 1958 expansion was constructed according to the plans drawn by Joseph R. Pelich, Hedrick and Stanley, and Preston M. Geren, Associated Architects. Renowned architect Walter Netsch of Skidmore, Owings and Merrill of Chicago was the designer of the 1982 addition. In 2013, in conjunction with the Rees-Jones Hall project, a complete renovation and small expansion of the 1982 addition was launched, with Cannon Design as the design architect, Hahnfeld Hoffer Stanford the architect of record, and construction by Linbeck.

The most recent project was completed in 2015 and added almost fifteen thousand square feet. It restored the library's main entrance from its somewhat awkwardly situated south side, of 1982 vintage, to one with the sort of grandeur that originally graced the building. Mary Couts Burnett Library's front steps and majestic pillars rightly cast it as the centerpiece of intellectual pursuits on campus, as should be the case at any institution of higher education. It also enhances an already grand vista down University Drive. The front façade was inspired by and recapitulates the architecture and reflection pool of the original 1925 building. Costing $34 million, the extant 81,236 square feet also underwent extensive renovations.

RIGHT
Mary Couts Burnett Library as it appeared in 1959. Courtesy of Mary Couts Burnett Library.

RIGHT
Mary Couts Burnett Library with its then-new south entrance, 1983. Courtesy of Mary Couts Burnett Library.

ABOVE
Mary Couts Burnett Library, 2015, shortly after major renovations were completed. Note the resemblance of the front and associated landscaping to the original building (see p.172). Photograph by Amy Peterson. Courtesy of TCU Marketing and Communication.

On the east side, glass and steel rise through the three-story atrium featuring an amphitheatre where the phrase "Knowledge is Power" appears in twelve languages, which numerically correlated with those spoken by the student body at the time of the project's completion. Other features include:

- "the Wave," a seating area under the lobby steps, space inspired by the Harry Potter Books;
- a dimensional wall graphic that engages viewers outside a private theatre;
- a technology sandbox, which provide students, faculty, and staff the opportunity to try out new devices and software;
- two third-floor study areas for graduate students;
- reservable group study rooms named for famous creators and thought leaders;
- a Fab lab with 3-D printing;
- the "Lizard Lounge," offering a casual meeting environment for graduate students and faculty and conveniently located near the new rendition of the Bistro Burnett;
- the Sumner Academic Heritage room, a comfy living room that showcases the university mace, portraits of TCU chancellors, faculty publications, and photographs of the recipients of the prestigious Chancellor's Award;
- new offices, reading room, conference room, and an expanded temperature and humidity-controlled vault for TCU Special Collections Department and its collections.

The architects successfully blended the old and new; for example, pews from the 1800s church where TCU's founders Addison and Randolph Clark convened have been restored and sit in the Lizard Lounge, which also houses shelves displaying pictures and fun artifacts from the university's history. The renovation has merited several well-deserved recognitions, including TEXO's "Best Building Award," Engineering News-Record's "Best Project Winner for Higher Education Research," and the United Masonry Contractors Association's "2016 Golden Trowel Award."

These renovations continued a trend that began at least twenty years earlier with the recognition that the library's study spaces were outstripped by the growth of the student body and, perhaps more importantly, that students desire an environment

The "Knowledge is Power" steps on the east end of Mary Couts Burnett Library, 2019. Photograph by Jeffrey McWhorter. Courtesy of TCU Marketing and Communication.

that is not completely bereft of food, drink, and quiet conversation. To that end, in the late 1990s the Burnett Bistro Café was added to the library. A few years later classical music was piped into parts of the library. The library still has several quiet zones, but this is most definitely not your mother's library. As stated in an article in *TCU Magazine*, "We don't shhhhhh anymore." Most of the wooden desks were replaced with more ergonomic furniture, often with armrests. Computer workstations were added throughout the building. To make room, a substantial portion of the library's collection was moved offsite to climate-controlled storage spaces. At present, close to 50 percent of the print collection (almost seven hundred thousand volumes) are offsite, having been moved to the TCU-owned, seventy thousand-square-foot building on Bolt Street that includes the library's Annex, a high-density shelving facility located two miles south of campus. Books and periodicals can be readily retrieved if requested.

Among the library's special collections are the papers of former Speaker of the United States House of Representatives Jim Wright. An exhibit highlighting Speaker Wright's career is located just outside of Special Collections on the third-floor east side of the building. In addition, the library is repository for the archival records and audio- and videotapes of the Van Cliburn International Piano Competitions, the Amon G. Carter papers, the American Hymnal Society holdings, the George T. Abell Collection of Antique Maps, and the William Luther Lewis Collection. This last contains works, many of which are first editions, of eighteenth- and nineteenth-century English and American writers. Premier in the collection is one of only two copies known to exist of the complete edition of nine quartos of Shakespeare printed by Thomas Pavier in 1619. An especially fine reproduction of *The Book of Kells* is on view to the public inside the offices of Special Collections on the third floor. The volume was a gift of Mrs. W. A. Moncrief, a member of a family whose community and institutional support continues to be generous.

Leaving the library, retrace your way down the front entrance steps and follow the pavement west, turning right at the first intersecting walk toward the religion center located in buildings immediately north of the library. On the way you may want to stop and rest in the shaded pleasance that lies just between the far west end of Lowden Street and University Drive. Complete with a tranquil water feature, this small park area, which was landscaped in 1987 and has since been incorporated into Veteran's Plaza, was a gift of the TCU House of Student Representatives in honor of Mary

Evans Beasley, wife of the late Theodore P. Beasley. The Beasleys generously support-ed numerous programs on the campus throughout many years. The commemorative stone in the garden simply, but eloquently, says of Mary Evans Beasley that she is "a friend of students."

Religion Center: Robert Carr Chapel, Moore Building, Beasley Hall, Harrison Building

In 1953, in a significant departure from tradition, architect Joseph R. Pelich designed the religion center complex along Georgian Colonial Revival lines, the single instance of this style on the campus. Tradition and traditionalists were further outraged by the selection of the masonry color. TCU President Sadler, weary of being asked why the new buildings were "red" rather than the usual buff, said: "In the first place they are not red; they're pink. The architects felt that this shade of brick would harmonize with the other buildings, and would be more appropriate for a chapel." Viewing the religion center now with its centerpiece, the Robert Carr Chapel, and trying to imag-ine it cream-toned and red-roofed, one would have to agree that the choice of style and brick was just right.

Preliminary plans to relocate Brite College of the Bible from what is now the Bailey Building had called for a dual-purpose unit. One section would house the graduate studies of Brite and the other would accommodate undergraduate religion studies, as well as provide classroom space for other AddRan College courses. A large contribu-tion and promise for complete funding from San Angelo rancher and oil man Robert G. Carr made it possible to add the beautiful chapel. Today the complex consists of the central chapel, the Moore and Harrison Buildings that house Brite Divinity School, and Beasley Hall, providing offices and classrooms for the Department of Religion. An enclosed cloister along the back of the chapel joins the Robert Carr, Beasley, and Moore. The Harrison Building, situated behind the original complex relative to Uni-versity Drive, was added to the complex in 2011 to meet the expanded needs of Brite.

ABOVE
Robert G. Carr, 1970s. Photograph by Linda Kaye. Courtesy of Mary Couts Burnett Library.

ABOVE
Robert Carr Chapel flanked by Beasley Hall
and the Moore Building, 1954. Courtesy of
Mary Couts Burnett Library.

Robert Carr Chapel

Completed in 1954, Robert Carr Chapel, with its 137-foot spire, has become a TCU landmark and can be seen from high-rise windows in downtown Fort Worth. It was struck by lightning in April 1994, necessitating replacement of the small, urn-like structures that decorate the lower portion of the steeple. Although efforts by one of us (PH) failed to establish its veracity in printed word, TCU lore has it that no campus structure should eclipse the height of the chapel.

The chapel incorporates a number of design elements from American Colonial churches, recommended by the wife of the president, Mrs. Frances Sadler, who travelled throughout the eastern states studying both architectural and decorative styles. The results of her research and the high quality of her taste are reflected in the simple elegance of Carr Chapel. Ionic stone columns support the pedimented entrance portico; cornices here and elsewhere around the walls are underscored with deep dentils. The spire is an exact replica of the one atop the famous Old Lyme Church in Connecticut, and the appointments in the chapel interior continue the replication of early American structures. The brass chandeliers are after the design of those in St. Michael's Church in Charleston, South Carolina; the pulpit is patterned after those in King's Chapel of Boston and Christ Church in Cambridge. The arched heads of the Palladian windows that grace both the chapel and the cloister walls reflect the style of Mount Vernon and a church in Watertown, Massachusetts. Dark mahogany enhances the interior simplicity of this quiet place of worship.

The present organ, with its three keyboards and thirty-six stops, was built by the Ross King Organ Company of Fort Worth. It replaced, in 1979, the original two-keyboard, fourteen-stop Reuter organ. The chapel carillon, built by the Cincinnati firm of Verdin, was installed in

ABOVE
Robert Carr Chapel and the Beasley Hall,
2017. Photograph by Amy Peterson. Courtesy
of TCU Marketing and Communication.

ABOVE
The interior of Robert Carr Chapel
on the occasion of its 2017 rededication.
Photograph by Amy Peterson. Courtesy
of TCU Marketing and Communication.

1984, replacing an earlier one provided by Robert Carr. The carillon is electronic, not, as one would expect, a cast-bell mechanism. Through an architectural omission, the chapel tower will not accommodate the hoisting of bells, and architectural design further prohibits renovation for tower bells. But the Verdin carillon that plays the short measures of the TCU alma mater before striking each hour is a close approximation to cast bells, and the tonality is clean and clear.

The chapel underwent a substantial renovation in 2017 aimed at addressing accessibility issues as well as increasing its functionality and aesthetics. Among the changes were a major overhaul to the chancel that included installation of a movable pulpit, lectern, and communion table and chairs, each replacing their stationary forebearers. As well, the organ was raised to a place of greater prominence. The chancel was also extended slightly to allow inclusion of a grand piano, enhancing its acoustics relative to its previous location. A retractable screen was installed and lighting redone to better highlight the chancel. In the sanctuary, the two front pews were removed and two others altered, thus enabling facile wheelchair seating. The wooden pews were refinished and adorned with beige cushions. A dark purple (what other color would do?) runner now decorates the center aisle. The hardwood flooring was refinished to better match the sanctuary's wood accents. In addition, the restrooms were made ADA compliant. Finally, the building was topped with a new roof, and the walkways adjoining the chapel on its east and west sides were repaved. While the initial renovation plans met with some initial heartfelt resistance by some who held the chapel particularly near and dear, the final result has been universally praised.

The chapel is in constant use for student worship services, campus memorial services, and as a classroom for student preachers. It is also heavily booked throughout the year for wedding ceremonies. Before the COVID pandemic, the chapel annually averaged more than fifteen thousand guests, one hundred weddings, and four hundred events. In 2012 it was nominated as one of the best ceremony venues in the DFW area by the American Association of Certified Wedding Planners. Speaking of weddings, no account of Robert Carr would be complete without mention of Emmett G. Smith '54 MM, who held the Herndon Professorship during most of his forty-five years on TCU's faculty. Serving as the chapel organist beginning with its 1954 opening, he provided the music for over 2,600 weddings. Professor Smith hasn't seen it all, but certainly comes close in terms of his exposure to memorable wedding foibles.

Moore Building

The three-story Jo Ann and Wayne Moore Building was built in 1953 and named in the Moores' honor in 1997. It communicates directly with the chapel and is home to a portion of Brite Divinity School. Wayne Moore was a geologist, oilman, and rancher who served as chair of the Brite Divinity School Board of Trustees for twenty-three years. Mrs. Moore was a Midland civic leader, a member of TCU's Board of Trustees, and was active in the Christian Church (Disciples of Christ). The basement level includes a kitchen and a large community room, Weatherly Hall, named in honor of John F. Weatherly, whose family provided funds for the hall. In recognition of their support, the university conferred an honorary degree on Mrs. Maggie Weatherly, a member of the family and leading churchwoman of Panhandle, Texas.

ABOVE
Wayne Moore. Courtesy of Brite Divinity School.

ABOVE LEFT
The Moore Building in the religion complex, 2018. Photograph by Jeffrey McWhorter. Courtesy of TCU Marketing and Communication.

Theodore Prentice Beasley Hall

ABOVE
Theodore Presley Beasley.
Courtesy of Mary Couts
Burnett Library.

To the north of the chapel and also physically connected is Beasley Hall, also built in 1953, which houses the Department of Religion. Known for many years as the Undergraduate Religion Building, it was later renamed to honor Theodore Prentice Beasley. A member of the board of trustees and major benefactor to Brite, Beasley was nationally prominent in affairs of the Christian Church (Disciples of Christ) and was a business, civic, and religious leader in Dallas. He was recipient of many honors, among them the Lay Churchman of the Year award of the Religious Heritage of America, Inc. in 1952 and, in 1965, a citation from the National Conference of Christians and Jews. TCU conferred on him the honorary doctor of laws degree in 1968.

Beasley Hall underwent a relatively recent and substantial two-step renovation. Phase I, begun and completed in the summer of 2013, was a three-story, 3,100-square-foot addition to Beasley's east end. This introduced an elevator to the building and an additional exit stairwell to replace a 1953-vintage external fire escape. A new entry and study lounge was also added. Phase II took place in the summer of 2014. All nine classrooms were essentially gutted and reconstructed, and all twenty-three religion departmental offices were rearranged and rebuilt to better suit the needs of the departmental faculty and staff. In addition, restrooms were completely renovated to render them ADA compliant. The natural lighting, such a key element in the original building design, was maintained with the installation of large, multipaned colonial-style windows throughout the building. Hahnfeld Hoffer Stanford was the architect and the Linbeck Group the builder.

Harrison Building

Situated behind the Moore Building relative to University Drive, the twenty-five-thousand-square-foot W. Oliver and Nell A. Harrison Building joined the Brite physical plant in 2011. It is not to be confused with the Harrison that faces onto West Berry Street, the latter named for Brenda and Mike Harrison, although Mike is Oliver and Nell's son. The Harrison Building displaced a parking lot, which itself for years was partially occupied by a series of temporary buildings that once housed some Brite faculty and others from what was then the AddRan College of Science and Humanities. The Harrison Building was a welcome and much-needed expansion of Brite, as the fifty students and six faculty members of 1952 (when the divinity school moved into the Moore Building) had expanded to 240 and twenty-three, respectively, by 2010. Oliver Harrison was a Brite graduate and served for many years on the Brite Board of Trustees, including in 1952 when the board voted unanimously to admit Black students. The building cost $11.5 million, with an additional $3.5 million devoted to renovating the Moore Building. This was funded in part through the "Building a Brite future" capital campaign, which yielded a $1.5 million challenge grant from the J. E. and L. E. Mabee Foundation. The Georgian Colonial Revival style has allowed the building to harmonize with the rest of the religion center. The Harrison Building contains a mixture of classrooms, offices, a conference center, a series of breakout rooms, and the Walker Preaching Center, named for renowned Disciples of Christ minister Granville Walker (1908–1991). It is highlighted by thoughtful décor. In addition, wood and glass doors from the old Brown Lupton Student Center were incorporated into the building. The building also has a 1930's Reeder oil portrait of Colby D. Hall, Brite's inaugural dean. This visual reminder of one of TCU's and Brite's most important figures was moved from Special Collections and now hangs in the Brite president's conference room. If any one name may be said to have achieved legendary status in the history of Brite Divinity School, it is surely that of Colby D. Hall. Educated at Add-Ran, Transylvania, the College of the Bible, and Columbia University, Dr. Hall became dean of Brite College in 1914 and served in the post for an astonishing thirty-three years. He also served as dean of the university from 1920 until 1943. We will return to a further discussion of his accomplishments when we tour Colby Residence Hall.

The land on which the religion center stands was bought in the early 1920s from landowners Robert L. Green and John L. Cassell. Until sometime in the 1930s, Lowden Street was named Cassell Boulevard. Several large homes which stood on the property were converted to residences for women when Jarvis Hall, the only campus provision for women, was at capacity. A two-story brick home on the northeast corner of Princeton, once owned by the Green family, was used by the university from around 1948 to 1975, first by the development office and then by the Speech and Hearing Clinic of the School of Fine Arts.

ABOVE
Nell Harrison (left), seated
with Chancellor Sadler, 1965.
Courtesy of Mary Couts
Burnett Library.

RIGHT
The religion complex as
viewed from the southeast,
with the Harrison Building
in the foreground, 2013.
of TCU Marketing and
Communication.

ABOVE
W. Oliver Harrison, 1970s.
Photograph by Linda Kaye.
Courtesy of Mary Couts
Burnett Library.

Brite Divinity School

The history of the divinity school parallels much of that of the university itself. From Thorp Spring days, the school continuously offered studies in the Bible, but it was not until 1895 that a charter was obtained for "The Bible Department." The first chair of that department, J. B. Sweeney, gave impetus to a plan that would establish and endow a Bible Chair and later a Bible College.

The precipitous event that secured the chair and the college for TCU is thought to be a baptism in 1897 near the small West Texas town of Marfa. Addison Clark, co-founder and president of the young school, had come by invitation to preach. Among the listeners that day were wealthy cattleman Luke Brite and his wife, Eddie, nee Edward McMinn Anderson. Inspired by the words of the Reverend Clark and by the thought of what the church could mean to themselves and to future generations, both husband and wife confessed publicly and were baptized the same day into the Disciples of Christ denomination. The Brites' story of the building of their western cattle kingdom, the hardships and tragedies they knew, their unshakable faith, and their steadfast generosity is told more fully in the book-length *Brites of Capote* by Noel Keith and in an article entitled "The Brite Legacy" by Jane Pattie.

Suffice it to say that when asked for his support in developing the divinity program at TCU, Lucas Charles Brite hesitated only long enough to "talk over [the] proposition with Mrs. Brite," and within two weeks the College of the Bible was assured of $25,000 to be used for a suitable building to house its program. In subsequent actions, the Brites donated $25,000 to endow a chair of English Bible and a total of $37,750 toward the Bible building. Over protest from the donors, the college was designated Brite College of the Bible. It was incorporated in 1914 as a unit separate from TCU and hence has an independent governance structure.

Mr. Brite was elected chairman of the Brite College Board of Trustees in 1926 and served in that capacity until 1941. On September 4 of that year, Brite died following an emergency appendectomy. Mrs. Eddie Brite finished the unexpired term of her husband on the Board of Trustees of Brite College and the university board as well, her tenure on both lasting up to her death in 1963.

In 1963, the name of Brite College was changed to Brite Divinity School. It has been accredited by the American Association of Theological Schools since 1939 and is the largest Christian Church-Disciples of Christ seminary in the nation. Brite of-

ABOVE
Lucas Charles Brite. Courtesy of Mary Couts Burnett Library.

ABOVE
Edward "Eddie" McMinn Brite. Courtesy of Mary Couts Burnett Library.

fers nine advanced degrees as well as several certificates. Because of its relationship with TCU, Brite uses many of TCU's services. In 2019, Brite and TCU reaffirmed an agreement that articulates the university's contractual commitment to provide a variety of support services. It has been and continues to be a truly symbiotic relationship.

The Creative Commons

With the TCU Music Center at its physical nexus, the Creative Commons draws on the expertise, passion, and talent resident in the flanking and contiguous Fine Arts Building, Mary Couts Burnett Library, J.M. Moudy Visual Arts and Communication Building, and Rees-Jones Hall. The Commons is an open area designed so that students and faculty may draw inspiration from green spaces, the gentle flow of water, and common areas. The Creative Commons and its resident buildings provide concrete evidence of TCU's commitment to providing first-class facilities for the fine arts as well as its institutional belief in the importance and power of the fine arts to enrich humanity.

TCU Music Center

Directly east of the Harrison Building is the TCU Music Center. You can enter this magnificent building from the north side into the elegant Keith & Linda Reimers Mixon Lobby, which provides immediate access to the world-class 717-seat Van Cliburn Concert Hall at TCU, which is designed to rival well-known venues such as Fort Worth's Bass Performance Hall in downtown Fort Worth. The Van Cliburn Hall at TCU is designed with electronically adjustable acoustics that will optimize a variety of performances. It also has a high ceiling to accentuate reverberation. The hall's name honors the legacy of Harvey Lavan "Van" Cliburn (1934–2013), the concert pianist long associated with Fort Worth. As a relatively unknown twenty-three-year-old from east Texas, Van Cliburn achieved international fame at the height of the Cold War by winning the inaugural 1958 International Tchaikovsky Piano Competition. He toured extensively throughout his career, playing for royalty, heads of state, and every president from Dwight Eisenhower to Barack Obama. The quadrennial and

eponymous Van Cliburn International Piano Competition, begun in 1962, was held for years in Ed Landreth Auditorium, a later stop on our tour. Beginning in 2022, the preliminary (thirty competitors) and quarterfinal (eighteen competitors) rounds will occur in the Van Cliburn Concert Hall at TCU before the last two rounds shift to the Bass Performance Hall. You may learn more about the inspiration for the hall by visiting the Van Cliburn Life and Legacy Exhibit, located on the TCU Music Center's second floor.

Walking the halls of the building, you'll notice the multiple practice rooms as well as a most interesting diversity of locker sizes and shapes, designed to accommodate various musical instruments. The Music Center also has a five-thousand-square-foot Band Rehearsal Hall, large enough to accommodate the entire Horned Frog Marching Band. In addition, the Ann Koonsman Orchestra Rehearsal Hall provides the first dedicated rehearsal space for the TCU Symphony orchestra in its one-hundred-plus-year history. Finally, percussion rehearsal rooms, individual practice rooms for students, faculty teaching studios, and a student lounge have been included in the building.

As you can imagine, sound abatement is critical, given the frequent concurrent individual and group practices mandated by a school of music whose enrollment doubled between 2005 and 2020. This has been achieved by pouring separate concrete slabs with foam separators in between. In essence, the Music Center was designed as if it were several conjoined buildings. The TCU Music Center's opening to faculty, staff, and students has largely addressed the acute problem generated by the School of Music's substantive growth, as it was formerly spread across four buildings (Landreth, Center, Music Building south, and Jarvis Hall) which spans the campus from north to south. However, the school remains in multiple buildings (Landreth, Walsh, and Jarvis) even after the Music Center construction. The new building is phase one of an envisioned two-phase comprehensive structure that would house the entire program.

The TCU Music Center was designed by BORA, a Portland, Oregon-based architectural firm. The $53 million price tag was paid in part through generous donations totaling just under $14 million from several donors. Dr. Richard Gipson, himself a renowned musician, served TCU for sixteen years as director of the School of Music,

followed by a four-year stint as dean of the College of Fine Arts. He was a passionate advocate for the college, working effectively not only to build partnerships with local arts organizations but also to expand college facilities, with the TCU Music Center his crowning achievement. When asked, Chancellor Victor J. Boschini summed up Dean Gipson's role nicely: "To say that we would not have our beautiful new Music Center without the work of Dr. Gipson would be an understatement. Richard worked tirelessly, both friend-raising and fund-raising to make this new facility a reality." The building was put into service in the fall of 2020, but the COVID pandemic delayed the grand opening until spring 2022.

ABOVE
Looking into the TCU Music Center with a bust of Van Cliburn facing the concert hall named in his honor, 2021. Photograph by Rodger Mallison. Courtesy of TCU Marketing and Communication.

ABOVE
TCU Music Center at dusk, 2021. Photograph by
Rodger Mallison. Courtesy of TCU Marketing and
Communication.

196 CHAPTER 7

Fine Arts Building

Exiting the Music Center, you can proceed northward into the main entrance of the Fine Arts Building, which serves as the creative hub for the Departments of Design and Fashion Merchandising. Opening in the fall of 2019, this thirty-three-thousand-square-foot facility includes nine state-of-the art learning spaces. Entering the building, you are immediately struck by its sleek, modern feel, with the architect's goal to inspire students and faculty alike. Walk around and peek into classrooms and laboratories loaded with specialized, discipline-specific equipment, including computer labs with software unique to the various industries for which students are training. On the first floor you can see a jury room (where students present their creations), an interior design studio, a Fashion Merchandising (FAME) classroom, a textiles-testing lab, a lighting lab, an apparels construction lab, a student open lab, a fashion computer lab, a graphic design lab, a design plotting room, and a photo studio. Costing $17 million, the building was designed by Cannon Design, and Linbeck carried out the construction.

Moudy Building

The J. M. Moudy Building for Visual Arts and Communication represents an even more radical break with traditional TCU architecture than the "pink" religion center. The extensive use of "raw" concrete, off-white masonry, and glass caused a controversy then, and years later still has its advocates and critics, although much more muted in recent years. Essentially two buildings (or at the very least separate and non-communicating wings of a single building), Moudy North houses several units of the College of Fine Arts, while Moudy South is home to the Schieffer College of Communication. The main entrance to both wings of the Moudy complex is through a three-story-high octagonal atrium under a protective canopy of tempered glass. The center of the atrium, which underwent a 2002 update to its shrubbery, seating, and artwork, is open to the sky and is landscaped with magnolia trees and native flora. Benches edge the wide walks near the periphery of the planted area. Intended as a "place where students, faculty, and visitors can sit and enjoy a few moments of rest," the atrium attracts colonies of birds that inhabit the upper reaches of the canopy. It also provides a venue for students to display large-scale artwork, which makes a walk through the atrium even more worth the while.

Following the desire of the donors, the building was named in honor of James M. Moudy (1916–2004), chancellor of the university from 1965 to 1979. Prior to his appointment as chancellor, he had served as dean of the graduate school and as academic and executive vice chancellor. He was the first TCU alumnus to be named its chief executive; his successor, William E. Tucker, was the second. During Moudy's tenure, first as vice chancellor for academic affairs and then as chancellor, six research-oriented doctoral programs were established, and the Honors Program begun. His emphasis on a strengthened academic program brought to TCU recognition of quality in the liberal arts and in the sciences. During his regime, also, chapters of Phi Beta Kappa and Sigma Xi were brought to the campus. In 1979, the year of Dr. Moudy's retirement, the school recognized his devoted and able leadership by conferring on him the honorary doctor of laws. The building named in his honor was dedicated in 1982.

Designed specifically for academic studies in art, journalism, radio-television-film, and speech communication, the two-part, $16 million structure was made possible by a gift from the Amon G. Carter Foundation, represented then by Amon G. Carter Jr., Ruth Carter Stevenson, and Katrine Deakins. The same foundation provided a

ABOVE
Chancellor James M. Moudy.
Courtesy of Mary Couts Burnett
Library.

LEFT
J. M. Moudy Visual Arts and Communi-
cation Building, 2022.
Photograph by Phil Hartman.

$1.5 million endowment for the building's maintenance in 1995. Mrs. Stevenson was responsible for choosing the Connecticut architectural firm of Kevin Roche, John Dinkeloo and Associates. The Moudy Building was the first Texas project of these architects, who were internationally noted for their "glass clad" designs.

In the conceptual design of the building, Roche's primary consideration was the already existing architectural environment and the site on the corner of University Drive and Cantey Street. Roche explained that his selection of plain uncolored brick related it to other campus buildings, and he purposely set back the south wing of Moudy so as to provide a view of the columnar entrance to the Carr Chapel. Roche was of the opinion that "what happens on that site [the northernmost entrance to campus grounds], will give one the first impression of what TCU is."

If you stand on the street curb squarely in front of the Moudy Building and face west, you can see at least a little of what TCU is and has been. You can see the classical columns of the 1911 Jarvis Hall clearly across University Drive to the left and the Georgian front of the 1949 Landreth Hall directly across the street. University Christian Church with its 1930s Spanish-style architecture is catercorner to the right across University Drive, and moving a fourth-turn to your left, you can see through and above the live oak branches to the colonial lines of the religion center with its towering chapel spire. Turning full round, you see close up the modern lines of the 1982 concrete-masonry-glass Moudy Building.

Moudy North has the Dean's Office of the College of Fine Arts located on its first floor. Also there is the J.M. Moudy Art Gallery with its regular displays of faculty, student, and community art work. High-ceilinged studios with an abundance of north light are features of the ceramics and sculpture facilities on the building's north side. Present within are huge kilns for firing all kinds of ceramics. Finally on the first floor, a 154-seat lecture hall is situated on the south side. The balance of the School of Art resides on the second floor with a similar abundance of natural lighting and discipline-specific technology. The school is joined by the departments of Art Education and Art History as well as a Visual Resources Library.

The College of Fine Arts offers thirty-three undergraduate degree options and twenty-four advanced degree programs. It is organized into Schools of Art, Music, and Classical and Contemporary Dance, and Departments of Design, Fashion Merchandising, and Theatre. The TCU community and indeed all of Fort Worth benefit from literally hundreds of annual performances and exhibitions offered by the

college, most open to the public and many without charge.

The south wing contains the Schieffer College of Communication, which separated from the College of Fine Arts in 2000 as a part of a larger college, school, and program reorganization. Four academic programs—Communication Studies; Film, Television and Digital Media; Journalism; and Strategic Communication—plus KTCU Radio, the Student Media program, and Roxo (the student-run advertising and public relations agency), and the dean's officer are housed in Moudy South. In 2013, the college assumed the name of Bob Schieffer, perhaps TCU's most famous alumnus. Bob '59 and wife Pat '61 have generously supported TCU by giving of both their time and financial resources. Born in Austin, Mr. Schieffer received his BA in journalism and English. After serving in the Air Force for three years, he worked for the *Fort Worth Star-Telegram* and, among other distinctions, was the first reporter from a Texas newspaper to be embedded in Vietnam. He spent the bulk of his career in our nation's capital, serving as a versatile and consummate anchor at CBS News, where his duties included hosting *Face the Nation* for almost twenty-five years. He also moderated three presidential debates. In addition to their strong interest in "his" college, the Schieffers served as honorary co-chairs of the successful seven-year, $434 million *The Campaign for TCU.*

Moudy South has undergone several significant renovations in recent years. The first, completed in 2010, created a 2,300-square-foot convergence center designed to expose students to the breadth of the field of journalism in the new millennium. Bringing together the TCU *Skiff*, TCU News Now, and the *Image* magazine operations in one newsroom, the $5.6 million expansion, with generous support from the Schieffers, provides a real-world environment for student learning. In 2014, a room on the first floor was dedicated to presenting various artifacts from Bob Schieffer's career, such as the notebooks used during the presidential debates he moderated. This is well worth a few minutes of your time.

The history of the student newspaper, the *Skiff*, deserves brief mention in a book describing the buildings on campus, in part because of its rather itinerate nature. Founded in 1902 in the room of an enterprising student, the *Skiff* temporarily roosted in two rooms of the Administration Building (now Dave Reed Hall) with the 1927 birth of the Department of Journalism. After a few years, the *Skiff*'s home moved to the cellar of the "little gym" (now Erma Lowe Hall) . . . and from there to the basement of Brite College (now the Bailey Building). In the 1940s, yet another move ensued, to the basement of Goode Hall (which stood on the site of Clark Hall). A 1952 relocation brought the student newspaper to temporary quarters in the World War II-vintage barracks known as "splinter village." Then on to Dan Rogers Hall in 1957, and finally to the Moudy Building in 1981. The hard-copy daily so many depended upon for campus news has largely been replaced with an online version, TCU360, but a printed weekly version of the *Skiff* is distributed during the fall and spring semesters.

In addition to the Schieffer Room, the first floor is occupied by the Department of Film, Television and Digital Media as well as KTCU The Choice (88.7), TCU's student-run radio station, which joined the FM airwaves in 1964 with a weekday format primarily of indie rock, alternative, EDM, and local artists. One of us (PH) particularly enjoys *Curtain Up!*, a Sunday morning journey into the world of musical theatre hosted by Dr. Harry Parker, longtime chair of TCU's Department of Theatre. The dean's office joins the Departments of Journalism and Strategic Communication as well as Roxo on the second floor. Roxo is the college's advertising and public-relations agency, providing training opportunities to students and quality product to over one hundred businesses and organizations across Texas. The Department of Communications Studies occupies the third floor.

Also on the East campus . . .

As TCU took root after its 1910 move to Fort Worth, the area surrounding campus took on an increasingly residential feel. By the 1920s, most of the homes that lined Lowden and Princeton Streets, along with other streets north and east of the campus, were occupied by faculty and staff of TCU. Beginning in 1924, the university began to purchase the land and, as a result, the campus has expanded considerably to the east. Still, the fact that TCU is largely bounded by private residences lends the campus a small-town, endearing charm, if nothing else through osmosis. A significant number of residences immediately proximal to the buildings on campus have long since been cleared and now serve as parking lots, which many students would argue remain in short supply (particularly between the "prime-time" class hours of 9 a.m. to 2 p.m.). However, several structures, while not a formal part of our tour, deserve mention:

Secrest-Wible

Located on Merida Avenue just off Berry Street, the Secrest-Wible Building is home to extended education, and, until recent years, risk management, a portion of information technology, and some business services. In 2018, a significant portion of the building was renovated to accommodate the TCU Opera Program. The building now contains a one hundred-seat rehearsal studio theatre, faculty offices, and a classroom.

Formerly housing Shannon Funeral Home, the building was named in honor of E. Leigh Secrest and Howard Wible. Dr. Secrest, who passed away in 2016, was a Phi Beta Kappa graduate of MIT with a PhD in theoretical physics. Joining TCU in 1965, and in his capacity as the president of the TCU Research Foundation and dean of the graduate school, he was a prolific fundraiser and was instrumental in raising TCU's research profile. Howard G. Wible (1920–2015) enjoyed a twenty-seven-year career at TCU, beginning in TCU's Evening College before joining the full-time faculty in the Neeley School of Business. He was appointed vice chancellor for Student Life in 1968 and became the vice chancellor for Academic Affairs and provost in 1972. He also served as acting chancellor in spring 1974 while then Chancellor Moudy was on leave with a grant from the Danforth Foundation.

Campus Police Building

Built in 1997, the 5,197 square foot Campus Police Building is located on Lubbock Avenue just off Berry Street. The TCU Police Department's mission is to provide a safe learning environment for students, faculty, staff, and visitors through mutual respect and shared responsibility of community policing. The TCU Police do a superb job in fulfilling their mission statement.

TCU Press

Moving to its present location on the corner of Sandage Avenue and West Bowie in 2001, TCU Press has traditionally published historical and creative works related to the American Southwest and Texas . . . including this book!

Leibrock Village

Opening in 1999, Leibrock Village includes five buildings (Beasley, Abell-Hanger, Moore, Hill, and Mabee). The village is named in honor of former Brite Trustee Robert Leibrock and his wife Prudie. It sits on a 3.7-acre block bounded by West Louden Street, McCart Avenue, West Bowie Street, and Sandage Avenue. In addition to common areas, the buildings consist primarily of unfurnished one- and two-bedroom apartments rented by Brite Divinity School students, although one apartment is furnished and used to house campus visitors. In addition, TCU has rental opportunities for graduate students located immediately to the east and west of Leibrock Village.

And soon to come

The board of trustees has approved the design for two residence halls on the east campus with an accompanying dining project, with the goal of completion by fall 2024. They are to be situated immediately east of the Hays Business Commons.

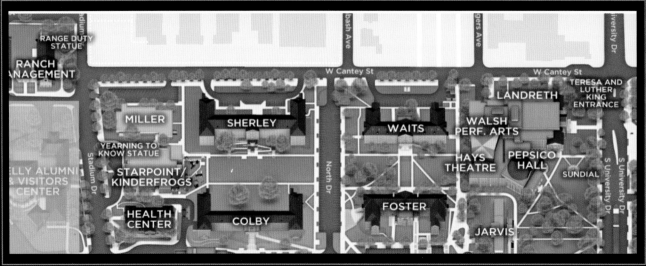

CHAPTER 8

The North Portion of the West Campus

I t is now time to cross University Drive at the Cantey Street intersection and work your way through the northern portion of the west campus. We'll begin at the complex that is Landreth Hall and the Walsh Center.

Ed Landreth Hall

Built in 1949 at a cost of $1.5 million, what is now designated as Ed Landreth Hall would claim several "firsts." It was the first classroom building to be added to the campus since 1914, when Brite College was constructed, and the first permanent structure built for instructional purposes since 1921, when the gymnasium was built. Initially calling for a domed structure with a decorative cupola atop, the plan was altered to the present style when it was evident funds would not be available for the more elaborate building. Even then, it had to wait three years for full funding.

Completed, the building was the largest of its kind in Texas, if not in the South, and was the only structure in the nation providing complete teaching space and equipment for all the arts under one roof. In fact, additional space made it possible to add new programs, some of which would grow to become popular and productive units of the present College of Fine Arts.

OPPOSITE
Map showing the campus structures discussed in this chapter.

ABOVE
Ed Landreth Hall, 1947. Courtesy
of Mary Couts Burnett Library.

The building was designed by the team of architects that had responsibility for the many buildings erected from 1949 through 1965—Wyatt Hedrick, Preston Geren, and Joseph Pelich. The exterior style resembles the earlier columned campus buildings, but instead of prominent freestanding structural elements, the columns are engaged. In addition, the entrance façade with its steps mounting from each side reflects neo-Georgian architecture rather than the earlier classical look. Pelich later patterned the remodeling of Reed Hall in the same style, sans columns.

The exterior of Landreth is a bit more ornate than other campus buildings of the same vintage, using stone carvings liberally. Most are generic, having little or no symbolism, but one bears special notice. In the pediment over the outer entrance to the Buschman Theatre is a particularly appealing rendition of ladies, clad in classical attire, engaged in terpsichore. The extensive use of the cast stone is given brief relief in the Tennessee Tavernelle rose marble panels on either side of the north and south entrances to the main hall. Dr. T. Smith McCorkle, dean of fine arts from 1942 to 1955, is given credit for planning and overseeing the construction of the interior space of Landreth Hall. His portrait, along with that of Ed Landreth, is displayed in the foyer of the building.

The building is actually composed of three main units. The first is an auditorium that seats 1,200. It occupies the central position of Ed Landreth and extends up through the three floors above the basement level. It can be most directly accessed through the front, University Drive-facing door. A foyer enables faculty to congregate indoors before processing in the fall and spring convocations that punctuate academic years. The acoustics in the main auditorium are especially fine, having been enhanced in 1973 from the original "dead" sound surface treatment. Following instructions from David Nibbilen, an acoustician from the Möller Company of Hagerstown, Maryland, the renovation included the addition of hard plaster and curved surfaces to provide enough reflective surface for good sound travel. The auditorium also received a $500,000 renovation in 2000, gaining new curtains and carpeting, catwalks, and aisle lighting. The project was completed by PMK, a Dallas-based company specializing in acoustics and theatre. The auditorium houses a concert pipe organ, one of the largest in the South. Built by the Möller Company, the four-keyboard organ has sixty

ABOVE
Ed Landreth Hall, 2010. Photograph by Carolyn Cruz. Courtesy of TCU Marketing and Communication.

stops and was valued in the 1990s at $492,000. For many years the auditorium was home to the quadrennial Van Cliburn International Piano Competition. In addition, Landreth Hall houses smaller organs for teaching and practice and many Steinway pianos. The second component of Ed Landreth consists of faculty and staff offices, studios, classrooms, and practice rooms that flank the great hall on three sides. Faculty and staff from both the Departments of Music and Theatre are housed in these offices.

The building's third component is the Jerita Foley Buschman Theatre and Box Office, which lies on its northwest side. Rededicated November 17, 2005, the renaming of the formerly innominate University Theatre honors Jerita Foley Buschman '46, longtime friend of the Department of Theatre, who donated $550,000 shortly before her death. Her gift provided the stimulus for a $1.2 million project that included substantial renovations to the theatre itself, as well as creation of a large acting studio on the third floor, four faculty offices on the second floor, and a north-facing lobby with an entrance off Cantey Street. The 175-seat Buschman Theatre provides an intimate setting for campus drama, including for a ten-year period (2009–2018) the summer Trinity Shakespeare Festival, a professional collaboration of Actors Equity Association actors with TCU students, joyfully and skillfully managed and directed by faculty members T. J. Walsh and Harry Parker.

E. A. "Ed" Landreth, for whom the building is named, was an active member of the TCU Board of Trustees from 1940 to 1960, when he was voted honorary life membership. In 1941, university leaders recognized the need to enlarge the physical plant and "thoroughly equip" the small but growing college. Plans for expansion were approved, and in the words of Dean Colby Hall, "all that was lacking to get it started was the person to be the sparkplug for raising the money." Such a man was found in Ed Landreth, a Fort Worth oil man, "a Methodist, and one who had attained the reputation of being able to elicit money from Fort Worth citizens in large sums and leaving them happy about it." Mr. Landreth enthusiastically threw himself into the work and as a result of his efforts, the women's residence hall, Foster Hall, was completed before the interruption of the war years. After World War II, he was co-chairman of an expansion that undertook to raise $5 million for new buildings on campus, of which the building bearing his name was the first. Initially, the auditorium in the fine arts building was named in his honor; later the whole building was designated Ed Landreth Hall. In 1947, the university granted the honorary doctorate to this energetic and devoted TCU advocate.

Mary D. and F. Howard Walsh
Center for Performing Arts

The fifty-six thousand square foot Mary D. and F. Howard Walsh Center for Performing Arts was dedicated March 29, 1998, close to the opening date of the world-famous Nancy Lee and Perry R. Bass Hall in downtown Fort Worth, yet another architectural gem. As stated by then Chancellor William Tucker, the Walshes "are among the very best friends of Texas Christian University, and have been for a solid generation." Their $3.5 million gift significantly defrayed the $12 million cost of the building, for which Thos. S. Bryne, Inc. was general contractor and Malcolm Holzman of Harry Holzman Pfeiffer Associates was the architect. A successful oilman, businessman and rancher, F. Howard Walsh '33 (1913–2016) played varsity tennis at TCU and served as a trustee from 1968 to 1983. Mary D. Fleming Walsh (1913–2005) was a prominent Fort Worth arts patron. Honorary doctor of laws degrees were conferred on the couple in 1979, the same year they received the TCU Alumni Association's Royal Purple award. Each of their five children attended TCU, and son F. Howard Walsh Jr '63 also served as a TCU Trustee.

Facing onto University Drive, the original façade was once favorably described in a *TCU Magazine* article as "an undulating rhapsody of bricks, mortar and steel designed to reflect the fabric of TCU's traditional architecture but with a few twists and turns in the melody." However, like the Moudy Building, its departure from the conventional TCU architectural style continued to rankle some to the point that the Walsh Foundation provided $2.6 million in 2014 to reconfigure the building's front with a new porch, pillars, and veranda. The front, east-side entrance takes you into the Brown-Lupton Lobby, which has been employed for receptions and performance intermissions. Take a peek into the 215-seat Marlene and Spencer Hays Theatre. Its three-sided stage provides a versatility much appreciated by those in the performing arts. The theatre bears the same name as the Neeley School's Commons, reflecting the Hayses' commitment to both business and the fine arts. You can then walk down the open staircase or take

ABOVE
F. Howard and Mary D. Walsh, 1979. Courtesy of Mary Couts Burnett Library.

PAGE 214
Walsh Performance Hall with Ed Landreth in the background, 2021. Photograph by Rodger Mallison. Courtesy of TCU Marketing and Communication.

the nearby elevator to view the 325-seat PepsiCo Recital Hall, which provides a more intimate setting than does Ed Landreth's 1,200-seat auditorium or the new 717-seat Van Cliburn Concert Hall at TCU in the TCU Music Center. The multilevel PepsiCo Recital Hall has a unique design that includes a false ceiling and shell-within-a-shell design with openings in the walls. The latter allows sound to escape and then reflect back in, enriching the recital hall's acoustics. The Walsh Center's lower level also contains the John Giordano Piano Wing, named for the Music Director Emeritus of the Fort Worth Symphony Orchestra, a position he held for twenty-seven years as not only music director but also as its conductor. Included are piano studios and practice rooms, a music library, and dressing rooms. The Broyles/Breeden Instrumental Rehearsal Room is also situated on the lower level, as are choral rehearsal halls. The latter eliminated the need for various choral groups to practice at University Christian Church, as was necessary prior to the building's completion. In addition to the 2014 front facelift and renovations mentioned above, substantial work was carried out in 2013 to the Hays Theatre, including adding a light and sound control booth, reconfiguring the balcony to improve sightlines, and creating more effective lighting positions. As well, a tension grid added above the stage improved accessibility and safety for rigging. Finally, there were renovations in the theatre scenic studio, including the addition of two offices to the north mezzanine.

Forget your wristwatch? Then you should most definitely reverse course and walk towards the plaza between PepsiCo Hall and University Drive to learn the time of day.

TCU Sundial

Located on the plaza between Ed Landreth Hall and the Walsh Center of Performing Arts, the TCU Sundial was unveiled and dedicated on May 5, 2015. Utilizing the movements of the earth around the sun, this impressive instrument tells time to the nearest minute, sunlight permitting, of course. Created by William Andrewes, an English-born and educated clockmaker and designer, the TCU Sundial successfully combines the classical elegance of the mid-1700s with the latest developments of modern technology. The TCU Sundial was created expressly for the university's exact latitude and longitude and is situated on a plaza bearing a map of the world. Interestingly, there were few other places on campus where the sundial could be in-

LEFT
TCU Sundial with Walsh Performance Hall in the background, 2021. Photograph by Jeffrey McWhorter. Courtesy of TCU Marketing and Communication.

stalled, because most sites, at various times of the day, are at least partially shaded by buildings and trees. At a cost of approximately $725,000, the sundial and plaza were commissioned by Joseph I. O'Neill III of Midland, in honor of his wife Marion Jan Donnelly O'Neill.

Residence Halls on the North Side of Campus

Four residence halls, for many years housing exclusively women, lie immediately west of Landreth Hall. In addition to Jarvis Hall, they provided non-sorority housing for over one thousand residents on the main campus. All were built on an E-plan, Foster and Waits being the smaller of the four, and all are almost identical in architectural style. Architects Wyatt Hedrick, Preston Geren, and Joseph Pelich, who had been retained by the university to participate in the expansion program that spanned the years from 1941 to 1958, designed all four dormitories. As discussed previously, all

TCU residence halls, including these four, underwent extensive renovations toward the beginning of the new millennium. In some cases, the buildings were reduced to support beams, floors, and the exterior walls, broadening design options and allowing creation of residence halls more attuned to the desires of millennials and subsequent generations.

Foster was the first built (1942) and its "vaguely Classical-Colonial-Revival style," as described by the Tarrant County Historical Survey, would become a model for most of the residence halls built on the campus in the two decades hence. Foster was the first TCU building to have the red-tiled hipped roof with a gabled portico over the central entrance, and of course, the TCU brick was used to harmonize with the rest of the campus. Directly north of and facing Foster, Waits Hall was erected in 1948. Colby Hall Residence Hall came in 1957, and finally Sherley in 1958. When viewed as mere buildings, the four residence halls seem an undistinguished matched set of red-topped, yellowish boxes. They stand unique, however, in time, and name, and in the memories created and cherished by past residents of now seventy-plus years.

You can view the four by walking westward from the TCU sundial around behind the Hays Theatre, and then continuing along the open grounds uniting them.

Foster Hall

Foster Hall was named as a memorial to R. Houston Foster, president of the university's board of trustees and chairman of the building and grounds committee at the time of his death in 1941. He had been a board member since 1932 and a trustee of Brite College of the Bible since 1926. It was Foster who, in 1933, wrote the initial document that defined a tenure policy for the university. Foster was a 1904 graduate of TCU, a distinguished attorney, a Christian leader, and lay teacher. He and his wife, Bess Coffman Foster, were both active in TCU affairs and in church stewardship in Fort Worth. In recognizing the strength of his leadership, President Emeritus E. M. Waits eulogized Foster at the building's dedication: "His untimely death was an irreparable loss to the university, and city, and the state. His devotion and loyalty and high chivalrous deeds are enshrined in this memorial, more lasting than bronze."

At a cost of $8.1 million, Foster was extensively renovated by Linbeck Construction Corps in the spring and summer of 2000. Various structural changes reduced

ABOVE
Foster Residence Hall, 2010. Courtesy of TCU Marketing and Communication.

the total number of rooms by about a dozen, but with a gain of study rooms, laundry rooms, and kitchens. Wiring, pipes, heating, and cooling were also completely replaced. The residence hall now has a mixture of suite-style rooms, doubles, and triples (some with in-suite bathrooms). The hardwood floor and columns in the lobby remain, thus retaining much of the charm of the original building. With a capacity of 222, Foster is now coed and houses first-year students.

Waits Hall

Waits Hall was named in honor of Edward McShane Waits, president of the university from 1916 to 1941. At the time of his appointment, he was pastor of the Magnolia Christian Church in Fort Worth and had been secretary of the TCU Board of Trustees for five years. During Waits's term of office, TCU was elected to membership in the Association of American Colleges and the Southern Association of Colleges and Secondary Schools. He led the school through the Depression years between 1929 and the mid-'30s, personally knocking on the doors of Fort Worth's business community to solicit desperately needed funds to keep the college going and to meet its faculty payroll. It was during his time, too, that the school's enrollment rose from 367 students to over two thousand, and faculty increased from twenty to over one hundred.

Described by all who knew him as a wise, kind, and gentle man, "Prexy," in the words of his colleague Dean Colby Hall, "was known for the beauty of his phraseology and the prolificity of his poetical quotation, but not for rushing to the termination of a speech." Students of his day will recall his slow eloquence and distinctive southern Kentucky pronunciation as he conducted mandatory three-times-a-week chapel in the old Ad Building's auditorium. Memorable, too, is his discussion of TCU's name. After extolling the greatness of Texas and the high purpose of a university, he explained that the middle word "Christian" gave dignity and meaning to the other two. Prexy's alma mater, Transylvania University in Kentucky, granted him the honorary doctor of laws degree in 1923, as did TCU, followed in 1924 by Austin College in Sherman, Texas. A nearby street was named after him also.

Waits Hall joined Foster in the renovation queue in 2001 with a nine-month, $9.2-million makeover that completely refurbished the building, retaining only the original floors, support pillars, and external walls. The halls were widened, a five-room suite was added to the second floor, and two loft apartments were added on the third floor. As with Foster Hall, there are a variety of two- and three-resident living options. In 2003, a portion of the basement was converted into nine sound-proofed practice rooms, providing much-needed space for music majors. Waits Hall has a 230-resident capacity and is open to all first-year students.

Colby Hall

Colby Hall, the third residence hall in this area, is named for longtime Dean Colby D. Hall. The residence hall is called by Dean Hall's first name to avoid the awkward moniker "Hall Hall." Colby Dick Hall was discussed earlier in conjunction with the history of Brite Divinity School, but an account of his contributions to TCU deserves further elaboration. With the possible exception of the founding brothers Clark, no other figure has cast such a long shadow on the history of TCU. For sixty-seven of his eighty-eight years, Dean Hall's life paralleled that of the university. In the introduction to Hall's historical account of the first seventy-five years of the university, then President Sadler wrote: "to tell the story [of TCU] with insight, understanding, comprehensiveness, and real meaning, demand[s] a writer who has known, lived and loved Texas Christian University. . . . Those who read this volume should understand that in a very real sense they are reading the autobiography of the writer."

Colby Hall attended Add-Ran University in Waco from 1896 to 1899. After receiving his BA from Transylvania and his MA from Columbia, he returned to the Waco area and in 1906 was listed as the educational secretary for Texas Christian University; three years later he was listed as the "minister of University Church" that met on the campus. When the university moved to Fort Worth in 1910, Mr. and Mrs. Hall, the former Beatrice Tomlinson, moved also with their daughter, Bita May, who became TCU professor emeritus of French, Spanish, and Italian. Holding faculty positions as professor of Latin and of English Bible, Colby Hall was elected the first Dean of Brite College of the Bible in 1915, a post in which he served until 1947. In 1911, he also accepted the role of the first pastor of a small campus congregation that would grow into University Christian Church.

In 1920, realizing his particular leadership qualities, the school asked Hall to step into the recently vacated position of dean of the university. This he did, in addition to retaining the deanship of Brite, and his influence as second officer of the university would extend over the next twenty-one years. In 1941, upon the resignation of President Waits, the board of trustees considered Dean Hall the likely successor to the presidency. He declined, however, citing his age as a precluding factor. In 1943, he asked to be relieved as dean of the university but stayed four more years at the Brite College helm. After retirement from his administrative duties, Dean Hall continued to teach courses in English Bible until 1950. He also served as president of the Texas

Christian Missionary Society (1948–1953) and the Texas Convention of Christian Churches (1950–1951). Texas Christian University, the school he "lived and loved," acknowledged its indebtedness to this universally esteemed man with the bestowal of an honorary doctor of divinity degree in 1951.

Colby Hall—the building, not the icon for whom it was named—underwent a sixteen-month renovation that in many ways recapitulated the extensive makeovers of Foster and Waits. Closed during the 2014–15 academic year, Colby returned to service with new room floorplans that included wider, brighter hallways and a reconfigured front entrance. There are study rooms on each floor and corner-room suites with four bedrooms. Perhaps the biggest draw, however, is the basement lounge, dubbed "Colby Cave," with kitchenettes, theatre, and laundry rooms. Colby is home to 345 first-year female students.

Sherley Hall

While construction was in progress on the fourth of the women's dormitories, the trustees decreed that it be named Sherley Hall in honor of Andrew Sherley and the members of "a large family, all of whom have been and are active friends and supporters of the school." Spelling the name variously as Sherley and Shirley, the men and women of this early northeast Texas family have long been identified with TCU.

T. E. Shirley, an uncle of Andrew, was the first of the family involved in the school's affairs. A railroad man from Melissa, Texas, T. E. served on the TCU Board of Trustees from 1893 to 1917, and served as chair from 1899 through 1909. Called by Colby D. Hall "a man of spirit indomitable" and "financial savior," Shirley propelled TCU through the "seven lean years" in Waco (1895–1902) by taking a leave of absence from the H&TC railroad to devote his time to the job of raising money to discharge the school's indebtedness. He was, in fact, the first to contribute to the campaign with the then-great sum of $1,000. It was also as a result of his solicitation that the first designated dormitory for women was built on the Waco campus in 1902.

Andrew Sherley served on the board of trustees from 1920 to 1945 and on the Brite College Board from 1921 to 1945. As was his relative before him, he was a tower of financial and moral strength during more of the university's lean years in the '20s and

'30s. Finding himself in financial difficulties during the Depression, he made good on an earlier pledge of $100,000 by deeding to TCU a number of farms in Grayson and Collin Counties, with the provision that Brite College share in the funds.

A son of Andrew, W. M. "Bill" Sherley continued the family's interest in TCU, serving as a board member from 1949 to 1965, when he was given honorary status. He was most active as chairman of the Board Athletic Committee and was instrumental in pushing forward the building of the Daniel-Meyer Coliseum.

Yet another member of the Sherley clan was a faculty member for forty-four years, from 1927 until 1971. Miss Lorraine Sherley was feared and revered by English students who had the privilege of attending her lectures in Interrelation of the Arts and her courses in Shakespearean drama and the Age of Shakespeare. Miss Sherley was an early and steady contributor to TCU programs, and a significant part of her estate was left to her alma mater upon her death in 1984. An additional endowment established a chair for the Lorraine Sherley Professor of Literature.

Sherley Hall joined the renovation progression in 2008. To the tune of $16 million, the residence hall bears the distinction of being the first TCU building to receive LEED Gold Certification from the United States Green Building Council's Leadership in Energy and Environmental Design. The stunning lobby boasts a marble-tiled

ABOVE LEFT
T. E. Sherley. Courtesy of Mary Couts Burnett Library.

ABOVE CENTER
Andrew Shirley. Courtesy of Mary Couts Burnett Library.

ABOVE RIGHT
W. M. "Bill" Shirley. Courtesy of Mary Couts Burnett Library.

ABOVE
Sherley Residence Hall, 2019.
Photograph by Jeffrey McWhorter.
Courtesy of TCU Marketing
and Communication.

entryway, large-screen televisions, and soft seating. Study lounges anchor the building's corners, displacing the covered stairwells to the building's exterior. The basement features a baking kitchen and a thirty-five-seat mini-theatre with a ten-foot screen and surround-sound stereo. Sherley's floor plans include six "super suites," each housing nine students. The residence hall is home to all first-year students with a capacity of 355.

Miller Speech & Hearing Clinic

As you leave the residence-hall area to continue the tour west toward Stadium Drive, take the sidewalk northward to West Cantey Street. The church directly across the street from Sherley Hall is University Baptist which, like University Christian Church (UCC), has no official affiliation with TCU, although like UCC, it serves a significant campus membership. The brick schoolhouse immediately to the church's west is Alice E. Carlson Applied Learning Center, named for the first woman to serve on the Fort Worth School Board. It was built in 1926, a time when neighborhood children attended classes in two rooms in the basement of the Bailey Building (then Brite College of the Bible). Alice Carlson was the first public school in the TCU area, and many a faculty child was taught within its walls. W. G. Clarkson, the same architect who designed the original Mary Couts Burnett Library and University Christian Church, was responsible for Carlson's Spanish Colonial Revival style. Declining enrollments ultimately precipitated the building's closure as an elementary school, and for nine years it was used by the district as office space. It was reopened in 1992 as an applied learning center, with K-5 children from across the district.

Situated at the southeast corner of the intersection of Cantey Street and Stadium Drive is TCU's Miller Speech and Hearing Clinic. A recessed drive marks the entrance off Cantey to the more than eleven-thousand-square-foot building, which was designed by Albert Komatsu and dedicated in 1976. The facility of the Davies School of Communication Sciences and Disorders, the building houses undergraduate and graduate programs in speech-language pathology as well as deaf and hard-of-hearing studies. In addition, the department offers a specialized graduate track focusing on assessment and treatment of bilingual speakers. The building also serves as a community outpatient clinic for clients with hearing problems, language delay, and other

communication disorders. It is a learning laboratory for students pursuing a degree in communication sciences & disorders, as students evaluate and treat individuals with communication and swallowing impairments. These patients attend regular therapy sessions conducted by undergraduate and graduate student clinicians under the supervision of faculty.

Founded as a speech-correction program by Dr. Dorothy Bell in 1949, the programs in communication sciences and disorders began in cramped quarters in Landreth Hall and would move twice to temporary buildings before an anonymous donor made possible a permanent home. As Chancellor James Moudy pointed out at the time, "anonymity has a special beauty," but it also has a fleeting presence. It was soon known that the principal donors to the cost of constructing the facility were Mr. and Mrs. Clarence B. Smith. Wilma (Miller) and Bennie Smith are alumni of TCU, she with a master's degree in music education and he with a degree in communication.

They were looking for an appropriate gift to the university when they heard of the speech and hearing program's critical need for adequate space and equipment. The name of the clinic honors her parents, the late W. C. "Jack" Miller and his wife, Maude Y. Miller. Miller was the founder and operator of Miller Veterinary Supply Company for sixty years, until the time of his death in 1991 at the age of ninety-one. Wilma and Bennie Smith continued to support the clinic's program with financial contributions for equipment and scholarships. Dr. Moudy's dedicatory remarks still apply: "The . . . facility . . . [is] an illustration of what happens when concerned people look at community needs and seriously evaluate their personal ability and willingness to invest and sacrifice in meeting those needs." A brick bench to the left of the clinic entrance recognizes Dorothy Bell's long and dedicated service (1949–1977) to TCU, and a full-length photo of Dr. Bell graces the east wall of the reception room.

ABOVE
Maude Young and Wilmer Clay "Jack" Miller. Courtesy of Mary Couts Burnett Library.

As one moves through the interior halls and rooms, the special nature of Miller Clinic is apparent. At the heart of the one-story building is an island of small rooms designed for one-on-one therapy. All are soundproof and seemingly isolated, but the surrounding hallways are equipped with one-way windows and listening apparatuses that allow faculty, students, and parents to monitor ongoing therapy sessions. Peripheral to this central section are classrooms for adults and children, evaluation rooms, two audiological testing suites, and faculty research offices throughout the building.

Miller Clinic is a bright and cheerful place, with primary blues, reds, greens, and yellows predominating. Specialized equipment is present throughout the building for use in testing, evaluating, teaching, and research. In 2014, the building was expanded with the addition of the Davies Graduate Workroom, providing an additional 890 square feet of much-needed space. This addition came from a generous donation by Trustee Marilyn Davies in appreciation for the education her daughter, Morgan, received while an undergraduate student in the Deaf and Hard of Hearing Studies program. Mrs. Davies continued her support of the programs in 2014 with a $5 million gift that established an endowment, prompting the department's renaming to the Davies School of Communication Sciences and Disorders.

The Winthrop Rockefeller Building for Ranch Management

Since 1993 the Winthrop Rockefeller Building for Ranch Management has housed one of TCU's largely hidden gems. It is but a quick jaunt across Stadium Drive to the building. Prior to 1993, the Ranch Management Program, initiated in 1956, led a somewhat peripatetic existence on TCU's campus. That changed beginning in 1990, when a Winthrop Rockefeller Charitable Trust challenge gift of $1.05 million provided the impetus to raise the $2.1 million balance for construction and maintenance of the building occupying the southwest corner of Stadium Drive and West Cantey Street. The names of those making the gifts, 632 in all, are displayed on a plaque in the building's interior. With the abundant use of natural materials, from cream brick to the mesquite block floors, the front lobby provides access to faculty and staff offices to the south and a library, lounge, and amphitheatre-shaped classroom to the north. The lobby's ambiance is enhanced by artist Karen Holt's brilliantly hued 28" x 45" oil painting on canvas titled: "Nearby . . . there is peace." It was commissioned in celebration

of the program's fiftieth anniversary in 2005 and depicts two cowboys on horses wading a stock pond to round up cattle.

Ranch Management offers a bachelor's degree as well as a full-time, nine-month certificate program. The latter boosts over 1,500 proud graduates from well over thirty-five states and twenty-three nations. In addition to school days that typically consist of six hours in the classroom, students log over ten thousand miles to ranches, feed yards, experimental stations, stock brokers, and other businesses to learn the ins and outs of the trade. It is considered by many to be the premier program of its kind. Winthrop Rockefeller (1948–2006) was himself a 1974 graduate of the program, subsequently serving as a TCU Trustee and the lieutenant governor of Arkansas. The Ranch Management building bears his name as well as that of his late father, the former governor of Arkansas. The Rockefeller building is also home to the Institute of Ranch Management, an outreach and research entity that has established global partnerships related to resource management with private industry, institutions, and governments. Both the program and institute administratively reside in the College of Science & Engineering.

As you exit and walk south on Stadium Drive toward our next stop, the evocative statue entitled "Range Duty" will catch your eye. The six-foot six-inch, eight hundred pound bronze statue was commissioned by the Tartaglino Richards Family Foundation and dedicated to the class of 2009. It is marked by the following quotation from the nineteenth-century English social thinker John Ruskin: "The highest reward for a man's toil is not what he gets for it, but what he becomes by it." In this work, artist Star Liana York asks us to imagine the thoughts of a lone cowboy out on the cold, rainy, and blustery range preparing to brand cattle.

Starpoint/Kinderfrogs

Immediately north of the Miller Clinic and facing Stadium Drive is another Komatsu-designed structure. It is home to two laboratory schools, both operating under the auspices of the College of Education. KinderFrogs School is an early childhood education program predominantly serving young children with Down syndrome. Starpoint School is an individualized academic program for children ages six through

twelve with learning differences. Both also serve as a training site for teachers and prospective teachers.

The story of TCU's Starpoint is one of thoughtful caring and generous giving. It was the grandson of M. J. and Alice Snead Neeley who inspired this unique program. Russ Nettles had a learning issue for which his family sought help. They finally found this in New York City at a school directed by Mrs. Marguerite Slater, a pioneer in understanding learning differences and devising programs to address them. The New York school was named Star Point. The Neeleys, determined to help other children with similar issues, brought Mrs. Slater to TCU in 1966 to be principal of a new university-based school that would carry the same name. Mrs. Slater was succeeded after five years by her assistant, Laura Lee Crane, who retired in 1990.

The first Starpoint classes at TCU were held in the old Speech and Hearing Clinic in the "Green" house on Princeton Street, and after that in a wooden barracks building on the east campus—the same that subsequently housed the Counseling Center for a spell. With the Neeleys' continued support and the financial contributions of a host of others, the permanent facility was completed in 1978. Other benefactors included Mr. and Mrs. George T. Abell, Mrs. O. C. Armstrong, Mr. and Mrs. Mark B. Clifford, Mr. and Mrs. Gene E. Engleman, Mr. and Mrs. Ben Fortson, Mr. and Mrs. W. R. Gibson, William A. Hudson and estate of Edwin R. Hudson, and Mr. and Mrs. F. Howard Walsh, as well as the Davidson Family Charitable Foundation, the Hoblitzelle Foundation, and the J. E. and L. E. Mabee Foundation.

The genesis of KinderFrogs also makes for a heartwarming story. In 1999, a group of young mothers approached Jean Wiggin Roach, an icon in the Fort Worth world of philanthropy and wife to John Roach, former chair of the TCU Board of Trustees. The Roaches' generous support of TCU has warranted mention several times previously, including in conjunction with the John V. Roach Honors College. The mothers drew Jean's attention to the fact that there was no area preschool program for children with Down syndrome, despite a clear need, as evidenced by the fact that nearly one hundred infants with this genetic condition were born in Tarrant County the previous year. The absence of a dedicated pre-school program was disadvantaging these vulnerable youngsters when they started elementary school. Jean proposed to the chancellor that TCU create a full-time preschool to address this void. The concept was embraced by him and other TCU administrators, but with the proviso that sufficient funding be raised. No problem, as Jean spearheaded an effort that yielded a $1.5

million challenge grant plus other significant funding. KinderFrogs opened in 2000 and has been thriving ever since. In recognition of this and many other benevolent activities, Jean was a recipient of a 2022 Tri Delta Women of Achievement Award.

The exterior style and use of material is in keeping with TCU architecture; the one-story flat-roofed aspect belies the space within. The interior is designed to reduce distraction for the children who come here each year to learn. Central in the interior is a large open space with a staired pit for sitting, watching, listening, playing, and resting. School begins here with morning assembly. Four classrooms with workrooms and locker rooms are located north and south of the central space. Primary colors—red, blue, and yellow, plus green—predominate; each of the four classrooms use one of the colors as a theme. A gymnasium, kitchen and lunch room, library, and a classroom for the university's education students occupy the eastern portion of the building. Along the west front are the reception area, the director's office, and a teachers' work area and lounge. Here are located portraits of the benevolent Neeleys and the innovative Marguerite Slater. A grant in 2009 from the Morris Foundation, supplemented by private donations, and school fund-raisers allowed for a $750,000 expansion to the building. The renovations converted the existing gym into a classroom, added a multi-purpose room with more storage space, and therapy/tutoring offices.

The life-size bronze in front of the low, modest building is a jewel that shines from this place especially designated for children with learning differences. The statuary was commissioned in 1990 by M. J. Neeley in honor of his family and particularly his wife, Alice Snead Neeley. Based on a photograph of Mrs. Neeley's mother, Mary Brazelton Snead, and the two Neeley daughters, Marian and Kathleen, the work is entitled *Yearning to Know*. It was sculpted by artist Randolph Johnston to depict the eternal bond of love and the spirit of teaching and learning. In dedicating the statue to the memory of his late wife, M. J. Neeley asked, "What greater thing could I do to recognize her love and her love for the family?"

It is a peaceful place, this Starpoint, that invites special children to learn in special ways.

Brown-Lupton Health Center

Brown-Lupton Health Center, built in 1963, was designed by Preston Geren in the one-story buff brick pattern conforming to the predominant TCU architectural style. Some health service had always been offered to TCU students, but not until after the health center was built in 1963 was full medical care provided. The first infirmary on the campus was established in 1942 and was located in the northeast corner of Jarvis Hall until 1948, when it was moved to the first floor east of Waits Hall. Under the general but usually absent direction of a physician, the facility was staffed by professional nurses. In 1962, Sam P. Woodson Jr., manager of the Brown-Lupton Foundation, presented a check to the university in the amount of $192,000 for the erection of a health center building.

The Health Center's mission is "to promote, maintain and restore the student's physical and mental health." This is accomplished by offering a variety of services to TCU students, including primary care, sexual health services, a full-service allergy clinic, psychiatric care, and nutrition consultations. In 1973 Dr. John Sanford "Jack" Terrell (1935–2012) was hired as the first full-time physician, also serving with distinction as the center's director until his 2007 retirement. Dr. Jane Torgerson is the current medical director with a staff of six that includes three other physicians, two PAs, and a registered pharmacist to provide medical needs. In addition, there are fifteen employees in the nursing division, two in psychiatry, and one in nutrition.

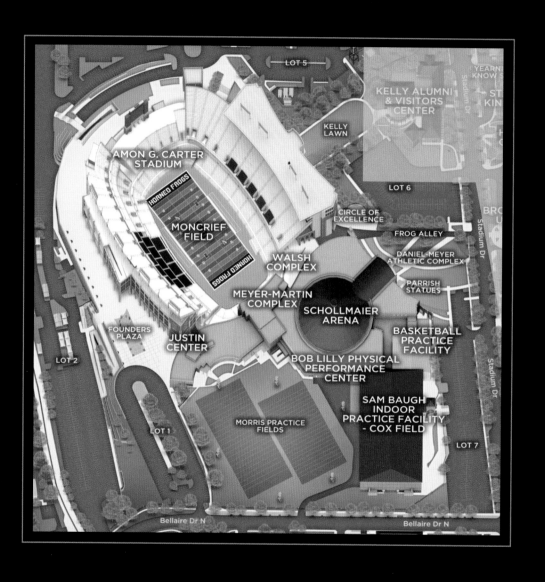

CHAPTER 9

Athletics

::

I f you began your walk at the Kelly Alumni Center, your tour of the main campus is completed. Should you opt to continue, visiting the athletic complex and the Worth Hills campus, you may elect to retrieve your car—particularly around Worth Hills— for the distances are somewhat longer and the route includes a steep hill or two. We will first pass by Amon G. Carter Stadium, then the Ed and Rae Schollmaier Arena, followed by a walk past practice facilities, first for basketball and then for football. We'll then circumnavigate the roughly mile-long sidewalk (or streets, depending upon your mode of transportation) that encompasses Worth Hills, along the way passing residence halls and intramural fields as well as the playing fields for TCU's NCAA soccer (women's), baseball (men's), track (men's and women's), and tennis (men's and women's) teams. Our home stretch passes by Facilities Services and Greek Village.

Former Director of Intercollegiate Athletics Chris Del Conte was fond of describing athletics as the front porch to the university. And what a glamorous front porch it has become, thanks in part to rich traditions, current successes, and, to be sure, facilities that have been lavished with extensive attention, particularly over the past twenty years.

OPPOSITE
Map showing the campus structures discussed in this chapter.

Amon G. Carter Stadium

Football came to TCU before the turn of the nineteenth century. The Waco college fielded its first team against Toby's Business College of Waco in 1896, a year before the school colors and mascot were chosen. Since that time, the purple and white Fightin' Frogs' fortunes have waxed and waned. In the early years in Fort Worth, the athletic teams played as a member of the Texas Intercollegiate Athletic Association, becoming members of the Southwest Conference in 1923. Often competing with a roster of only sixteen to eighteen men chosen from a total enrollment of some one hundred and fifty, "little TCU" began to make itself known in the region.

The first football arena that provided spectator seating was Clark Field on the east campus, now the site of the eastern portion of the library and Rees-Jones Hall. Encouraged and inspired by a 1929 Southwest Conference championship under the direction of Coach Francis Schmidt, TCU began to plan a modern permanent home for its champions in a natural bowl of land on a recently purchased tract to the west of the main campus. This early stadium was the design of architect Wyatt C. Hedrick. As originally planned, east and west stands would have a seating capacity of twenty thousand. Only the west stand, however, was built initially. Constructed entirely of reinforced concrete, the arcaded exterior and blocky end bays were part of the 1930 structure.

In this new home, the Horned Frogs would make history. They played their first game in the new stadium, then unnamed, on October 1, 1930, soundly defeating a University of Arkansas club by a score of 40 to 0. In 1932, they again snared the Southwest Conference championship with a perfect record against all other conference schools. But the real glory days were yet to come. The legendary Leo R. "Dutch" Meyer became head coach in 1934 and steered the Frogs not only to national recognition but also to a coach's dream—the designation of No. 1 in the nation in 1935 and again in 1938. The year 1935 featured the "Game of the Century"—even though almost two-thirds of a century was yet to transpire—between 10-0 SMU and 10-0 TCU. Passing was the name of the game in those years, and two of the passers, Slingin' Sammy Baugh and little Davey O'Brien, are still regarded as gridiron heroes in the history of collegiate football. Retiring as athletic director in 1963, the "Dutchman's" association with TCU began when he was a public-school student in Waco and a water boy for the TCU football team on which Milton Daniel played. Their association

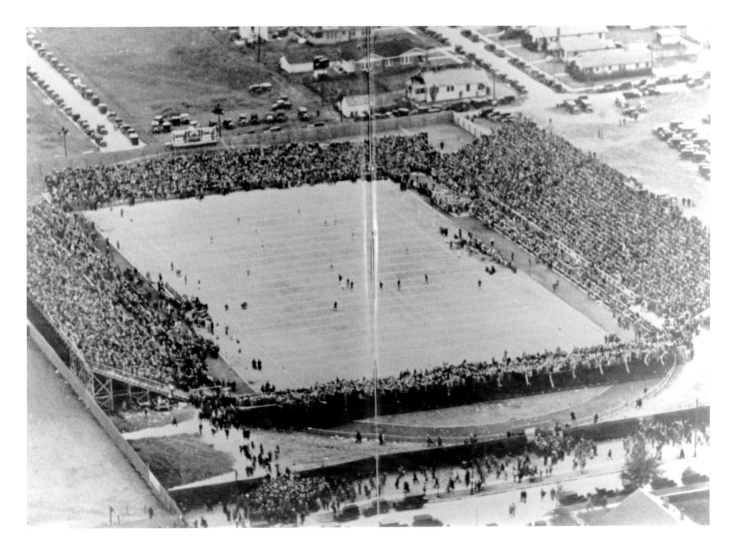

ABOVE
Looking south at Clark Field, which stood
on the east campus behind Mary Couts
Burnett Library, 1930. Courtesy of Mary
Couts Burnett Library.

continued when Meyer entered TCU in 1917, the one year that Daniel was the Frogs' football coach. As a student athlete at TCU, Meyer lettered in three sports—football, basketball, and baseball. After his 1922 graduation, he became the basketball coach at Fort Worth's Polytechnic High School, returning to TCU the next year as coach of freshman football, basketball, and baseball. With the exception of that one year, Dutch's entire adult life was spent in some phase of athletics at TCU. Coaching varsity baseball in 1933, he saw his team win TCU's first Southwest Conference championship. From 1934 through 1952, he was head football coach, his teams winning three Southwest Conference championships, two national championships, and seven bowl game bids . . . and this in a day before bowl games became a dime a dozen. Whatever the contest, he meant to win, whether it was dominoes, bridge, fishing, baseball, or football. Certainly his most enduring utterance, borrowed from the Civil War era, is: "Fight 'em till Hell freezes over, then fight 'em on the ice!"

Alas, the glory years of the 1930s through the 1950s gave way to a period when gridiron success was not so regular for the Frogs. There were fewer highlight games, such as the one in 1961 when TCU toppled the number-one-ranked University of Texas, prompting their coach to utter the enduring quip comparing TCU to a cockroach falling into food and ruining it. To a certain extent, this lean period influenced TCU's 1996 exclusion from the Big 12 Conference coincident with the dissolution of the Southwest Conference. From there it was on to the Western Athletic Conference, Conference USA, Mountain West Conference, and a pledge to join the Big East before the Big 12 finally came calling in 2012. The Frogs' leap back to a Power Five conference was made possible primarily by two factors: the success of TCU athletics, most notably that of the football team, and systematic upgrades of the university's athletic facilities, the latter made possible by substantial monetary investments by many loyal donors. Numerous individuals, both internal and external to TCU, positively influenced TCU's athletic resurgence, but in the opinion of Eric Hyman, TCU director of athletics from 1997 to 2005, two names head the list. They are Provost William "Bill" Koehler, who was mentioned in Chapter 7, and Malcolm Louden, who will be discussed in the subsequent chapter. Provost Koehler's support of athletic endeavors was critical both operationally and symbolically. Malcolm Louden not only made substantive financial contributions himself, but his passion for TCU athletics was infectious, prompting others also to provide the resources necessary to upgrade facilities. To borrow from the parlance of another sport, TCU went from

bogey to birdie golf with the occasional eagle mixed in. Just as Dutch Meyer, Sammy Baugh, and Davey O'Brien call to mind the successes of days long past, so too do names such as Gary Patterson, LaDainian Tomlinson (now a member of TCU's Board of Trustees), and Andy Dalton, to mention only three, elevate the pulses of more recent Frog fans. Further, under the leadership of Chancellor Victor J. Boschini, who will be discussed in the last chapter, TCU's success in the intercollegiate athletics realm has continued.

Indeed, and with all due respect to his predecessors such as Jim Wacker and Pat Sullivan, one could be hard pressed to deny that Gary Patterson's tenure as coach encompasses much of TCU's second golden era of gridiron glory, which includes the exploits of Heisman runner-up Max Duggan and national coach-of-the-year Sonny Dykes. Nor the postulate that he was critical to TCU's sustained excellence during this time period. One could also argue that Dennis Franchione set the stage, because not only did he put TCU's football fortunes on the ascension, but he appointed a well-travelled assistant coach named Gary Patterson as TCU's defensive coordinator. A native of Rozel, Kansas, Patterson began his coaching career in 1982 at Kansas State University. He assumed the Frogs' head coaching duties in 2000 in the Mobile, Alabama, bowl game and went on to be the winningest coach in TCU history, leading the Frogs to six conference championships and nine bowl-game victories while compiling a 181-79 (69.6 percent) record. Contrast the twenty-one-year, 181-win "Patterson era" with the twenty-one years from 1971 to 1991 when TCU won a *total* of 68 games, including a run of eight straight years of two or fewer wins per season. Patterson's teams won ten games or more a remarkable eleven different seasons. There are numerous highlights in the Patterson era, but many would rank the Frogs 2011 Rose Bowl victory over the University of Wisconsin as number one. And speaking of numbers, the 13-0 Frogs finished that season ranked second in the nation. Along the way Patterson was the recipient of multiple conference and national coach-of-the-year awards. Known as a defensive wizard, Patterson's 4-2-5 defense was integral to the Frogs leading the nation in total defense multiple years. Gary Patterson was also a larger-than-life ambassador for TCU and Fort Worth. Along with wife Kelsey, he invested considerable effort in the Gary

Patterson Foundation, whose mission was and remains to support children in and around Fort Worth. A bit later on our tour you'll pass statues commemorating Dutch Meyer, Davey O'Brien, Gary Patterson, and James Cash, four Frogs O' Fame of the first order.

The current version of "the Carter" bears little semblance to the structure that debuted in 1930, with several expansions through the years. The east stands and end zone seating were erected during 1947 and 1948. Expansions in 1951 and 1953 increased the stadium's seating capacity to thirty-three thousand and then to thirty-seven thousand. It was in this construction phase that the carved stone all-sports murals were placed above the arcaded east front. In 1956, a second deck—along with a press box some eighteen stories above the floor—was added to the west stands, dwarfing the 1930 structure and upping the seat count to 45,627. For roughly fifteen years the upper deck featured a thirty-foot-by-thirty-foot "flying TCU logo," visible across campus, which was replaced in 1995 by a more traditional design. The lighting was upgraded in 1983. In 1991, the fiberglass seats and wood planks in the nine-thousand-seat upper deck were replaced by aluminum benches complete with backs and arms. In 1992, the playing field returned to natural grass, specifically a seedless Bermuda hybrid, replacing the Astroturf that was installed in 1973. In addition, the field's crown was raised from twelve inches to eighteen inches. The drainage system was updated at the same time, replacing more than 1.5 miles of pipe. It took 2,500 tons of gravel and 5,000 pounds of sand, a total of approximately 300 truckloads, to restore the field, which in 2003 was dedicated at the TCU-Vanderbilt game as the W. A. Monty and Tex Moncrief Field, honoring two of TCU's staunchest supporters. Speaking of turf, TCU received a pair of 2021 Field of the Year awards from the Sports Turf Manager's Association for Moncrief Field and the Garvey-Rosenthal soccer field, a later stop on our tour. Given to Sport Field Manager Andrew Siegel, this annual award spotlights individuals and programs excelling in providing quality and safe playing surfaces. In 2002 the David E. Bloxom Sr. Foundation donated a state-of-the-art scoring and video center beyond the north end zone.

These renovations paled by comparison to the complete makeover that commenced immediately after the 2010 season. A crowd gathered to witness the demolition of the west grandstand on a chilly December 5th morning. A series of thunderclap booms signaled the destruction of the support columns, starting on the north side and moving southward. Then, seemingly in slow motion, the upper-deck grandstands came

tumbling down. To paraphrase a 1974 movie, eighty years of history was "gone in thirty seconds." The east side was subsequently demolished in less dramatic fashion using a two-ton wrecking ball and a trio of high-reach excavators, reducing tons of concrete, brick, and mortar to rubble and clearing everything but the bottom twenty rows of the lower bowl. The majority of the debris was hauled off and recycled, ultimately finding its way back into the east stands. The majority of the construction was finished before the 2011 season, but the west upper deck was not completed until 2012. Still, the wait was well worth it.

At a cost of $165 million (including $105 million to rebuild the west grandstands and add a second level to the north end zone), the project was entirely donor funded.

It represented the first substantive upgrade to the stadium since 1956. Thirty-four donors made major contributions to the project, most notably six original donors who cumulatively gave $105 million. Located outside the stadium's west entrance, Founders Plaza serves to recognize these individuals themselves or whoever they've chosen to recognize. They are: Addison Clark (provided by The Cox Family of Midland, TX), Randolph Clark (provided by the Amon G. Carter Foundation), John and Jane Justin (provided by the Jane & John Justin Foundation), Hunter & Shirley Enis and Dick & Mary Lowe, William A. "Monty" Moncrief and William A. "Tex" Moncrief Jr., and Clarence Scharbauer III. This edifice consists of one-half dozen limestone markers with the individuals' likenesses cast in stone busts. Founders Plaza rests on forty-four thousand square feet of grounds that feature a giant map of Fort Worth streets and landmarks. TCU hired Austin Construction to build the stadium, and HKS Sports & Entertainment Group, whose credits include the Dallas Cowboys' home AT&T stadium, served as the architects. A time capsule is buried in the stadium with mementos that include a jersey worn by Andy Dalton, a baseball cap from TCU's appearance in the 2010 College World Series, and ticket stubs from the Rose and Fiesta Bowl games.

Seating forty-six thousand, the Carter boasts thirteen concession stands and sixteen restrooms. Two hundred and forty grandstand lights, two video boards, and 268 flat-screen televisions enhance the viewing experience. Don't try to count them, but the 791,520 bricks blend nicely with the 66,000 tons of concrete that went into the structure. The west side press box, named in honor of legendary sportswriter Dan Jenkins '53 in 2017, is among the largest in a collegiate stadium, seating 132. The 23,000-square-foot Champion's Club Suite accommodates 2,400 ticket holders on the west side on Level 2, just below the eighteen Champions Club suites, which each seat twenty-four people. One level down, the Founders Suites each have a kitchenette and a glass door leading to seating for fourteen. Each suite is accessed from the eight-thousand-square-foot Founders Club immediately off the main concourse. The Founders Club has a centrally located stacked-rock fireplace flanked by a full bar with two permanent buffet dining areas. The east-side grandstands were also updated and include a giant mural celebrating the stadium's milestones. Both the home (located in the conjoined Walsh Complex in the south end zone) and visitors' locker rooms (located in the north portion of the west stands) were also completely refurbished. Except for the standalone KTCU tower, the 163-foot, three-inch lighting stanchions topping it make Amon G. Carter the tallest ground-to-top structure on campus.

It should be noted, however, that the steeple atop Robert Carr Chapel, although checking in at 130 feet, three inches, is still the highest point on campus owing to the gentle downward east-to-west slope from Robert Carr to the Carter.

Beginning June 2018, the east stands underwent a $113 million upgrade, again facilitated by private donations. The result was the creation of the Legends Club and Suites, sitting atop the east bleachers, with over 1,050 club seats, over 130 televisions, forty-eight loge boxes, twenty-two luxury suites. and two private clubs. The Frogs' locker room was refreshed at the same time, with updated graphics and cosmetic improvements. This significant addition to Amon G. Carter Stadium came under the

ABOVE
Amon G. Carter Stadium, 2017.
Photograph by Sharon Ellman.
Courtesy of TCU Athletics.

OPPOSITE
Amon G. Carter Stadium, 2019.
Courtesy of TCU Facilities Services.

leadership of TCU Director of Intercollegiate Athletics Jeremiah Donati, who became TCU's eighth such director in 2017.

The stadium has occasionally been described as the Camden Yards of collegiate football, paying homage to the home of baseball's Baltimore Orioles. It is a compliment that speaks to the Carter's sublime blend of new-time amenities baked into a structure that oozes with old-school charm. Then Director of Intercollegiate Athletics Chris Del Conte remarked: "It will be first-class in every respect, but equally important, it will honor the glorious past of our program." And it does so nicely. In addition to home games for the Frogs, Amon G. Carter Stadium has served as the site of the Armed Forces Bowl game since 2003.

The stadium was nameless until 1951, when the board of trustees voted officially to designate it Amon G. Carter Stadium in honor of the *Fort Worth Star-Telegram*'s publisher and entrepreneur. Stories with Amon G. Carter as the central character are legion. He was, after all, "Mr. Fort Worth." Many of the most colorful tales have to do with his exuberant support of the TCU athletic programs, especially in the '20s, '30s, and '40s, when the Fightin' Frogs were riding high on victory in football, and the baseball team was no slouch. Some said that Carter never had time for anything but a winner, and that was the reason the Frogs were "his" team. Others said that TCU's good fortune was to be in Fort Worth and be a winner, and that was the reason he touted them.

Carter's finest hour came when Davey O'Brien won the Heisman Trophy in 1938. He chartered a plane to transport Davey and an entourage of TCU officials and friends to New York for the award ceremony and arranged to have a Knickerbocker stagecoach with six white horses and thirty men of the Staten Island Sheriff's Horse Guard meet his party. With Dutch Meyer and TCU President Waits inside the coach and Davey on the driver's seat beside him, Carter took the reins and drove down Wall Street, waving his big Shady Oaks Stetson hat and yelling "Hooray for Fort Worth, West Texas, and TCU!" One can only imagine the modest Davey's thoughts amid all that hoopla.

With all the moral and financial support that Amon Carter gave, one wonders why it took so long to give his name to the Frogs' battlefield. It was Amon Carter who led an effort in 1923 to find contributors to a $50,000 fund to help clear the university's indebtedness. It was Amon Carter who headed the fund-raising campaign to erect the football stadium for the school after the championship of 1929. In fact, almost single-handedly (some say heavy-handedly), he raised the $450,000 necessary for its construction, paid for the electric scoreboard himself, and was an active consultant on the stadium's design. It was probably no mistake that when the west stands had been completed, they ran up sixty-one rows, one more than SMU's Owenby Stadium in Dallas.

Circle of Excellence

As you arrive at the southwest corner of Amon G. Carter Stadium you'll encounter the Circle of Excellence, built and dedicated in 2013 to mark the fiftieth anniversary of Greek life at TCU. The Circle celebrates the campus leadership and distinction in TCU's classrooms achieved by members of TCU fraternities and sororities.

ABOVE
Circle of Excellence, 2013.
Photograph by Glen Ellman.
Courtesy of Glen Ellman.

Frog Alley

"The Pride of TCU" marching band enters Amon G. Carter Stadium, 2021. Photograph by James Anger. Courtesy of TCU Marketing and Communication.

Immediately south of the Circle of Excellence and extending to Stadium Drive is Frog Alley. This portion of the tour is well worth reprising during a home football game, as it is the epicenter of pre-game excitement. Opening two hours before the game's start, Frog Alley features live music, bounce houses, and much more. Shortly before kickoff, TCU's award-winning marching band and spirit team parade into the stadium. You can't help but notice an eight-foot tall, 1,900-pound frog who crouches fiercely as if guarding Amon G. Carter Stadium. Steve Gray, Bill Shaddock '73, and Ricky Stuart

'96 funded the project, commissioning New Braunfels artist Paul Tadlock to craft the piece. It was installed in 2013 and subsequently relocated to the entrance to Schollmaier Arena in 2018 in advance of the east-side stadium project. There are certainly many universities with birds, lions, tigers, and even cow mascots, but TCU prides itself as having its singular, and singularly fierce, reptilian mascot.

Walsh Athletic Complex, Meyer-Martin Academic Enhancement Center, Justin Athletic Center

Reversing direction from the Circle of Excellence you can walk westward between Amon G. Carter Stadium and Schollmaier Arena. Your attention will gravitate naturally to the picturesque view of Moncrief Field and the stadium, but it's worth looking southward to the Walsh Athletic Complex. Dedicated in 1996, this $2.5 million complex was named in honor of Trustee F. Howard Walsh and his wife Mary D. Fleming Walsh, whom we discussed in conjunction with the performing arts center that also bears their names. The facility is highlighted by a 7,200-square-foot weight-and-conditioning area and represented an important early step in TCU's concerted effort to upgrade its athletic facilities. Twelve years later, the Dutch Meyer Athletic Complex and Abe Martin Academic Enhancement Center were added immediately to the west of the Walsh Complex. Perched atop the Meyer-Martin Complex are six stadium boxes with 250 club seats that are situated above and behind the south endzone stands. These were made possible by gifts from Patti and Larry Brogdon, the Amon G. Carter Foundation, Alice and Brad Cunningham, Shirley and Hunter Enis, the Four Sevens Operating Co., Ltd., the Luther and Teresa King Family Foundation, Luther King Capital Management, Mary and Dick Lowe, the W. A. and Elizabeth B. Moncrief Foundation, Jean and John Roach, and Duer Wagner III. Among other things, these six stadium boxes served as templates for the eventual renovation of the stadium's west side. Named for two legendary coaches, the forty-thousand-square-foot Meyer-Martin Complex facility cost $13 million. It includes a large gameday lounge enjoyed by those with priority seating at basketball and football games. Also included are a player's lounge, team meeting room, a computer lab, and academic tutoring and work rooms. Thanks to the generosity of the Jane & John Justin Foundation, the weight room was subsequently moved in 2011 and named the Bob Lilly Physical Performance Center,

honoring TCU and Dallas Cowboys legend Bob Lilly. The vacated space became the new football locker room. Immediately past the Meyer-Martin Complex and even with the west grandstands of Amon G. Carter Stadium is the John Justin Athletic Center, which was completed in 2000 and houses all football offices, video labs, and meeting rooms, as well as a Heritage Center. Made possible by a gift from the Justin Foundation, the name recognizes late trustee John S. Justin Jr. '41, who was a former mayor of Fort Worth as well as the founder and longtime CEO of Justin Industries, which includes Justin Boot Company and Acme Brick Company. He was a proud supporter of Horned Frog athletics for over half a century and was instrumental in TCU's acquisition of the Worth Hills area, which we'll visit shortly.

As long as you've come this far, you may elect to continue a few more steps on to Founders Plaza, which was discussed a bit earlier. Either way, you can now double back and get a taste of the facilities that support TCU's men's and women's basketball teams. To do so, turn right at the Circle of Excellence and make your way a short distance to Schollmaier Arena. You're in for a real treat.

Ed and Rae Schollmaier Arena and Ed and Rae Schollmaier Basketball Complex

A new coliseum for the TCU basketball program was in the university's long-range building plans for at least fifteen years before funds were finally available to begin construction in 1961. For twelve of those years, Coach Byron "Buster" Brannon carried architects' plans on recruiting trips, promising prospects that if they signed with the Frogs, they would have a swanky new court on which to play. Although Brannon continued as head coach through the 1966–1967 season, only a few of his recruits would ever bounce a ball on the hard maple floor of the facility. And although Buster coached the Frogs to four Southwest Conference titles, he never won one in what was early called "Buster's House." That honor was left to his successors, including Johnny Swaim, Jim Killingsworth, Billy Tubbs, and most recently Jamie Dixon.

When TCU moved from Waco to Fort Worth in 1910, the upstairs gymnasium of the First Baptist Church in the city was home court. In 1921, the "little gym" (now Erma Lowe Hall) was built, which provided a campus court until 1926 when a larger facility, the wooden "big gym," was constructed. The popularity of the sport and the condition of the "barn," as the big gym came to be called, forced the Frogs in the mid-'40s to seek another place to play.

In 1947, Fort Worth's City Council voted an improvement to the city's large-capacity Will Rogers Coliseum—a portable hardwood basketball floor that could be laid on the arena surface, thus providing space not only for the university's games but for high school contests, as well. The first game in Will Rogers, a mile north of the campus, was between Poly High and Paschal High, followed the same evening by the first conference game of 1947 between TCU and Texas A&M. The "barn" continued as a practice gym until it burned in 1953.

With so many events taking place in the versatile Will Rogers, it became increasingly difficult to schedule basketball. In the 1955 season, TCU and the high schools began playing in the newly built Public Schools Gymnasium located to the east of the Will Rogers complex. Then, finally in 1961, the Frogs came home to the spacious Daniel-Meyer and, but for two years, have stayed home ever since.

The May 3, 1946, *Skiff* shows a picture of a planned "Field House" in the squared boxy style then common to basketball gyms. As it turned out, of course, the now common circular arena with a center playing court and domed roof was ultimately built. In 1959, a tentative sketch of that design was published in the *Skiff*. Fort Worth-based Joseph Pelich was chosen as the final architect, ground was broken in March 1961, and the building was completed by the Cadenheard Company, also from Cowtown, in December of that year at a cost of $1.4 million. The Amon Carter Foundation was again a major contributor. Even before the building was completed, the board of trustees named it the Daniel-Meyer Coliseum, in honor of Milton E. Daniel and Leo R. "Dutch" Meyer. This was the second posthumous honor for Daniel: a men's dormitory had been named after him in 1957.

"DMC," as it came to be known, underwent a number of upgrades through the years. In 1964, an Ex-Letterman's Club Room was added facing north, its windows overlooking the south end zone of Amon G. Carter Stadium. Tastefully furnished in purple and white, the room is used primarily for club meetings and for entertaining recruits. A 1970 expansion improved dressing rooms, added new training rooms, and provided player access to the stadium by means of a tunnel leading from the coliseum's lower-level dressing area. In 1994, the sound system was upgraded, and Dr. Pepper provided a new scoreboard, valued at an estimated $425,000. Remarked the irascible Coach Billy Tubbs at the time, "The scoreboard might not win us one game, but it may help draw the recruits to come to the coliseum to watch the team." In 1997 the 7,166 green, orange, and yellow chairs were removed and replaced with more color-appropriate purple-and-gray seats. A new men's locker room and player's lounge was added in 2002, with similar facilities built for the women cagers one year later. A new playing surface replaced the original floor that same year. Upgraded lighting, a $1.5 million four-panel LED scoreboard, and a new sound system graced the building in 2004, 2007, and 2010, respectively.

There have indeed been some memorable games played in DMC, including the Frogs' 1981 four-overtime conquest of a University of Houston squad that included future NBA star Clyde Drexler. Or how about future coach Jamie Dixon's 1986 last-second, thirty-five-foot heave, resulting in a win over the University of Texas and securing a regular-season Southwest Conference co-championship for the Frogs? And let's not forget Sandora Irvin's record-setting sixteen-block effort in 2004 against the University of Alabama-Birmingham. Yes, that was sixteen rejections in one game, perhaps not surprising, given that she finished her TCU career as the NCAA leader in career blocked shots and was named to the Associated Press and Kodak first-team All American teams. Indeed, the highlight list could go on and on, and they are not confined to basketball. DMC served as a concert hall to, among others, Simon & Garfunkel, Joe Cocker, Jefferson Airplane, and the Grateful Dead (kids, ask your parents or grandparents about these musicians). The arena is also the site of TCU graduation exercises, including in 1968 when President Lyndon B. Johnson gave the commencement address. It still sees regular action for a plethora of high school commencements as well as those of TCU.

The upgrades described above are dwarfed by the complete overhaul of 2013 to 2015, relegating the Frogs to play home games in a local high school gym for two years. It was worth the wait. The new name—Ed and Rae Schollmaier Arena—honors the couple who provided a $10 million lead gift toward the $72 million price tag. Ed Schollmaier (1933–2021) was CEO of Alcon Laboratories for twenty-five years. He was a rarity among CEOs, working for a single company that he saw grow from $36 million to $2 billion in sales during his tenure. Serving on TCU's Board of Trustees, he and his wife Rae (1934–2015) were courtside regulars at TCU basketball games for decades. An empty front-row seat during the 2021–2022 season provided a reminder of the impact Mr. and Mrs. Schollmaier had on the fortunes of TCU basketball. And the names Milton Daniel and Dutch Meyer have not been completely relegated to the history books, as the entire athletic complex encompassing Schollmaier Arena, the Walsh Complex, the Meyer-Martin Complex, the Justin Center, and the Sam Baugh Indoor Practice Facility now collectively constitute the Meyer-Martin Complex.

Let's enter the arena, which you'll notice has a façade that architecturally complements Amon G. Carter Stadium and the TCU campus, in marked contrast to the rather drab DMC. You'll be greeted by a spacious lobby opening into the Jane and John Justin Hall of Fame, which provides a visual celebration of the twenty-two varsity sports and 250-plus Frog greats enshrined in the TCU Athletic Hall of Fame, which is managed by the TCU Block T Association. Wander about and take in a plethora of TCU's most prestigious sports hardware. Rose Bowl trophy? Heisman trophy?

ABOVE
Jefferson Airplane performs in Daniel Meyer Coliseum, November 1, 1970. Courtesy of TCU Marketing and Communication.

They are two of literally hundreds of such tangible signs of Horned Frog athletic accomplishments through the years. You can easily spend hours in the Hall of Fame, but let's press on to the arena proper, which is built with upper and lower levels divided by a concourse circumscribing the arena that includes a plaza overlooking Amon G. Carter Stadium. Widened in the Daniel Meyer-to-Schollmaier conversion, the concourse abounds in concessions stands that serve much more than popcorn and hotdogs (not that there's anything wrong with a game-day dog) and spacious restrooms. Life-sized team photos adorn the concourse walls. Eighteen entrances off the concourse provide access to the arena proper. The arena floor was lowered four feet from the arena's DMC days to improve sight lines and situate some sections closer to the floor. At floor level are new locker rooms with dark-stained wooden lockers, recapitulating the spaciousness and amenities of those in the football locker room. Also present are team lounges with a twenty-five-seat theatre-style video room. There is a well-appointed club area, the Stuart Family Courtside Club, created for the original project donors. To the north of the Hall of Fame and up one level are office suites housing various athletics support staff. At 173,571 square feet, Schollmaier Arena is 68,794 square feet larger than DMC but with a seating capacity reduced from 7,166 to 6,800. But as they say, there's not a bad seat in the house . . . or even mediocre one, for that matter. An additional one thousand chairs can be comfortably placed on the covered playing surface, allowing for special events such as commencement exercises. And speaking of playing surfaces, you might notice the subtle lizard-skin pattern on the Walsh Family Court floor. In addition to men's and women's basketball, TCU's volleyball team calls Schollmaier Arena their home.

Physically connected to the south portion of the Hall of Fame is the Ed and Rae Schollmaier Basketball Complex, completed in 2003 at the cost of $5.8 million. It was made possible by $1.5 million lead gift from the Schollmaiers that complemented those from forty-five other donors. Its Connor Uni-Force Floor, same as that in the coliseum, provides a flexibility that makes jumping (and landing!) easier on the legs. The twenty-two-thousand-square-foot facility has office space for coaches, conference rooms, media rooms, a weight room, locker rooms for the coaches, and a lobby. Its six baskets make for more efficient practices.

ABOVE
Ed and Rae Schollmaier Arena.
Photograph by Rodger Mallison.
Courtesy of TCU Marketing
and Communication.

ABOVE
Fall commencement in Schollmaier
Arena, 2021. Photograph by
Peter Matthews. Courtesy of
Glen Ellman.

OPPOSITE
The Jane & John Justin Hall of Fame.
Photograph by Rodger Mallison. Courtesy
of TCU Marketing and Communication.

ABOVE
The Parrish statues, featuring (from left to right) Dutch Meyer, Davey O'Brien, James Cash, and Gary Patterson. Photograph by James Anger. Courtesy of TCU Marketing and Communication.

Parrish Statues and
Walk of Excellence

We are now ready to exit Schollmaier Arena and continue south. You can angle to the southeast, slightly away from the practice facility, allowing you to pause at the Parrish Statues, provided through the generosity of TCU alums Sue and Bill Parrish. The first three life-sized bronze statues were dedicated in April 2016. Sculpted by David Alan Clark, the statues honor three legendary Horned Frogs whose exploits were chronicled earlier in this chapter. They are two-time national championship coach Leo R. "Dutch" Meyer, 1938 Heisman Trophy winner Davey O'Brien, and TCU's all-time winningest football coach Gary Patterson. A fourth statue commemorating basketball great James Cash Jr. '69 was dedicated November 2022. Cash was the first Black student-athlete at TCU and the first Black basketball player in the Southwest Conference, where he graduated as one of five players in school history with at least 1,000 points and 800 rebounds. He was named First Team All-Southwest Conference in 1968, leading the Frogs to the conference championship. He went on to earn master's and doctorate degrees at Purdue, subsequently joining the business faculty at Harvard in 1976. In 1985 he became the first Black faculty member to be granted tenure in the Harvard Business School.

Sam Baugh Indoor Practice Facility
and Cox Field/ Sheridan and Clif Morris
Practice Fields

Continuing to the south, either through the parking lot or on the sidewalk along Stadium Drive, you will pass by the Sam Baugh Indoor Practice Facility and Cox Field. Completed in 2007 at the cost of $7 million—$3 million from the Jane and John Justin Foundation and $4 million from the Cox Family of Midland, Texas—the eighty-thousand-square-foot, climate-controlled structure sits on the site of TCU's old baseball field and boasts an eighty-yard field with two ten-yard end zones. The HVAC system underwent a significant upgrade in 2013, thanks to the generosity of TCU Trustee Brad Cunningham '89 and his wife Alice, who provided a gift of $1 million.

Massive vinyl banners are displayed on the north and south walls, including one of the facility's namesake, Samuel (Sammy) Adrian Baugh '35, who quarterbacked TCU to its first national championship and went on to lead the Washington Redskins to NFL championships in 1937 and 1942. He was named NFL player of the year in 1947 and 1948. Touted as a strong recruiting arrow in the quiver, this world-class facility has served as a practice site for the Dallas Cowboys, Pittsburgh Steelers, and most recently the New Orleans Saints. In addition to football, the practice facility has been utilized by the baseball, track and field, and cross-country track and soccer teams.

Situated directly west of the Sam Baugh Indoor Practice Facility-Cox Field are the Sheridan and Clif Morris Practice Fields for outdoor use by the football team. In 2000 the fields were named in honor of Clif Morris, CEO of AmeriCredit, and his wife Sheridan, a Fort Worth community volunteer.

Ames Observatory

As you continue past the indoor practice facility you will come to the former site of the Ames Observatory. As early as 1948, the idea of an observatory on campus began receiving some consideration. At that time, Charlie M. Noble, a TCU instructor of anatomy, was an enthusiastic supporter of the idea. The large planetarium at Fort Worth Museum of Science and History is named for her.

In 1956, *Fort Worth Magazine* published an article proposing an "astronomical center" for the campus. The center was to include a twelve-inch catadioptric telescope, other smaller telescopes, a spectroheliograph, a planetarium, laboratories, and classrooms. That plan was never realized, but in 1961 a $50,000 gift from C. B. Ames, then director of Fish Engineering Corporation of Houston and father of TCU student Dick Ames, did make possible the smaller observatory and a large part of its equipment, including a twelve-inch compound telescope with a clock-drive mechanism for rotational purposes. Sadly, the dome was never able to rotate properly, and the classroom was ultimately turned into storage, its fate sealed by subsequent erection of nearby multistory apartments and athletic venues as well as maturing trees that progressively blocked its view of the heavens. The coup de grace was delivered by the tennis court lights installed at Bayard Friedman Tennis Center, which were a source of considerable light pollution. Originally scheduled for demolition in 2003, the working parts and dome of the observatory were instead donated in 2004 to St. John's School, a preparatory academy in Houston, thanks to conversations between TCU physics professor Dr. C. A. Quarles and a St. John's faculty member. Dedicated four years later, it now sits atop a hill outside tiny Hunt, Texas, in the Hill Country, about ninety miles northwest of San Antonio, Texas.

If you're at the intersection of Bellaire Drive North and Stadium Drive, we are now ready to walk (or drive as the case may be) around Worth Hills, Worth Hills Village (formerly known as "the Greek"), and more of the athletics complex.

CHAPTER 10

Worth Hills

The Past

In 1961 TCU acquired the 106 acres of land that now comprise the Worth Hills portion of the campus. It was previously home to a municipal golf course, formally named Worth Hills Golf Course but locally dubbed "Goat Hills" because of its rough and rolling topography. Opened in 1923, Goat Hills was Fort Worth's first public course, although private clubs Glen Garden and Rivercrest preceded it. It was memorialized in a 1965 article in *Sports Illustrated* entitled "The Glory Game at Goat Hills," by sportswriting legend and TCU alum Dan Jenkins '53, who described the wild and woolly brand of golf perpetrated on the course by a fictional cast of characters who were loosely based on Jenkins and his playing partners. TCU's proposal to the Fort Worth City Council to buy the property set off a spirited debate among the citizenry, with primary opposition coming from the TCU-Westcliff Homeowner's League, many members of whom owned homes bordering the course. In a citywide election, however, TCU won the right to purchase Worth Hills, thereby gaining much-needed ground for future expansion. With money from the sale, the city built a new municipal course near Benbrook Lake to appease the golfers who lost their home course.

The Worth Hills area of the campus was often called "the Greek" because the university-owned and managed residence halls for the social fraternities and sororities

OPPOSITE
Map showing the campus structures discussed in this chapter.

were located there. Although initially opposed by a majority of students, faculty, and alumni, Greek associations were brought to the campus for the first time in 1954. Now, about half of TCU's undergraduates belong to nationally recognized chapters.

The buildings on the northeast portion of Worth Hills underwent a virtually complete replacement between 2012 and 2015. Gone are the residence halls, designed by Preston Geren and Joseph Pelich and built in the 1960s through the early 1970s, which were characterized by both unremarkable architecture and increasing wear and tear, particularly those that housed rambunctious fraternity members. Three of those buildings were rectangular; four were T-shaped. All retained the main campus tones of buff brick, red roof, and white cast-stone trim. The sororities, however, added a touch of individualism and a splash of color by mounting over their entrance doors canvas canopies emblazoned with the Greek chapter letters. Gone but not forgotten are:

- Tomlinson Hall, named in honor of T. E. Tomlinson, who was a member of the board of trustees from 1907 to 1941 and was chairman when the decision was made to move TCU to Fort Worth. Tomlinson Hall was home to the Kappa Sigma, Sigma Chi, Phi Delta Theta, and Lambda Chi Alpha fraternities.
- Martin-Moore Hall was situated immediately west of Tomlinson Hall and was named for TCU alumnus Othol "Abe" Martin, head football coach from 1953 through 1966, during which time he led TCU to three SWC titles in the 1950s. The second namesake is Jerome A. Moore '23, who served as the first dean of TCU's AddRan College of Arts and Sciences from 1943 to 1973. Martin-Moore Hall housed Phi Kappa Sigma, Phi Gamma Delta, Delta Tau Delta, and Sigma Alpha Epsilon fraternities.
- Beckham-Shelburne Hall was home to the Pi Beta Phi, Chi Omega, Delta Gamma, and Kappa Alpha Theta sororities. Namesake Sadie Beckham began her tenure in 1920, first as matron of Jarvis Hall, then as dean of women. Coincident with her 1937 retirement she became only the second woman to be elected a member of the board of trustees. Beckham passed the reins to her assistant, Elizabeth Shelburne, who served in that position for twenty-four years, until she finished her career as supervisor of the health facilities, a position she held until 1968.

- Moody Hall was named in honor of W. L. Moody Jr. of Galveston, who with his wife established a foundation in 1942 to assist religious, charitable, scientific, and educational organizations in Texas. On more than one occasion, the university has been a recipient of grants from the Moody Foundation. Moody Hall provided space to Zeta Tau Alpha, Kappa Kappa Gamma, Alpha Chi Omega, and Delta Delta Delta sororities.
- Frances Sadler Hall was named for the wife of M. E. Sadler, TCU's chief executive officer from 1941 to 1965. Two more sororities, Kappa Delta and Alpha Delta Pi, were housed here. It was Mrs. Sadler who was singularly responsible for the interior design of the Carr Chapel. A woman of quiet dignity, she served as a strong and faithful First Lady. In ill health for many of her later years, Frances Sadler died in 1971.
- Mary Lipscomb Wiggins Hall, built in 1972, was the last of "Worth Hills v.1.0." It was named after one of the ten members of the 1896 graduating class of Add-Ran Christian University of Waco. Both of Mrs. Wiggins's daughters completed their degrees at TCU in Fort Worth. One of the daughters, Ruth, had a further tie to the university through her marriage to the late Judge A. D. Green, a TCU alumnus and member of the board of trustees. The $1.4 million Wiggins estate was bequeathed in equal parts to the TCU and Brite College corporations. Wiggins served as a non-Greek women's residence hall.
- Brachman Hall was constructed in 1970 as an "experimental" dormitory. It was designed as a modern adaptation of the European tradition of the "residential college" in which the ultimate emphasis is on living and learning. Built in a T-shape, Brachman housed men in the north section and women in the south. Included in the unit were classrooms, seminar rooms, faculty offices and living quarters, and common rooms for coeducational study and social activity. Called simply "New Hall" during its first year of operation, the building was officially dedicated and named the Solomon and Etta Brachman Hall in 1971. Brachman was a local businessman whose philanthropy was generously extended to TCU. In 1959, he was given honorary membership in the TCU Alumni Association and in 1968 he was awarded an honorary doctor of laws degree by the university. Brachman was demolished in summer of 2015 to make room for a parking garage, which we'll pass by a bit later. The Brachman name remains memorialized on campus in the form of the Brachman Auditorium in the BLUU.

Worth Hills residence halls under
construction, 1964. Courtesy of
Mary Couts Burnett Library.

The Present

King Family Commons

Beginning in 2010, and in short order, it was out with the old and in with the new. We will begin with six buildings that are laid out along Stadium Drive and then West Berry Street as you amble southward. The first of this half-dozen is King Family Commons. Dubbed "BLUU2" or "KFC" by students, its name recognizes the philanthropic efforts of Trustee J. Luther King Jr. and his wife Teresa, the couple discussed in connection with the residence hall on the Campus Commons that also bears their names, as well as that of their sons, Trustee J. Bryan King and Mason King. Opened in January 2015 at the cost of $21 million, the two-story structure was designed to complement the BLUU in terms of both providing dining options and study spaces, with over one-third of the building devoted to the latter. Jon Pontius, project architect at KSQ Architects of Tulsa, Oklahoma, stated that the intent of the building was to feel like a second living room. Mission accomplished. With more than thirty-nine thousand square feet of open space, the open floor plan gives the interior a relaxed aura. Students can choose from four dining options, including The Press (that features coffee, snacks, paninis), O'Brien's Grill (named for Davey O'Brien), the Tex-Mex themed Caliente's, and Magnolia's (which has an ever-changing menu highlighted by fresh-made salads, a wok station, and made-for-you pasta). The dining area's appeal is enhanced by a high, classic barrel-vault ceiling, providing an abundance of natural lighting. The second-floor balcony projects into another double-volume space, visually integrating the two floors. There are also meeting rooms that include the Greek Room, which provides meeting and storage space for all Greek letter organizations. The office for Fraternity and Sorority Life is also located on the second floor. An outdoor amphitheatre, complete with power and external speakers, extends from the east entrance to provide an opportunity for medium-sized gatherings on temperate days. Exterior seating shaded by large umbrellas is located on the south side of the building.

OPPOSITE
Interior view of King Family Commons, 2021.
Photograph by James Anger. Courtesy of TCU
Marketing and Communication.

ABOVE
King Family Commons, 2018. Photograph by
Jeffrey McWhorter. Courtesy of TCU Marketing
and Communication.

Clark, Marion, Hays, Richards, and Arnold Residence Halls

Non-Greek students reside in the next five buildings on the tour. These residence halls brought TCU's capacity to over 4,300 on-campus beds, an increase mandated by the student body's continued growth as well as the increased proportion of students desiring to live on campus beyond the currently mandated two years. KSQ Design, an architectural firm specializing in educational buildings, and Beck Construction were responsible for the planning and construction, respectively. All four buildings have LED lighting, study rooms at the ends of each floor, and expansive lower levels that include laundry facilities, kitchens, and lounge space. Neutral paint shades dominate the walls and furnishings, providing a calming effect. Casters make the bedroom furniture easily movable, allowing for flexibility in room-to-room layout. Like the residence halls on the Campus Commons, the building emphasizes common and community-learning spaces such as study lounges and reading nooks. All four buildings have a variety of floor plans, with a few one- and two-bedroom suites and predominantly three- and four-bedroom suites. To varying degrees the exteriors have the now-familiar colonnaded walkways and arches in front, highlighted by a distinctive curved façade. Interestingly, something is missing in a significant number of the rooms; namely, telephone wiring, and as a consequence, landlines. How far we've come from the days of old when telephones were absent dorm rooms but for a very different reason!

Opened August 2013, Pamela and Edward Clark Hall sits proximal to the King Family Commons. Sometime referred to as "new Clark" to distinguish it from "old Clark" on University Drive, its name recognizes the loyal philanthropic support of Pam Williams Clark '82 and Edward "Eddie" A. Clark '80. Mr. Clark, a TCU Trustee, is owner and chairman of the board of Professional Turf products, which distributes Toro equipment for the south-central United States. He lettered as the quarterback of the Horned Frogs football team. Mrs. Clark served the same company in accounting and human resources. Both received bachelors' of business administration from TCU in 1980 and 1982, respectively. Mrs. Clark was a member of Zeta Tau Alpha. The Clarks have three children, one of whom (Hannah) is a TCU graduate.

Also opened in 2013, Marion Hall is situated to the southeast and is connected to Clark Hall by a grand archway. It is named for Anne Burnett Windfohr Marion (1938–2020) and her husband John Marion in recognition of the extraordinary philanthropic support of TCU by the Marions and the Burnett Foundation. Anne Marion served as president of the Burnett Foundation, Burnett Companies, and Burnet Ranches L.L.C. She joined the board of trustees in 1979 and was appointed an honorary trustee in 1992. She was given the TCU Alumni Association's Royal Purple Award in 1985. John Marion worked for many years for Sotheby's, first as an auctioneer before ultimately ascending to the company's presidency. Together the Marions were the driving force behind many projects, most notably the Georgia O'Keeffe Museum of Santa Fe. The Burnett Foundation's ongoing support of TCU includes a $50 million naming gift to the Anne Burnett Marion School of Medicine.

Marion Hall is TCU's largest residence hall, checking in at 81,549 square feet. The total capacity of Clark and Marion Halls is 396 residents. They were built at a cost of $34.1 million. Both are coed, housing first-year students as well as those with advanced classifications.

Located directly south of Marion Hall, the sixty-one-thousand-square-foot, $16.7 million Marlene Moss Hays Hall opened in 2014. We have previously discussed the contributions of Marlene Hays and her husband Spencer Hays in conjunction with our traipse through the Spencer and Marlene Hays Business Commons, home to the Neeley School of Business. As with Clark and Marion Halls, the 163 inhabitants of Hays Hall are both male and female students who are primarily sophomores and juniors. Richards Hall and its sister Arnold Hall both opened in August 2019 and collectively house three hundred students, again both males and females but in this case all with junior and senior standing. Richards Hall is located immediately south of Hays Hall and runs north-south, while Arnold Hall stands perpendicular to Richards, completing the fivesome of new residence halls. Built as one project at a cost of $55 million, Richard and Arnold Halls share a similar architecture, departing somewhat from that of other TCU residence halls of recent vintage; specifically, the traditional TCU building materials have a more linear configuration as opposed to the sweeping arches and curves of, for example, Clark and Marion Halls.

Richards Hall is named in honor of the generous philanthropic support of the Richards family, whose relationship with TCU began with the 2004 enrollment of Stewart Richards, followed by his brother David in 2008. Their mother, trustee emeritus

ABOVE
Hays Residence Hall, 2022. Photograph
by James Anger. Courtesy of TCU Marketing
and Communication.

PAGES 284-285
Arnold Residence Hall (left) and
Richards Residence Hall (right),
2019. Courtesy of TCU Marketing
and Communication.

Nancy Tartaglino Richards, served on the Chancellor's Advisory Council beginning in 2009. She and her business partner Lisa Barrentine underwrote and endowed the TCU Value and Ventures Competition® in the Neeley School of Business, which has grown into one of the largest annual international business plan competitions. She is founder of Dallas-based First Preston HT. Multiple members of the Richards family have made substantive gifts to TCU.

The naming of Arnold Hall recognizes the Arnold family, whose gift helped fund the residence hall that bears their name. They have also generously supported Children's Medical Center Dallas and Plano. Ashley and Gregg Arnold are parents of four children, three of whom are TCU graduates. Mr. Arnold, a TCU Trustee, is chairman and CEO of TAC-The Arnold Companies, a privately owned petroleum marketing and aviation services company. Mrs. Arnold has served on the board of Children's Health Dallas and has also been involved with Meals on Wheels and Family Legacy, a foundation that aids Zambian children.

Athletic fields on Worth Hills

Garvey-Rosenthal Soccer Stadium

As you continue along the boulevard that is West Berry Street you will pass Frog Pond, complete with its two pedestrian bridges. Long used as a retention pond for water runoff from the neighborhoods south of Worth Hills, Frog Pond faced an uncertain future as recently as 2015, when its chief function was seemingly as a target for golf balls hit from the fraternity lawns. It is now considerably spiffed up and, among other things, the two pedestrian bridges provide easy access to Amon G. Carter Stadium on game days. Continuing on past a gated parking lot, West Berry veers back to the west after its brief north-south stint, passing by one of two recreation fields that sees extensive use by various intramural sports. Climbing the hill allows you a sweeping view of the soccer complex, consisting of Garvey-Rosenthal Soccer Stadium, Jane Justin Field House, and Jane Justin Field. These constitute the home pitch and associated facilities for TCU's women's soccer program, which began in 1986 under the direction of TCU alum and head coach David Rubinson. The twenty-six years under Rubinson and then Dan Abdalla brought modest success during a time when the Frogs underwent a somewhat nomadic journey from conference to conference. Eric Bell's hire coincided with the Frogs' entry into the Big 12 Conference. The Frogs earned their first conference championship during the 2021–2022 season, going undefeated in conference play and advancing deep into the COVID-delayed NCAA tournament. In 2021–2022, Coach Bell and the Frogs added their second consecutive Big 12 Conference Championship.

With 1,500 seats, the Garvey-Rosenthal Soccer Stadium has a press box and workout spaces. Fans can enjoy matches from a covered porch. Opened in 2000, the stadium was made possible by a $300,000 gift from Manny and Rosalyn Rosenthal and a $250,000 donation from James, Shirley, and Richard Garvey and the Garvey Texas Foundation. Lights were added in 2006, expanding the playing-time options considerably. A new LED scoreboard followed shortly. The Frogs play on the Jane Justin Field, named in honor of the late Jane C. Justin '43, a Fort Worth civic leader, author, and advocate for children with special needs. Perched behind the north goal is the Jane Justin Field House, a 2010 addition to the soccer complex. It was funded by a $1.5 million donation from the Jane and John Justin Foundation, which incidentally

ABOVE
Garvey-Rosenthal Soccer Stadium
and Jane Justin Field House. Courtesy
of TCU Athletics.

constituted the largest gift ever to TCU earmarked expressly for women's athletics. The five-thousand square-foot fieldhouse has home and visitor locker rooms, an official's locker room, a training room, a coach's office, and a lounge area. Its wraparound viewing terrace provides a bird's-eye view of the action.

Charlie and Marie Lupton Baseball Stadium

Continuing westward you will pass a parking lot, one of several favored tailgating areas, before encountering Charlie and Marie Lupton Baseball Stadium and its associated structures. TCU and baseball go way back together, to 1896 to be precise. Dutch Meyer's success as a coach extended from the gridiron to the diamond, as he led TCU to a SWC championship in 1933, a feat he replicated in 1956 during a brief second stint as the Frogs' baseball coach. Additional SWC championships were garnered in 1966, 1967, and 1994, the last occurring under the seventeen-year direction of head coach Lance Brown, a TCU as well as SWC hall-of-famer as both a TCU player and coach, who notched 517 wins, a school record at that point. TCU continued as a national power during Jim Schlossnagle's eighteen years at the helm, with thirteen regular-season and/or conference-tournament championships, including four appearances in the College World Series (2010, 2014–2017), and a total of 770 victories. The Frogs enjoy a strong fan base, as the average attendance has ranked first or second among private schools every year since 2011.

Beginning in 1962 and for forty-one years hence, the Frogs threw, caught, and batted at the TCU Diamond, a utilitarian structure located south of Amon G. Carter Stadium. In 2000, the "Here's the pitch" fund-raising campaign commenced, yielding $7 million from more than 220 donors. This culminated in the 2003 opening of the 2,200-seat Charlie and Marie Lupton Baseball Stadium. Built to Triple-A Minor League standards, Lupton Stadium brought TCU into the "major leagues" of college baseball in terms of its facilities. The intimate feel, complete with four skybox suites and a cantilevered roof system, not only positively impacted recruiting but was most certainly a factor in attracting multiple regional and super regional post-season tournaments. The stadium is named for Charles A. and Marie Lupton, who owned the Coco-Cola bottling franchise in Fort Worth and whose last name provides the "L" in the BLUU (Brown Lupton University Union). The Brown-Lupton Foundation made the naming gift to the ballpark. The Frogs play on Williams-Reilly Field, which

ABOVE
TCU baseball field, 1966. Photograph
by Linda Kaye. Courtesy of Mary Couts
Burnett Library.

RIGHT
Charlie and Marie Lupton Baseball
Stadium, 2022. Photograph by
Phil Hartman.

recognizes current Trustee Roger Williams, TCU alum and former baseball coach, who lettered for TCU from 1968 to 1971, as well as philanthropist Michael Reilly, a commercial real-estate developer in the metroplex. Lifelong friends, Williams and Reilly were teammates at Arlington Heights High School, just a few miles to the north. In 2006, thanks to lead gifts from the T. J. Brown and C. A. Lupton Foundation, Inc. and the William and Catherine Bryce Memorial Fund, a thirty-six-by-ten-foot scoreboard was added, complete with a twenty-one-by-ten-foot digital video monitor and a four-by-fifty-seven-foot ribbon displaying player statistics. A second scoreboard, this one measuring forty by twenty feet, was added in 2016. Upper-deck seating was increased in 2010, a $1 million project increasing the stadium's capacity to nine thousand. The year 2013 saw an array of new construction projects, including new fences (which were moved in an average of ten feet to counteract the prevailing southerly breezes, thus rendering the park more hitter friendly), new warning tracks, and a newly excavated hill on the right-field side of the stadium. Thanks to lead gifts from the T. J. Brown and the C. A. Lupton Foundation, Inc., and the William and Catherine Bryce Memorial Fund, in 2016 the stadium received an $8 million, two-story expansion to create player's and coach's locker rooms, lounge areas, team rooms, and second-floor coaches' offices with balconies overlooking the field, as well as a large classroom that can also serve as a media room. In addition to 7,440 square feet of added space, renovations were made to the 12,800 square feet of the existing stadium.

On October 3, 2014, the $2.5 million, twenty-thousand-square-foot G. Malcolm Louden Player Development Center for Baseball was dedicated. It includes a nine-thousand-square-foot hitting facility with four eighty-foot batting cages and indoor pitching mounds. Yet another game changer, the Louden Center allows practices to run unimpeded by the vagaries of Texas weather. Stated the Director of Intercollegiate Athletics Chris Del Conte at the dedication: "Malcolm Louden has been an unbelievable friend and supporter of our athletics program. We are truly grateful to Malcolm for his passion for TCU and for enhancing the student-athlete experience in our baseball program." Malcolm Louden '67 would make the short list of virtually any compilation of TCU's most ardent supporters, particularly of all things athletic. A generous donor of his time and financial resources, he served on the board of trustees for many years while managing the Walsh Companies for over thirty-five years.

The baseball complex also includes "Paul's Patios," situated by the right-field outfield, which consists of four donor patios complete with built-in grills and fixed seating, thus providing the opportunity to enjoy games from a unique vantage point. Paul's Patios is named for baseball letterman Paul Sorrels '42.

Robert and Maria Lowdon Track and Field Complex

Both the women's and men's TCU track and field teams have a rich heritage, which has been built primarily on their acumen in sprint events. The opening of Lowdon Track and Field Complex has helped sustain that tradition, providing an excellent training facility for both the cross country and the track and field teams. Located at the corner of West Berry and Bellaire Drive West, it took less than a year from the facility's 1999 opening to be recognized as an "Outstanding Track Complex" by the United States Tennis Court and Track Builder's Association (yes, there is such an organization). The $1.8 million facility was made possible through a $1 million gift from Robert and Maria Lowdon, as well as $300,000 from Dick Williams and $500,000 from Ken Huffman. A nine-lane Benyon surface was installed in 2011, which optimizes sprint times. In addition to the track, the facility has an outstanding area for throwing and jumping events.

Class of 2012 Gates . . . and other entrance structures as well

You can view the Lowdon Complex as you walk up Berry Street and turn right onto Bellaire Drive West, which takes you past the Class of 2012 Gates. This welcoming edifice, illuminated at night and an architectural mimicry of many of the more recent additions to campus, was a gift from the family of David Joseph Richards to honor the Class of 2012. There are other "gates to TCU," including the brick-and wrought-iron entry Ray Gate on Stadium Drive at West Berry. It was designed by Michael J. Bennet '78, an architect and CEO with Bennett Partners, Architecture Interiors Planning, whose handiwork includes mixed-used developments such as WestBend, MOLA at the Fort Worth Zoo, Frost Tower, the Woodshed Smokehouse, and the refurbishing of Erma Lowe Hall, an earlier stop on our tour. Funding was provided by TCU Trustee Jerry Ray '58 and his wife Betty Herring Ray, an Austin community leader. The Ray Gates were constructed and dedicated in the fall of 2005. Last but not least is the Teresa and Luther King Entrance, situated at the southwest corner of University Avenue and West Cantey Street. This welcoming structure bears the name of Teresa Carter King, a Dallas community leader, and her husband Dr. Luther King Jr. '62, MBA '66, who served as chair of TCU's Board of Trustees. The Kings were discussed in conjunction with the Campus Commons and King Family Commons. Collectively these structures demarcate and highlight the three most frequently employed entrances to campus. Each signals that the visitor is entering the land of the Horned Frogs.

ABOVE
The Ray Gates in front of the Wright
Admission Center, 2022. Photograph by
James Anger. Courtesy of TCU Marketing
and Communication.

Continuing north, you'll pass by the Justin Fields, situated on the corner of Bellaire Drive North and Bellaire Drive West. Added in 2016 through the generosity of the Jane and John Justin Foundation, these fields are used primarily for TCU's nationally recognized Sport Club Program, which plays sanctioned matches in rugby, lacrosse, soccer, and ultimate frisbee, to name a few sports.

Bayard H. Friedman Tennis Center

Tennis anyone? If so, grab your racquet and walk or drive into the parking lot a few paces to the east on Bellaire Drive North. You've entered the Bayard H. Friedman Tennis Center, a world-class facility completed in 1976 at the cost of over $2 million. Home to TCU's men's and women's tennis teams, the facility won national awards by *Tennis* magazine and the United States Tennis Association in 1990 and 1998, respectively. In addition to serving as home to TCU's tennis teams, the center hosts other tennis events, including the Fort Worth Pro Tennis Classic. It is also open for public play.

Funded by the Mary Potishman Lard Trust, and in fact named Potishman Lard for almost twenty years, the center now bears the name of Bayard H. Friedman (1926– 1998), CEO of Fort Worth National Bank, former mayor of Fort Worth (1963– 1965), and chair of TCU's Board of Trustees (1979–1990). Mr. Friedman was a longtime tennis enthusiast and could be frequently seen at the center which, since 1999, bears his name. Designed by Jack Kamrath of MacKie and Kamrath Architects of Houston, in consultation with the Tennis Planning Consultants of Houston and Chicago, the outdoor courts were sculpted out of the natural hills and valleys of the Worth Hills property. Among other things, the recessed courts provide partial shelter from the sometimes blustery Texas winds.

Six courts to the north serve (pun intended) the TCU varsity tennis program and for championship tournaments, with stadium seating for 1,500 spectators. They are reverently named the Bernard J. "Tut" Bartzen Varsity Courts, paying homage to TCU's head tennis coach from 1974 to 1998. Accumulating over five hundred wins along the way, Tut Bartzen (1927–2019), himself a top-ten singles player from 1953 to 1961, transformed the program into a juggernaut, as evidenced by eight conference crowns and NCAA final four appearances in 1989 and 1996. The Frogs have had over twenty-five All-Americans since the team's 1974 inception. They continue to excel in the post-Bartzen era, routinely achieving high national rankings, winning conference

ABOVE
Bayard H. Friedman. Photograph by Linda Kaye. Courtesy of Mary Couts Burnett Library.

OPPOSITE
Aerial view of the Bayard H. Friedman Tennis Center with Lupton Stadium in the background, 2009. Photographed by Paul Moseley for Epic Helicopters. Courtesy of TCU Sports Department.

titles (including the years 2016 through 2018), advancing deep into NCAA tournaments, and, most recently, winning the 2022 NCAA Indoor Tennis Tournament.

At the heart of the center, on the mall between the outdoor courts, is a clubhouse with a retail shop that offers a complete line of tennis equipment, apparel, and accessories. Men's and women's locker rooms are available for use by all patrons. Around the walls of the retail shop are pictures representing the tennis teams' accomplishments in collegiate competition—a TCU Tennis Hall of Fame of sorts.

Sixteen outdoor courts flank the clubhouse to the south and are open to all tennis enthusiasts. A seventeenth court, bifurcated by a concrete wall, is located on the east end of the complex, allowing for solo practice. The varsity tennis teams' building marks the south apex of the grounds, serving as home office to the coaches of the men's and women's tennis teams and also providing locker facilities for both. Finally, to the east of the team building are five indoor courts that allow for year-around tennis. Completed in 1980, the $500,000 cost of the indoor facility was again borne by the Mary Potishman Lard Trust.

Facilities Services,
the Worth Hills Parking Garage,
the Bat Flight facility, and Worth Hills
Information Technology Offices
and Chiller Plant

A steep hill awaits as you head east on Bellaire Drive North to complete your tour of campus. To the right sits a building labeled Physical Plant. Built in 1966, it houses TCU's Facilities Services, whose mission is to provide the physical and educational environment necessary for academic excellence and realization of the mission, vision, and core values of the university. This essential campus unit and its 315 full-time employees oversee the entirety of TCU's grounds, including the 125 major buildings (which comprise over 5.1 million square feet) and the institution's 302 acres.

Directly to the west is the Worth Hills Parking Garage, completed in 2016. With approximately 1,200 parking spaces, this six-level garage primarily serves the residents of Worth Hills. The Worth Hills Parking Garage is TCU's largest structure, checking in at 391,441 square feet. Speaking of parking garages, you likely began your tour at the Frog Alley Parking Garage, TCU's first such structure, which was completed a year earlier and accommodates 984 vehicles. The two garages blend with the surrounding buildings, both in terms of their architecture and building materials. Somewhat amusingly, the perceived absence of convenient parking has been perhaps the second-most commonly levied student complaint—behind only tuition increases—in the *Skiff*, TCU's student newspaper, for at least forty years. Interestingly, as recently as 1994, the board of trustees formally rejected the notion of building parking garages on campus. Even when the plan was approved in 2001, construction experienced a series of delays, precipitated primarily by construction costs. As one can imagine, it's a bit more difficult to successfully solicit donations for a parking garage than an academic building, residence hall, or athletic facility, perhaps explaining why the two structures bear geographical names only.

The Worth Hills Information Technology (IT) Offices and Chiller Plant is tucked behind the Worth Hills Parking Garage and is accessible by Pond Drive, which forms the entrance to the Worth Hills Village. The building opened in 1964 and was expanded to its current 20,140 square feet in 2015. TCU's IT Division strives to provide the campus with superior technology and a robust infrastructure designed to meet the needs of a growing student and employee population. Once occupying only a fraction of the Sid Richardson basement, IT's footprint has enlarged considerably over the past forty years. The conjoined Chiller Plant supports the Worth Hills area.

Turning to the north, we find the Bat Flight Facility tucked among the creek-bottom trees, with Amon Carter Stadium looming to the east. Nicknamed the "Batatorium," this 2,040-square-foot structure was completed in 2016. It supports research efforts conducted by faculty and students in the Departments of Biology and Environmental Sciences, who employ high-speed videography to better understand bat navigation.

Worth Hills Village

Worth Hills Village consists of eleven new residences that house thirteen sororities and twelve fraternities. They replaced the aging housing structures built in the 1960s and last renovated in the early 2000s. This project was supported by literally hundreds of donors from each sorority and fraternity. TCU worked with Tulsa-based architectural firm KSQ for the development of the Worth Hills Village. Construction was by the Beck Group. Phase one began in 2016 and phase two was completed in 2018.

The structures feature TCU's custom combination of clay roof tiles and buff brick, along with cast stone and stucco. Checking in at four stories, the buildings mimic Greek architecture with elements such as round columns and wide porches that are arranged in patterns, creating a unique façade for each building. Currently unnamed (save for placeholder designations FA1-FA3, FB1&FB2, SA1-SA5, SB1) and ranging from 27,462 to 50,361 square feet, the eleven buildings are smaller than other residence halls, but they interconnect to create a sense of community that is enhanced by landscaping and a parklike setting. The total living capacity is 757, with eleven hall directors and twenty-five resident assistants provided by Fraternity and Sorority Life. Each sorority was given the opportunity to personalize their area's interior, with TCU footing most of the bill but chapters paying for certain specific design elements. Major outdoor architectural features include the Divine Nine, Obelisk, and a memorial tribute to the original Worth Hills residence halls that once stood there. Housing is a combination of doubles, suites, and apartment style, consistent with other new TCU residence halls. The project earned the 2018 Project Achievement Award from the Construction Management Association of America, North Texas Chapter. In 2018, TCU became the first university to have pillars erected representing the National PanHellenic Council (NPHC), an entity that includes African American organizations. There is a pillar for each organization on campus, each including the Greek letters, open motto, and founding date. The specific fraternity and sorority occupants of Worth Hills are as follows: SA1 (Sigma Kappa and Zeta Tau Alpha), SA2 (Alpha Chi Omega and Pi Beta Phi), SA3 (Kappa Kappa Gamma and Kappa Alpha Theta), SA4 (Delta Gamma), SA5 (Chi Omega and Alpha Delta Pi), SB1 (Gamma Phi Beta, Delta Delta Delta, Phi Mu), FA1 (Delta Tau Delta and Kappa Sigma), FA2 (Phi Delta Theta and Pi Kappa Phi), FA3 (Sigma Nu and Sigma Phi Epsilon), FB1 (Phi Gamma Delta, Sigma Alpha Epsilon, and Phi Kappa Sigma), and FB2 (Beta Theta Pi, Lambda Chi Alpha, and Sigma Chi). Each of the chapters are indicated by name on the outside of their respective buildings. In addition, two of the sorority chapter houses are named: "The Big 6 Kappa Alpha Theta House" (named for the "Big 6" of Susan Abbey, Mary Johnson Draper, Kathleen Terrell, Carol Tobin Kingwell-Smith, Mary Walker Gaertner, and Kerry Wallace Scarbauer) and the Tri Delta House (named for alumna Jean Wiggin Roach, Amy Roach Bailey, and Lori Roach David). The Tri Delta Phi Lambda Chapter house naming was made possible by a gift from John V. Roach '61, MBA '65.

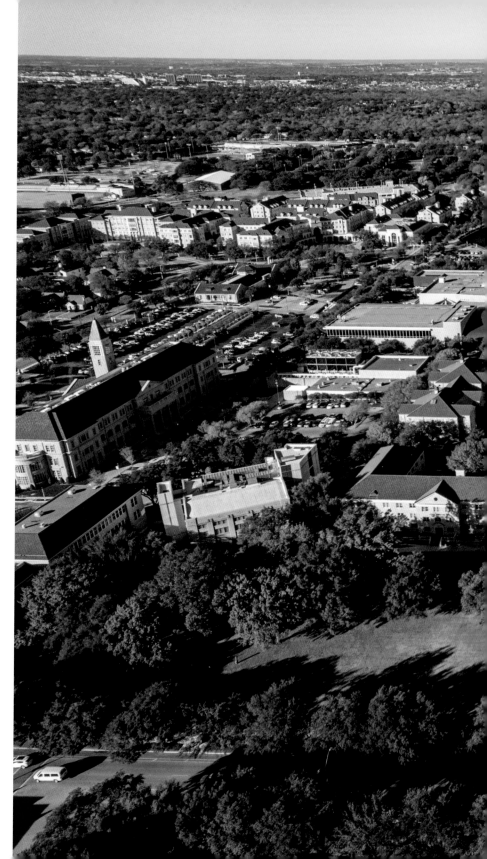

RIGHT
Aerial view of the west campus, athletic complex, and Worth Hills Village, 2022. Photograph by James Anger. Courtesy of TCU Marketing and Communication.

CHAPTER 11

Some Closing Miscellany

(Campus beauty; A bit about bricks; Streets around campus;
Sustainability; The School of Medicine; Master planning;
and the campus through the decades)

Campus beauty

TCU's campus is graced with some magnificent trees, mostly live oaks, that are integral to its beauty. But if one runs the clock back to 1910 and the decision to relocate the campus to the windswept hills that stood as an outpost to Fort Worth, there was but a single scruffy tree to be found on the hardscrabble prairie. Instead, Johnson grass and horned toads were the predominant life forms. That orphan tree was located near the University Drive-West Cantey intersection and has long since disappeared. Various accounts have it that E. M. Waits planted two magnolias, still standing, at the entrance to the Administration Building (now Reed Hall) shortly after he became president in 1916, and that he took pride in watching their growth during his twenty-five-plus years at TCU's helm. His effort was preceded by a live oak, planted by the class of 1912, which initially stood in solitude but now comingles with others to the northeast of Reed Hall. The campus took on a different look in 1913, when local businessman W. C. Stripling donated one hundred trees for planting on campus. Following that arboreal infusion, Arbor Day in 1915 was celebrated when a professor asked every student and faculty member to contribute a tree, yielding an additional four hundred. Many of the now-stately live oaks on campus were obtained from ranches near Glen Rose as seven- and eight-footers in the 1940s and 1950s. They

OPPOSITE
Aerial view of the west campus, athletic complex, and Worth Hills Village, 2022. Photograph by James Anger. Courtesy of TCU Marketing and Communication.

were planted under the loving direction of Buck Fielding (1929–2009), director of building maintenance, whose TCU tenure at his 2001 retirement stood at a remarkable fifty-four years. Fast forward to 2021 and TCU's fifth-straight annual recognition by the Arbor Day Foundation for its dedication to preserving the diverse species of approximately 3,200 trees that now contribute to campus beauty. Live oaks dominate, but red and pin oaks, pecan and sweetgums, elms and others adorn campus . . . over forty species in all. In some cases, such as the "Julie tree" by the Moore Building, plantings serve as memorials to students or faculty. Others honor the living. Dendrophiles (tree lovers) may opt to take the stroll prescribed in the Spring 2021 issue of *TCU Magazine*, aptly entitled: "What trees are on campus?" This "tree tour," which clusters mainly around Sadler Hall and the Tom Brown/Pete Wright Residential Community, was one of many brainchildren of Provost Nowell Donovan.

ABOVE
The first tree to be planted on campus, 2018. Photograph by Carolyn Cruz. Courtesy of TCU Marketing and Communication.

But of course the beauty of TCU's campus is the sum of more than stately trees, statues, monuments, buildings, and congruent architecture. The shrubbery, grass, and even more so the flowers combine to render the land of Horned Frogs a veritable botanical wonderland. A tip of the hat to the grounds crew for making this happen. They utilize the TCU greenhouses, located behind the Physical Plant building, to grow various plantings that both hold visual appeal and can withstand the climatic extremes of North Texas weather. The begonias, impatiens, geraniums, petunias, dianthus, marigolds, zinnias, snapdragons, and caladiums are then transplanted around campus into rototilled flower beds, over eleven thousand square feet in all, amended with peat moss and red lava sand. This is in addition to over fifteen thousand square feet of perennial flower beds. The spring plantings, especially the tulips, are particularly striking. These bulbs are planted annually and then discarded after vividly decorating campus. The expense of maintaining this wonderland is not borne by TCU's operating budget but instead comes from an endowment initiated in 1987 by board of trustees' member Mary Evans Beasley, which now exceeds $1.74 million.

A Bit about Bricks and Roofs

Whether by happenstance or design, the buff brick has been as central to TCU's architectural identity as any other element. Recalling the conflagration of the main building that precipitated TCU's move to Fort Worth, the Clark brothers likely selected brick and reinforced concrete simply because these materials wouldn't burn. Speculation has it that buff brick was chosen because it was the least expensive at the time. Fort Worth-based Acme Brick has supplied this essential building block for the past few decades.

TCU gained another key element to it architectural ethos during the construction spurt of the 1940s; namely, that of the red tile roof. Interestingly, this was mandated by the raw-material shortages extant during World War II and in the years immediately following; specifically, it was impossible to roof the residence halls with traditional asphalt-based shingles because they contained a petroleum byproduct. To paraphrase Mick Jagger: "You can't always get what you want, but if you try, you get what you need." Most would agree this necessity proved fortuitous indeed.

Streets Around Campus

The genesis and evolution of Berry Avenue and University Drive were touched upon in Chapter 6, but it's now well worth mentioning a few additional streets whose histories inculcate with that of TCU:

- **Cockrell Avenue**, **Greene Avenue**, and **Rogers Avenue** were paved and, perhaps, named during the early 1920s. Up to that time, the TCU neighborhood—the "hill"—had been outside the city limits of Fort Worth, connected to the city by a route that led from Forest Park Boulevard to Eighth Avenue to the streets of downtown. In fact, University Drive was still an extension of Forest Park Boulevard. Rogers bears the name of R. L. Rogers, a real-estate developer. Dr. R. M. Greene owned and lived on extensive property east of the campus. Rogers and Greene sold a number of vacant lots, with the proceeds covering two-thirds of the cost of the streets' paving. Dr. Greene subsequently willed TCU much of his estate. He had earlier sold the land on which the library stands for the bargain price of $15,000. Cockrell is named for Dr. Egbert R. Cockrell and his wife Dura Brokaw Cockrell. He was a professor of history, political, and social science, and she the head of the art department. Dr. Cockrell went on to become the president of William Woods College in Fulton, Missouri. (On a personal note, both authors lived on Rogers at one time or another, just a stone's throw or two from campus. In fact, one of us (JS) grew up in the TCU neighborhood.)

- **Shirley Avenue** most certainly pays homage to T. E. Shirley, who served on the board of trustees from 1893–1917 and who also has a residence hall named in his honor (as noted previously the spelling varies between Sherley and Shirley). Perhaps Shirley should occupy a more prominent place in our collective consciousness, as a motion was made in his first year as board chair to discontinue the school owing to its indebtedness. He refused to honor the motion, subsequently devoting himself full time to raising money, including a $1,000 personal contribution, to address the debt. As a result, TCU exists today.

- **McPherson Street** was named for Chalmers McPherson, a Waxahachie minister, whose photo occurs in the prologue of this book in conjunction with the original layout of campus. He was a member of the board, endowment secretary of the university, and taught in Brite College of the Bible until his death in 1927.

- **Waits Avenue** bears the name of Edward McShane Waits, president of TCU from 1916 to 1941. Like T. E. Shirley, a residence hall is named in his honor. His accomplishments are many, including leading TCU through the Depression years, a time when, incidentally, faculty took a series of pay cuts totaling 43 percent.

Construction That Promotes Sustainability (LEED Certification)

While construction can negatively impact the environment, TCU has actively sought to minimize the harmful effects, as evidenced by the increased number of LEED-certified buildings on campus. Leadership in Energy and Environmental Design (LEED) guidelines were created and are monitored by the US Green Building Council. Following the international baseline for sustainable buildings, projects may be certified as silver, gold, or platinum, based upon nine criteria such as materials and resources, indoor environmental quality, and water efficiency. As of 2022 there are thirty-two LEED-certified buildings on campus, including twenty-five with gold status. Virtually all new projects have either been granted a LEED certification or have made application for it.

The Anne Burnett Marion School of Medicine

In 2015, TCU and the University of North Texas Health Science Center (UNTHSC) announced plans to initiate an allopathic (MD-granting) medical school. Dr. Stuart Flynn was appointed the founding dean in 2016, and the first class of sixty students matriculated July 2019. In 2021 TCU assumed sole ownership of the medical school. In addition to many clinical sites in Tarrant County, the first classes met on

UNTHSC's campus on Camp Bowie Boulevard and on TCU's campus, and, beginning in 2022, in temporary quarters south of TCU campus. That is set to change in 2024, as construction began in fall 2022 on a major building project in Fort Worth's Near Southside neighborhood. Standing at four stories, the approximately one-hundred-thousand-square-foot medical education building will be the academic hub for the School of Medicine's 240 medical students as well as for hundreds of faculty and staff. The building will feature flexible classrooms and ample study/collaboration space. The third floor will be home to a functional anatomy lab, simulation lab, and clinical skills space. Other spaces will include a grand forum space, café, library, fitness area, and student lounge. Los Angeles-based CO Architects will serve as the design architect, with Dallas-based Hoefer Welker the architect of record. The construction will be carried out by the Linbeck Group.

Interestingly enough, the Burnett School of Medicine became TCU's second medical school. In 1911, TCU assumed operation of the Fort Worth School of Medicine at its downtown location. Operations ceased in 1917 at a time when, in the aftermath of the Flexner Report, medical education became significantly more standardized in the US and, consequently, the number of medical schools contracted by well over 60 percent.

Master Planning

Master planning very likely presaged TCU's existence, at least in a formal sense. It certainly preceded the Fort Worth campus, as the January 1910 *Skiff* depicted visions of a ten-building campus even before construction began on the first two buildings (the Administration Building—which became Reed Hall—and Jarvis Hall). Created by Fort Worth architects Waller and Field, the sketch (shown in the prologue) articulated the university's "accepted layout" for its future campus. The intent was for the buildings and curved, tree-lined walkways to reside in "perfect harmony." Of course, like best-laid plans, there were numerous departures from the original good intentions. There doesn't appear to be a subsequent campus master plan for another eighty-one years, at least one of any prominence. In fact, a formal blueprint of campus didn't exist until the 1980s. A largely *ad hoc* process changed when a master plan was completed in 1991 under the direction of Will Stallworth, a thirty-year veteran of the Air Force who flunked retirement and was appointed head of TCU's Physical Plant. Stallworth quickly realized the need for such a comprehensive plan, one that addressed aspirational needs as well as the realities of campus maintenance. The plan he developed envisioned a more pedestrian-friendly central campus, with clearly marked entrances to the university. Two interrelated major goals were: first, addressing parking issues through the construction of parking structures; and second, limiting vehicular access to the extent possible. Despite best intentions, the facilities master plan was slow to translate into action, in large part because TCU was in a lean fiscal period. Specifically, when William Tucker arrived as chancellor in 1979, the endowment stood at a mere $53 million (versus over three-quarters of a billion dollars upon his 1998 retirement). Even more challenging, TCU was struggling to maintain enrollment. Specifically, total enrollment had dropped from 7,340 in 1968 to 5,874 in 1978. Moreover, a relative paucity in the number of applications (only 1,560 in 1981) mandated that only 184 be rejected. Contrast that the university's situation in 2022, during which around 20,000 applicants vied for an entering class of approximately 2,500. Further, the endowment was in excess of $2.4 billion. Indeed, resources were modest at best in the 1970s and 1980s, and difficulties were compounded by a struggling economy in the late 1980s. As a consequence, TCU was forced to move most projects, save essential maintenance, to the back burner. Not surprisingly, the TCU campus of the 1980s was visually a far cry from its current splendor, instead punctuated at regular intervals by bare ground in shady areas, exposed rocks here and there, and tired-looking fire hydrants with faded purple paint.

Momentum built gradually but perceptibly, as evidenced by "The Next Frontier," TCU's first comprehensive fund-raising campaign that spanned 1992 to 1997. The $100 million goal was eclipsed as 26,111 donors contributed $126.1 million. A significant fraction of the income from that effort went to "mortar and brick" rather than "people and programs." Around the same time efforts such as the Berry Street Initiative, discussed in Chapter 6, both upgraded Berry Street and better integrated TCU into its surrounding environs. The stage was set nicely for the 1999–2000 "Commission on the Future of TCU," initiated by then Chancellor Michael "Mick" Ferrari. The commission comprised seventeen task forces, composed of five hundred campus and community leaders, that took a comprehensive and aspirational look at TCU. It was Chancellor Ferrari's dream to transform TCU from a solid regional institution to one of truly national prominence. Among the outcomes was a $150 million investment in the campus, upgrading more than one hundred classrooms and laboratories and beginning the process of refurbishing residence halls. Four major construction projects were completed during this time, a prelude to the building flurry that led some to dub TCU as Texas Construction University. This provided the momentum for another campus-wide strategic planning effort, spearheaded by Chancellor Victor J. Boschini and Provost Nowell Donovan, named Vision in Action (VIA). Phase one of VIA was approved by the board of trustees on November 2005 and included development of the Campus Commons (including the BLUU and four residence halls), as well as expansion of the physical plant of the College of Education. Over the next fifteen years, led by Chancellor Boschini and Provost Donovan, VIA matured into a strategic plan entitled "Vision in Action: Lead On," a collection of goals and recommendations that was presented to the board of trustees, the Chancellor's Cabinet, and the Provost's Council in April 2019.

Appointed in 2003, Dr. Boschini is TCU's tenth chancellor. He has been praised for a leadership style that is student-focused, which is well-suited for a student-centric institution such as TCU. A nationally recognized leader in higher education, he has served as the Big 12 Conference's representative on the NCAA Presidential Forum and has chaired the National Association of Independent Colleges and Universities (NAICU). The campus has been physically transformed during his tenure as chancellor, a transformation that includes not only substantive upgrades to literally every building on campus but also the construction of fifty-seven new buildings, including twenty residence halls (counting Worth Hills Village). Indeed, a walk of the campus is now a very different experience than when he assumed the reins from Chancellor Ferrari.

The 2017 Facilities Master Plan was an important adjunct to VIA-Lead On. Chaired by Provost Donovan, Vice Chancellor for Student Affairs Kathy Cavins-Tull, and Associate Vice Chancellor for Facilities and Campus Planning Todd Waldvogel, the Facilities Master Plan process sought the input from on- and off-campus constituents. The plan's intent was to "provide direction in facility planning to ensure future building honors the rich campus heritage yet remains adaptable to the evolution of the University's Strategic Plan." Further, "It is intended to guide development in a

ABOVE
Chancellor Victor J. Boschini and Provost Nowell Donovan, 2014. Photograph by Glen Ellman. Courtesy of Glen Ellman.

manner that enhances the mission, vision, and value of the University. Texas Christian University is a special place and this plan preserves and expands this legacy into the future." Perhaps the third edition of *Walking TCU* will comment on how this legacy was fulfilled.

The Campus Through the Decades

TCU's campus construction did not occur at a steady rate, but rather through a series of bursts followed by relatively quiescent periods. Logically enough, these mirrored fluctuations in TCU's financial health and growth of the student body through the years. This is evidenced in the figure on page 317, which depicts the square footage added on a per-decade basis. The 1910s and 1920s saw the construction of the original campus, followed by a largely dormant period of roughly twenty years. Post-World War II brought both increases in TCU's enrollment and the financial resources to add academic buildings, residence halls, and athletic facilities. As with the period from the Great Depression through the Second World War, the late 1970s through the mid-1990s were marked by comparatively little construction. This in turn was followed by an uptick that quickly morphed to a figurative tsunami, with construction projects totaling more than $1.2 billion over the past twenty years.

Three points are worth noting regarding the figure. First, the values reflect not only the addition of new buildings but the elimination of old ones. For example, the 140,809 square feet added by the BLUU was significantly counterbalanced by the loss of 97,961 square feet when the Brown Lupton Student Center (the Main) was demolished, thus adding only 42,848 to the total. Thus, the growth portrayed in the figure represents true growth in overall square footage; it is not inflated by ignoring collateral demolition. Second, the two parking garages were not included in the calculations. Collectively, they added 750,270 square feet to the university's footprint, almost one-third of the total square footage added in the last decade and more than the total square footage added between 1914 and 1955! Third, the pattern of growth in athletic facilities (which comprise 22 percent of the total square footage) largely mirrors that of non-athletic facilities, which are largely academic buildings and residence halls. Thus, academics and athletic fortunes appear interrelated, at least at TCU.

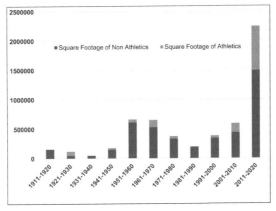

ABOVE
Aerial view of campus, c. 1925.
Courtesy of Mary Couts
Burnett Library.

LEFT
Net square footage of campus
structures added on a decade-
by-decade basis.

SOME CLOSING MISCELLANY   **317**

ABOVE
Aerial view of campus, 1942. Courtesy
of Mary Couts Burnett Library.

OPPOSITE
Aerial view of campus, 1966. Courtesy
of Mary Couts Burnett Library.

PAGES 320-321
Aerial view of campus, 2022. Photograph by
James Anger. Courtesy of TCU Marketing
and Communication.

ABOVE
Aerial view of campus, 2021. Courtesy
of TCU Facilities Services.

Epilogue

You have now visited the final location on this tour of Texas Christian University. Whether you followed from the outset or joined in along the way, it is hoped that the journey was pleasant and informative, and that you will take away with you some small part of the spirit that shaped the past and is guiding the present of this institution of teaching and learning.

Long years have been covered in this account, which has required a brevity that necessarily fragments significant times and foreshortens individual lives. It would be unseemly and sad to dismiss or take for granted the hardships, sacrifice, passion, strain, weariness, vision, despair, jubilation, dedication, commitment, and wonder that was theirs. May their lives and deeds not be diminished or ignored, but held up as a light for our path into the future.

Appendix
Chronological Building Sequence of Major Structures

1873
Add-Ran College opened, Thorp Spring.

1878
First building erected, displacing the original Thorp building.

1882
The left wing of the building added.

1892
The right wing complete, named "Jarvis Building."

1895
Christmas, moved to Waco.

1910
- March 22—Main Building destroyed by fire.
- September—school opens in downtown Fort Worth.

1911
- Administration Building (renovated 1961, renamed Dave Reed Hall).
- Jarvis Hall (originally a women's residence hall).
- Goode Hall (a ministerial and boys' residence hall) (demolished 1958).

1912
Clark Hall (men's residence hall) (demolished 1959).

1914
Brite College of the Bible (renamed Bailey Building).

1921
Gymnasium (renamed Erma Lowe Hall).

1923
Memorial Arch.

1925
Mary Couts Burnett Library (enlarged 1958, 1982, 2015).

1930

Stadium west (enlarged, 1948, named Amon G. Carter Stadium; enlarged, 1953, 1956; demolished and rebuilt, 2010, 2018).

1942

Foster Residence Hall (women's residence hall).

1947

Tom Brown Residence Hall (men's residence hall) (demolished 1998).

1948

• Waits Residence Hall (women's residence hall).
• Stadium east (Amon G. Carter).

1949

Ed Landreth Hall and Auditorium.

1952

Winton-Scott Hall.

1953

Religion center begun with what is now Theodore Prentis Beasley Hall, Robert Carr Chapel, and Jo Ann and Wayne Moore Building.

1955

• Brown-Lupton Student Center (demolished 2008).
• Pete Wright Residence Hall (men's residence hall) (demolished 1999).

1956

Upper deck, Amon G. Carter Stadium.

1957

• Colby Residence Hall (women's residence hall).
• Milton Daniel Hall (men's residence hall).
• Dan D. Rogers Hall (demolished 2018).

1958

• Sherley Residence Hall (women's residence hall).
• Clark Residence Hall (men's residence hall).

1960

M. E. Sadler Hall administration building.

1961

Daniel-Meyer Coliseum (converted to Ed and Rae Schollmaier Arena in 2015), Ames Observatory.

1963

Brown-Lupton Health Center.

1964

Worth Hills campus acquired; four residence halls built:
  Beckham-Shelburne Hall sorority house (demolished 2015)
  Frances Sadler Hall sorority house (demolished 2015)
  W. L. Moody Hall sorority house (demolished 2015)
  Tomlinson Hall fraternity house (demolished 2015).

1965

• Martin-Moore Hall fraternity house (demolished 2015).
• Worth Hills cafeteria (demolished 2015).

1969

Frog Fountain.

1970

Brachman Hall coed residence hall (demolished 2015).

1971

• Sid W. Richardson Physical Sciences Building.
• Annie Richardson Bass Building.

1972

• Cyrus K. and Ann Rickel Building (expanded 2001 and renamed University Recreation Center).
• Mary Lipscomb Wiggins Hall (women's residence hall) (demolished 2015).

1975

Miller Speech and Hearing Clinic.

1976

Mary Potishman Lard Tennis Center (renamed Bayard H. Friedman Tennis Center).

1978
Starpoint School.

1979
KTCU tower.

1982
James M. Moudy Visual and Communications Arts Building.

1988
Moncrief Residence Hall (athletics).

1989
Charles D. Tandy Hall.

1992
Winthrop Rockefeller Building for Ranch Management.

1996
Walsh Athletic Complex.

1997
- Dee J. Kelly Alumni and Visitors Center (expanded in 2018).
- TCU Bookstore (moved into new building 2008).
- Campus Police Building.

1998
- Tom Brown-Pete Wright Residential Community (Fish Hall, Walker Hall, Britain Hall, Mullins Hall).
- Mary D. and F. Howard Walsh Center for Performing Arts.

1999
- Institute of Behavioral Research.
- Robert and Maria Lowdon Track and Field Complex.
- Garvey-Rosenthal Soccer Stadium.
- Tom Brown-Pete Wright Residential Community (Mabee Hall, Herndon Hall, TB/PW Commons Building).
- Leibrock Village (Beasley House, Abell-Hanger House, Moore House, Hill House, and Mabee House).

2000
- John Justin Athletic Center.
- Secrest-Wible Building.

2001

TCU Press.

2002

William E. and Jean Jones Tucker Technology Center.

2003

- Steve and Sarah Smith Entrepreneurs Hall.
- Charlie and Marie Lupton Baseball Stadium.
- Varsity Tennis Team Building.

2004

Ed and Rae Schollmaier Basketball Complex (practice facility).

2007

- Sam Baugh Indoor Practice Facility and Cox Field.
- Betsy and Steve Palko Hall.
- J. E. & L. E. Mabee Foundation Education Complex.
- Kellye Wright Samuelson Residence Hall.
- Amon G. Carter Residence Hall.
- Teresa and Luther King Residence Hall.
- Mary and Robert J. Wright Residence Hall.

2008

- Meyer-Martin Athletic Complex (Dutch Meyer Athletic Complex and Abe Martin Academic Enhancement Center).
- Fort Worth Contemporary Arts Studio.
- TCU Campus Store.
- Brown-Lupton University Union.

2009

Clarence and Kerry Scharbauer Hall.

2010

- Jane Justin Field House.
- Mary Wright Admission Center.

2011
- Bob Lilly Physical Performance Center.
- W. Oliver and Nell A. Harrison Building (Brite).

2013
- Pamela and Edward Clark Residence Hall.
- Marion Residence Hall.

2014
- Rees-Jones Hall.
- The G. Malcolm Louden Player Development Center for Baseball.
- Marlene Moss Hays Residence Hall.

2015
- King Family Commons.
- Frog Alley Parking Garage.

2016
- Bat Flight Facility.
- Worth Hills Parking Garage.

2017
Worth Hills Village (Buildings SA1-SA5, SB1, FA2).

2018
- Worth Hills Village (Buildings FA1, FA3, FB1, FB2).
- Human Resources.

2019
- Fine Arts Building.
- Richards Residence Hall.
- Arnold Residence Hall.
- Spencer and Marlene Hays Business Commons (Tom and Marilyn Sumner Hall, Spencer Hays Hall, Kim and Bill Shaddock Auditorium).

2020
- TCU Music Center and Van Cliburn Concert Hall at TCU.
- The Harrison.

Bibliography

Note: The *Skiff* is TCU's student newspaper; *TCU 360* is the digital part of TCU student media. Where not clear from the title, article contents are indicated in parenthesis.

Abrams, Brian. "Filling station." *TCU Magazine*, Summer 2007, 54–55. (Dutch's)

Albertson, Sierra. "Tom Brown-Pete Wright apartments undergo renovation." *Skiff*, October 2, 2014, 3.

"Alumni center ground breaking set." *TCU Magazine*, Fall 1995, 28. (Kelly Alumni Center)

Alvarez, Diana. "Mabee complex to be dedicated." *Skiff*, September 14, 2007, 1.

Armstrong, Sally. "The cornerstone comes home." *TCU Magazine*, September 1992, 4-6.

"A bigger, better library." *TCU Magazine*, Fall 2015, 10–18.

"A grand opening." *TCU Magazine*, Fall 2006, 10. (Grand Marc)

"A new Colby Hall." *TCU Magazine*, Fall 2015, 11.

"A new Frog playground." *TCU Magazine*, Spring 2003, 26–29. (Rec center)

"A place to stay." *TCU Magazine*, Summer 2021, 55–56. (Hyatt place)

"A work of (performing) art." *TCU Magazine*, Summer 1998. Back cover. (Walsh Center for Performing Arts)

Baker, Emily. "Smith Entrepreneurs Hall to be dedicated Saturday." *Skiff*, April 2, 2003, 1, 3.

Baker, Steven. "Frogs on the right track." *Skiff*, September 29, 1999, 6. (Lowdon Track)

Bateman, Caressa, "Robert Carr Chapel nominated for best wedding venue in metroplex." *Skiff*, March 9, 2012, 1.

Blanc, Paulina. "Rees-Jones Hall fosters better learning for students." *TCU 360*, December 10, 2014, 22, 23.

Blanton, Jaime. "James Mattox Moudy: 1916-2004." *TCU Magazine*, Fall 2004, 56.

Blietz, Lena. "Updated classrooms introduced in the Bass Building." *TCU 360*, September 25, 2014, 12.

Boschini, Victor J., Jr. "Connecting our past, our future and one another." *TCU Magazine*, Spring 2019, 2. (Kelly Alumni Center)

Boser, Taylor. "Concert hall to honor the late Van Cliburn." *Skiff*, November 15, 2018, 2.

Brite Divinity School: An Historical Sketch. 1989, Box: 110b. Records of Brite Divinity School, RU 46. Archives and Special Collections, Mary Couts Burnett Library. https://archives.tcu.edu/repositories/2/archival_objects/32433. Accessed September 15, 2022.

"Carving a tradition." *TCU Magazine*, September 1999, 63. (TCU ceremonial mace)

Cervantez, Jessica. "Graduating seniors make their mark on campus." *Skiff*, February 1, 2001, 1, 6. (senior bricks)

Chapman, Joey, and Susan Woodell. "Up in smoke." *Skiff*, March 30, 2006, 1, 2. (bookstore fire)

Clark, Randolph. "Sketch of the Life of Elder J. A. Clark." Unpublished, c. 1920, TCU Library.

Coffman, Angie, and Monica Landers. "Trustees approve $5.2-million plan for Brown-Lupton." *Skiff*, November 23, 1989, 4, 5.

Collier, Caroline. "Love points the way to learning." *TCU Magazine*, Winter 2017, 37–45. (*Yearning to Know* statue)

Crabtree, Rob. "$7.5 million, two years, one fire later, bookstore is back." *Skiff*, January 15, 2008, 1, 2.

Crane, Jason. "Smoothie bar opens its doors." *Skiff*, February 10, 1997, 1, 2. (Smoothie King)

Cruz, Lexy and Kristin Barnes. "Sculpture captures SuperFrog in BLUU statue." *Skiff*, October 25, 2012, 4.

Day, John-Mark. "Refurbished Waits opens doors." *Skiff*, August 23, 2001, 1, 4.

Dodson, Dee. "2011 Alumni Awards." *TCU Magazine*, Summer 2011, 74. (J. Luther and Teresa King)

Droddy, Taylor. "Building awarded eco-friendly certification." *Skiff*, August 25, 2009. (Shirley Hall)

Edgemon, Richard. "TCU nearly finished with preparing for new administration building." *TCU360*, August 23, 2018, 12.

"First-class facilities." *TCU Magazine*, Fall 2008, 52–53. (Dutch Meyer Athletic Complex and Abe Martin Academic Enhancement Center)

"Flowing again." *TCU Magazine*, Winter 2007, 11. (Frog Fountain)

Gray, Mindy. "Walsh Center is a unique addition." *Skiff*, March 31, 1998, 1, 3.

Gutierrez, Michael. "New horned frog statue has horns dulled." *Skiff*, March 15, 2012, 3, 4.

Hall, Colby D. *History of Texas Christian University: a College of the Cattle Frontier*. Fort Worth: TCU Press, 1947.

Hawkins, Christy. "M.J. Neeley passes away." *Skiff*, November 17, 1996, 1, 2.

Hoffacker, Abby. "TCU Students try to navigate famously confusing Sid W. Richardson building." *TCU 360*, August 24, 2021.

Hopper, Kathryn. "$750,000 grant spurs expansion to Starpoint." *TCU Magazine*, Spring 2009, 23.

———. "For better or worse." *TCU Magazine*, Summer 2012, 46–47. (Emmet Smith/Robert Carr Chapel)

———. "Reed Hall reopens after 16-month redo." *TCU Magazine*, Fall 2010, 6.

———. "Scharbauer Hall to open in January for Honors, AddRan." *TCU Magazine*, Winter 2000, 12.

Horner, Alec. "New in 2014: Study room on

first floor of Moudy transformed into small Bob Schieffer memorabilia display." *TCU 360*, April 10, 2014, 7.

Howell, Braden. "Meteorite collection to open Saturday." *Skiff*, January 31, 2003, 1, 2.

Hughston, Heather. "Art & History." *TCU Magazine*, Winter 2021, 9. (We can, together art installation)

Hulme, Shelley. "Renovations to meet accessibility standards at Robert Carr Chapel." *TCU Magazine*, Fall 2016, 8.

———. "Worth Hills Greek Village gains new buildings." *TCU Magazine*, Fall 2018, 12.

Ito, Daichi. "What to expect from the new music center." *TCU360*, March 2020.

Johnson, Ben. "Lightning damages chapel." *Skiff*, April 28, 1994, 1.

Jones, Matt. "Foster Hall reopens, other renovations to follow." *Skiff*, August 23, 2000, 1, 4.

Katz, Chelsea. "Construction on Sadler Hall set to finish by July." *Skiff*, April 2, 2011, 2.

Kelton, Katie. "A Legacy set in stone." *TCU Magazine*, Summer 2021, 115–16. (Sid W. Richardson and Annie Richardson Bass)

Kokoruz, Aaron. "Music practice rooms open." *Skiff*, September 24, 2003, 1, 2. (Waits and Ed Landreth)

Ladner, Jim. "Moudy received endowment." *Skiff*, March 22, 1995, 5. (Moudy building)

Lynch, Greg. "Sadler renovations completed." *Skiff*, April 2, 1991, 4.

"Making a Marc." *TCU Magazine*, Spring 2005, 7. (GrandMarc)

Marino, Kelly. "Ed Landreth Hall renovated." *Skiff*, January 24, 2000, 1, 5.

Martin, Lisa. "Calling campus home." *TCU Magazine*, Summer 2021, 26–29. (overview of new residence halls)

Martino, Zach. "Brick by brick." *TCU Magazine*, Fall 2020, 5–6. (TCU buff bricks)

Masenda, Andrea. "Students vote to name frog after legendary horned frog, Ol' Rip." *TCU 360*, April 12, 2012, 6.

Massey, Abigail. "Indoor practice facility opens for use in 2015." *Skiffx360*, January 29, 2015, 15.

Master, Rachel Stowe. "Spencer Hayes '59." *TCU Magazine*, Spring 2017, 70.

McReynolds, Joey. "Walsh Performing Arts Center undergoes $2.5 million renovation." *TCU 360*, January 25, 2014, 11.

Meddaugh, Jeff. "New era of dorms to come." *Skiff*, October 17, 1997, 1, 8. (Tom Brown-Pete Wright)

Melton, Marica. "Greenhouse effect." *TCU Magazine*, Spring 2013, 36–37. (plantings on campus)

Mourer, Mark. "Goat Hills." *TCU Magazine*, Spring 2009, 78–79. (Worth Hills golf course)

"Movement of the earth and sun." *TCU Magazine*, Summer 2015, 9. (TCU sundial)

"New stone age comes to campus." *TCU Magazine*, Winter 2005, 13. (Froghenge)

"Oh give me a home." *TCU Magazine*, Winter 2006, 20–21. (Rockefeller building)

Potter, Matt. "Field named for longtime donor." *Skiff*, September 24, 2003, 8. (Amon Carter)

"Remembering their service." *TCU Magazine*, Winter 2005, 23. (Veterans Plaza)

Rubinson, Alison. "Buschman theatre dedicated." *Skiff*, November 18, 2005, 1, 2.

Salazar, Daniel. "Worth Hills 2.0." *TCU 360*, November 14, 2023, 8, 9. (new residence halls)

"School of Education gets new statue." *TCU Magazine*, Fall 2008, 5.

Severance, Emily, and Trisha Spence. "Honoring the brave." *TCU Magazine*, Fall 2021, 15. (Veterans Plaza)

Skiff Staff. "Preparation underway for tech center." *Skiff*, February 15, 2002. (Tucker Technology)

Smith, Emmet G., and Judith Oelfke Smith. "Congrats on Robert Carr Chapel." *TCU Magazine*, Summer 2017, 4.

Speer, Allison. "Putting down (new) roots." *TCU Magazine*, Fall 2006, 75. (trees on campus)

Summa, Andy. "Move off campus marks a new era for University store." *Skiff*, Octo-

ber 31, 1997, 4.

"Super structure." *TCU Magazine*, Summer 2007, 10. (Baugh practice facility)

Swaim, Joan Hewatt. "A TCU Cowboy." *This Is TCU* 30, no. 1 (March 1988), 38–39.

———. "Of Time and the Drag." *This Is TCU* 33, no. 3 (September 1990), 38.

———. "University Drive." *TCU Magazine*, Summer 2000, 40–41. (description of some neighborhood streets)

"The past stays with us." *TCU Magazine*, May 1991, 26–27. (Sadler lobby)

The *TCU Magazine* Staff. "Greener pastures for Amon G. Carter Stadium." *TCU Magazine*, Summer 2013, 53. (football field)

Triebwasser, Melissa. "Seal of Excellence," *Skiff*, September 4, 1997, 1. (Flag plaza in front of Sadler)

"Tucker Tribute." *TCU Magazine*, Winter 2002, 4. (Tucker Technology Center)

Van Meter, David. "The Clarks: putty in her hands." *TCU Magazine*, June 1992, 20–21. (Clark Brothers statue)

"Want fries with that? Frog Food." *TCU Magazine*, Winter 1999, 10. (Food options in the Main)

Wassenaar, Alisha. "Atrium being improved." *Skiff*, February 5, 2002, 1. (Moudy Building)

Waters, Rick. "A cathedral of knowledge." *TCU Magazine*, Winter 2016, 30–37. (Mary Couts Burnett Library)

———. "A century of partnership begins." *TCU Magazine*, Fall 2010, 42–49. (Fort Worth-TCU relationship)

———. "A model teacher-scholar." *TCU Magazine*, Summer 2004, 50. (Provost William Koehler)

———. "Amon G. Carter Stadium. 80 memories of 80 years." *TCU Magazine*, Winter 2010, 40–49 (Amon Carter, including implosion of original)

———. "A monument to school spirit." *TCU Magazine*, Summer 2012, 78–79.

———. "A new era for DMC." *TCU Magazine*, Spring 2014, 40–47.

———. "A new front door." *TCU Magazine*, Fall 2010, 33–39. (Wright Admission Center)

———. "At Student Memorial, a single flute." *TCU Magazine*, Summer 2013, 9.

———. "Celebrating a milestone in Berry Street makeover." *TCU Magazine*, Summer 2013, 10.

———. "Clark reopens with fresh look." *TCU Magazine*, Fall 2008, 11.

———. "Convergence lab opening new era for Schieffer School." *TCU Magazine*, Spring 2010, 10.

———. "Dee J. Kelly 1929-2015." *TCU Magazine*, Fall 2015, 69.

———. "Dr. Karyn Sue Brand Purvis." *TCU Magazine*, Spring 2016, 68

———. "E. Leigh Secrest 1928-2016." *TCU Magazine*, Spring 2016, 67.

———. "Fateful fire." *TCU Magazine*, Spring 2010, 38-49. (Fire to Main)

———. "Flower power." *TCU Magazine*, Summer 2007, 74–75.

———. "Gym dandy." *TCU Magazine*, Spring 2011, 82. (Erma Lowe)

———. "Harrison Building gives Brite more classrooms, offices." *TCU Magazine*, Spring 2012, 11.

———. "Howard G. Wible 1920-2015." *TCU Magazine*, Winter 2016, 68.

———. "Jarvis is new home to music, campus services." *TCU Magazine*, Fall 2008, 10.

———. "Lowe Hall opens as new home for Dance." *TCU Magazine*, Winter 2011, 12.

———. "Making his own legend." *TCU Magazine*, Fall 2005, 38–45. (Gary Patterson)

———. "'Milton Hilton' now the 'Ritz.'" *TCU Magazine*, Fall 2010, 11.

———. "New admissions building will use geothermal energy." *TCU Magazine*, Spring 2010, 11.

———. "Paulette Burns: 1949-2014." *TCU Magazine*, Winter 2015, 46.

———. "Remodeled Milton Daniel to open in August." *TCU Magazine*, Spring 2010, 10.

———. "Sherley reopens as greenest tech-iest residence hall." *TCU Magazine*, Fall 2009, 10.

———. "Starring role in twilight years." *TCU Magazine*, Winter 2004, 16–17. (Ames Observatory)

———. "Supreme court." *TCU Magazine*, Winter 2016, 42–45. (Schollmaier Arena)

———. "Tandy statue relocated to campus." *TCU Magazine*, Fall 2009, 11.

———. "TCU celebrates official Big 12 entrance." *TCU Magazine*, Fall 2012, 10.

———. "TCU hides time capsule inside stadium column." *TCU Magazine*, Winter 2011, 10. (Amon Carter Stadium)

———. "The 21st century TCU." *TCU Magazine*, Spring 2008, 28–37. (TCU master plan then and now)

———. "The classroom (R)evolution." *TCU Magazine*, Spring 2015, 28–36. (Rees-Jones Hall)

———. "The man Patterson passed." *TCU Magazine*, Fall 2012, 46–47. (Dutch Meyer)

———. "The state of our union." *TCU Magazine*, Fall 2008, 30–35. (the BLUU)

———. "We don't shhhhhhh anymore." *TCU Magazine*, Spring 2002, 18–23. (Mary Couts Burnett Library)

———. "Welcome Home: The Carter Is Ready." *TCU Magazine*, Fall 2012, 36–39. (Amon Carter Stadium)

———. "Worth Hills residence halls open." *TCU Magazine*, Fall 2013, 13.

Welch, Brenda. "Berry Street Initiative moves forward with road work." *Skiff*, January 25, 2012, 3.

Wiklund, Gabe. "Rec center recognized for unique design." *Skiff*, September 8, 2004, 1, 2.

Wilson, Beth. "Bagel joint hits TCU community with a bang." *Skiff*, March 25, 1997, 1, 4. (Einstein's)

———. "Beasley Hall receives new wing." *Skiff*, October 10, 1997, 2.

Wright, Mark. "Old school; new school." *TCU Magazine*, Fall 2007, 24–25. (College of Education)

———. "Sign of the times." *TCU Magazine*, Summer 2006, 30–31. (Record Town)

———. "Street smarts." *TCU Magazine*, Fall 2007, 38–47. (Berry Street initiative)

Yoest, Sarah. "Stage West theatre company moving near campus." *Skiff*, August 27, 1993, 1.

Youngman, Clayton. "Multipurpose building opens Monday." *TCU 360*, January 15, 2015, 6, 7. (King Family Commons)

———. "The Campus: Doing what didn't come naturally." *TCU Magazine*, March 1991, 19–25. (trees on campus)

Zuber, Molly. "Lowe Hall recognized for preserving history." *Skiff*, September 21, 2012, 3.

BOOKS

Clark, Joseph Lynn. *Thank God We Made It!: A Family Affair with Education*. Austin: University of Texas, Humanities Research Center, 1969.

Clark, Randolph. *Reminiscences: Biographical and Historical*. Wichita Falls, Texas: Lee Clark, Publisher, 1919; reprinted TCU Press, 1986.

Colquitt, Betsy. *Prologue: the TCU Library to 1983*. Fort Worth: Mary Couts Burnett Library, 1983.

Corder, Jim W., with photographs by Michael Chesser and Linda Kaye. *More Than a Century*. Fort Worth: TCU Press, 1973.

Flemmons, Jerry. *Amon: the Life of Amon Carter, Sr. of Texas*. Austin: Jenkins Publishing Co., 1978.

Fort Worth: Upper North, Northeast, East, Far South, and Far West. Tarrant County Historic Resources Survey. Fort Worth: Historic Preservation Council for Tarrant County, Texas, 1989.

Hall, Colby D. *The Early Years: University Christian Church, Fort Worth, Texas, 1873–1941*. Published by the church, 1983.

———. *History of Texas Christian University: a College of the Cattle Frontier*. Fort Worth: Texas Christian University Press, 1947.

———. "Source Material and Memoranda in Connection with the History of Texas Christian University, A College of the Cattle Frontier." 2 vols. unpublished, c. 1941, Special Collections, TCU Library.

Hammond, John H. *Jerome A. Moore: A Man of TCU.* Fort Worth: TCUPress, 1974.

Harris, Lucy. *The Harris College of Nursing: Five Decades of Struggle for a Cause.* Fort Worth: TCU Press, 1973.

Hartley, Julia Magee. *Old American Glass: the Mills Collection at Texas Christian University.* Fort Worth: TCU Press, 1975.

Keith, Noel L. *The Brites of Capote.* Fort Worth: TCU Press, 1950.

Knight, Oliver, and Cissy Stewart Lale. *Fort Worth: Outpost on the Trinity.* Fort Worth: TCU Press, 1990.

Mason, Mrs. Frank Miller. "The Beginnings of Texas Christian University." Unpublished Master's Thesis. Texas Christian University, 1930.

Monroe, "Cowboy" Louis. *The Life Story of "Cowboy" Louis Monroe.* Privately published, 1968.

Moore, Jerome A. *Texas Christian University: A Hundred Years of History.* Fort Worth: TCU Press, 1973.

Pirtle, Caleb. *Fort Worth: the Civilized West.* Tulsa, Oklahoma: Continental Heritage Press, 1980.

Starpoint, A Shining Place (for the Dedication of Starpoint School). Fort Worth: TCU Press, 1978.

Van Zandt, K. M. *Force Without Fanfare: the Autobiography of K. M. Van Zandt.* Edited and with an Introduction by Sandra L. Myres. Fort Worth: TCU Press, 1968.

Pattie, Jane. "The Brite Legacy." *The Cattleman* (March, 1990).

ADDITIONAL RESOURCES

Fort Worth Star-Telegram

The Horned Frog. Annual of Texas Christian University.

The *Skiff.* 1980–2021. A daily newspaper published under the auspices of the student body of Texas Christian University. The *Skiff* is currently published Thursdays during the fall and spring semesters.

TCU News Service releases.

TCU360. A part of TCU Student Media, *TCU360* is the official student-produced, online product of the Department of Journalism in the Bob Schieffer College of Communication.

Files in the Special Collections Department, Mary Couts Burnett Library, Texas Christian University.

Index

About the Authors

A graduate of TCU and the third generation of her family to be on the university staff, **JOAN HEWATT SWAIM** retired in 1995 as coordinator of bibliographic control for the Mary Couts Burnett Library after eighteen years of service.

PHIL HARTMAN served as head of TCU's pre-health professions program (now Institute) for twenty-two years before becoming dean of the College of Science & Engineering from 2012 until his 2021 retirement.